The McGraw-Hill
Guide to Starting
Your Own Business

The McGraw-Hill Guide to Starting Your Own Business

A Step-by-Step Blueprint for the First-Time Entrepreneur

Second Edition

Stephen C. Harper

McGraw-Hill
New York   Chicago   San Francisco
Lisbon   London   Madrid   Mexico City
Milan   New Delhi   San Juan   Seoul
Singapore   Sydney   Toronto

6 7 8 9 0 DOC/DOC 0 9 8 7 6

ISBN: 0-07-141012-0

The author believes that the material presented in this manuscript was accurate when the manuscript was submitted to the publisher. The rates, figures, and calculations have been provided as examples to the material and they are subject to change over time. Some of the calculations and financial projections have been simplified for the reader. The reader is encouraged to seek professional assistance when making financial calculations and addressing legal matters. The names of businesses used in the business plan part of this book are fictitious. Any similarities to actual businesses are coincidental and unintentional. Also, the material presented in this book is the product of the author's efforts. In no way is the University of North Carolina at Wilmington to be considered responsible or liable for its contents.

McGraw-Hill books are available at special quantity discounts to use as premiums and sales promotions, or for use in corporate training programs. For more information, please write to the Director of Special Sales, Professional Publishing, McGraw-Hill, Two Penn Plaza, New York, NY 10121-2298. Or contact your local bookstore.

Library of Congress Cataloging-in-Publication Data
Harper, Stephen C.
    The Mcgraw-hill guide to starting your own business : a step-by-step blueprint for the first-time entrepreneur / Stephen C. Harper.— 2nd ed.
    p. cm.
    Includes index.
    ISBN 0-07-141012-0 (pbk. : alk. paper)
    1. New business enterprises. I. Title.
    HD62.5 H3734 2003
    658.1'141—dc21   2002154295

 This book is printed on recycled, acid-free paper containing a minimum of 50% recycled de-inked fiber.

This book is dedicated to

America—the land of opportunity.

The entrepreneurs—whom I have met, worked with, and learned from over the years. They and other entrepreneurs throughout the country had the courage to venture out and create the standard of living we enjoy today.

My students, who demonstrate that the entrepreneurial spirit is alive.

My father, H. Mitchell Harper, Jr., who helped me realize you can't take it with you and that life is not a spectator sport.

The people who came up with the Schlitz slogan, "If you can only go around once in life, then do it with gusto!" the Michelob slogan, "Who says you can't have it all?" and the Nike slogan, "Just do it!" These slogans capture the essence of the entrepreneurial spirit.

Contents

Lessons for Starting Your Own Business

Fred DeLuca

Dr. Harper hits on so many of the lessons that I wish someone had taught me when I started out on this incredible journey of owning my own business. For me, it was the summer of 1965, and as a 17-year-old college student I knew little about running my own business. There were nowhere near as many resources for would-be entrepreneurs as there are today. My partner, Pete Buck, and I learned things as we went along, and we learned many things the hard way. However, after many challenges, a few pitfalls, and a lot of education, we realized our dream of being successful entrepreneurs. We have and continue to learn many lessons about business every day we operate. Thank you, Dr. Harper for helping all of us entrepreneurs in our quest for success.

1. Opportunity waits for no one.
Think about all the opportunities that are afforded you as you begin your planning for opening your own business. Look at the options from all angles, educate yourself but do it quickly—opportunity waits for no one. Take that first step.

Fred DeLuca is cofounder and president of Subway Restaurants. Subway Restaurants is the world's largest submarine sandwich franchise, with more than 17,500 locations in 71 countries. It is also the second largest fast-food franchise chain in the world and has recently surpassed McDonald's in the number of locations in the United States and Canada. Headquartered in Milford, Connecticut, Subway was cofounded by Fred DeLuca and Dr. Peter Buck in 1965. That partnership marked the beginning of a remarkable journey, which has made it possible for thousands of individuals to build and succeed in their own businesses.

In 1965, my opportunity came when I told a family friend, Pete Buck, that I was trying to find ways to finance my college education. Pete's idea—open a submarine sandwich shop. He would be my partner, loan me $1000 to get started, and that would be that. It was an opportunity I could not pass up.

2. *Do your homework.*

Learn and then learn some more. Resources are plentiful for business owners. I strongly suggest you do your research and look at all aspects of the business you want to own. Talk to others who share your dream or who are operating a similar business. Going into business can be as exciting as it is challenging.

In the case of Subway, Pete Buck and I traveled to other submarine or "Italian" sandwich shops in New England to see how they operated before we embarked on our journey.

3. *Be persistent and don't give up.*

In business there will always be obstacles in your path. One of the keys to success is how you handle them. Some people just quit while others keep working to find solutions.

At Subway, we have had our share of obstacles. For instance, our sales during the first day in business were fantastic but they declined steadily with each passing week. Within 6 months, sales were so poor that we considered just locking the door and throwing away the key to cut our losses. Instead we decided to stick with it, and we even took the unconventional approach of opening a second store before the first one turned a profit.

4. *Have a plan—but be flexible.*

Just because you have an idea and a strategy, don't hesitate to stray from the original plan if it means the difference between success and failure. *The year after we started we were faced with the fact that we were losing money and might have to close up shop. We did not want to fail. So, we thought of other solutions, and we came up with something we really liked: We decided to go forward and open a second store! We thought although there were some definite risks, there were benefits too. We would have more brand visibility: We could advertise more and get our message to more customers!*

5. *Be positive and have fun.*

Many great entrepreneurs tried and tried again until they got it right; they graduated from the school of hard knocks. If you truly believe in what you are doing, chances are you can and will be successful.

We believed in our dream and were so excited by the results of our second store opening that we decided to open a third store shortly thereafter. Eleven months after we first set out on our journey, we had three submarine sandwich shops open. Things moved along at a good pace and by the winter our sales in stores two and three began to trend like our first! Now, instead of having one low-volume money-losing store, we had three low-volume money losing stores!

We remained positive, and we knew that the key to our success was to stick with it, be innovative, find solutions, and continue to build our skills and our business to the point where, eventually, we would be out of the woods!

Today, with Pete Buck still my partner and thousands of other business partners in our worldwide network of franchises we still live by these rules—and yes, we still have fun doing it!

Preface

The McGraw-Hill Guide to Starting Your Own Business has been written for the same reason that most businesses are started—to fill a void in the marketplace. There are numerous books available about starting a business. However, few of these books are tailored to people who have limited experience and education in business. Some books are too simplistic. They try to be funny, offer few guidelines on how to actually start a business, and paint too rosy a picture. Other books assume that the reader has an MBA from Harvard and plans to start a high-technology business with venture capital and then make millions by taking it public.

This guide is written for the "first-timer." It encourages you to take an objective look at why you want to start your own business and whether you have what it takes to succeed. It also offers a step-by-step guide that goes from identifying business opportunities all the way to finding ways to finance your new business.

The first edition of *Starting Your Own Business* has been a best-selling book. It was the featured selection of Fortune Book Club the first month it was published. It was later featured in Business Week Book Club, Book-of-the-Month Book Club, and Money Book Club. While sales of the first edition have not slowed much in the last few years, McGraw-Hill and I decided that it was time to launch a twenty-first century edition that would capture many of the challenges that you may face in today's marketplace.

While every chapter of the new edition of *Starting Your Own Business* has been updated and improved, particular attention has been directed to five specific areas. First, Fred DeLuca, cofounder of Subway Restaurants, has shared his thoughts about starting a business in a foreword. Second, numerous examples of ventures that have succeeded—and why they succeeded—

have been provided. Third, the chapter on funding your business has been changed to reflect the reluctance of banks to provide loans to start-ups. Fourth, the epilogue features more than a hundred insightful do's and don'ts from entrepreneurs who started a variety of businesses. Fifth, an appendix has been provided that lists additional sources of information, including web sites.

By the way, the new edition does not get wrapped up in all the irrational exuberance exhibited by so many naïve people in the last few years. It is still targeted to first-timers who want to start a business that will beat the odds and that will make money the old-fashioned way . . . by earning it!

Acknowledgments

This book was partly the result of a faculty research grant provided by the Cameron School of Business at the University of North Carolina at Wilmington.* This grant made it possible for me to take some time off from my regular activities to write the book. Numerous people helped me put together the first edition. Eight people associated with UNC-Wilmington at that time deserve special attention. Jane Kenan, as an MBA candidate, provided considerable editorial and research assistance. Elaine Furguson, Carolyn Cook, Rhonda LaMarsh, Barbara Holder, Susan Ritz, Amy Brown, and Trudy Owen also provided editorial and secretarial assistance. I also want to thank all the people who have worked with me over the years in my "Starting Your Own Business" workshop. They include Dr. Earl Honeycutt; Ted Jans; Leslie Langer; Charles H. Craft III, CPA; Ernie Sewell; and David Lewis, JD. Charles, David, and Tom Long provided valuable editorial and technical assistance.

I also want to thank Ann Wildman, associate editor at McGraw-Hill, for encouraging me to put together this new edition and for providing timely assistance. Numerous other people also provided valuable assistance in the development of this new edition. Four graduate students were particularly helpful. Jeff Vito helped digitize the manuscript so that it could be updated and revised. Eason Bryan, Donald Peterson, and Lisa Eakins helped in the

*I would also like to thank Dan and Betty Cameron and Bruce and Louise Cameron for their support of the University of North Carolina at Wilmington. Their never-ending financial generosity and ongoing guidance have helped make it possible for me and other members of the faculty to grow professionally and enjoy our relationship with the university.

analysis of the insights generated during interviews with over 150 entrepreneurs. These insights became a valuable part of this new edition. The entrepreneurial do's and don'ts in the epilogue were the result of interviews conducted by my students over the last few years. The interviews were conducted by students enrolled in the Weekend Executive MBA program while I was a visiting professor at Duke University as well as the MBA and undergraduate students enrolled in my entrepreneurship classes at the University of North Carolina at Wilmington. I truly appreciate the time and effort they put into the interviews. The epilogue reflects only a fraction of their work and contribution. I also want to thank my daughter, Allison Farmer. She provided valuable assistance with designing the tables and figures. Fred DeLuca, cofounder of Subway Restaurants, deserves special thanks for writing the foreword to this new edition.

Introduction

Prepare to Boldly Go Where You Have Not Gone Before!

The fact that you opened this book indicates that you are contemplating starting your own business. You may be among those readers who are merely curious about what may be involved in starting a new business. Conversely, you may be among those readers who have already decided to start a business. All you need to do is to determine what type of business to start, how large it should be, where it should be located, how much money it will take, how it can be financed, and when will be the best time to start it.

Whether you are just toying with the notion of starting a business sometime in your life or are already at the point where you can't eat, drink, or sleep without thinking about starting your own business, you should recognize one thing right now: Starting a business, even a small one, is a major undertaking. It is not like taking up a hobby or going on a diet. Nor is it a glamorous form of semiretirement. Starting a business is a serious endeavor and one that requires considerable preparation. Someone once defined luck as what happens when preparation meets opportunity. This book is not about relying on luck; it is about being prepared.

Many people view starting a business as comparable to embarking on a glorious adventure, filled with challenge and excitement. Yet, if you ask people who started their first business in the last couple of years how they feel about it now, many of them will tell you that the honeymoon lasted only a few weeks, the marriage has involved considerable anxiety and self-sacrifice, and they continue to wonder whether they should get a divorce from the business!

Most of the people who have started a business will confess that had they known about all the time, skills, and frustrations it would entail, they would never have done it. Even the people who are glad they started their own businesses will tell you that it is not always a glamorous way of spending one's time and money. Numerous aspects of starting and managing a business are time-consuming, repetitive, and mundane. It involves risks and requires personal sacrifices.

Nevertheless, starting your own business offers you the opportunity to experience things that are not available when you are working for someone else. If you know yourself, understand the nature of the marketplace, have identified a market opportunity, have the ability to provide targeted customers with what they want, and possess the numerous skills and resources that are necessary to start and manage a new business, then you should be in a position to beat the odds. You may also find it personally and financially rewarding.

People who start their own businesses are different from most people. Someone once observed that entrepreneurs would rather work 60 or 70 hours for themselves than work 40 hours for someone else. Once you have your own business, you may find that you could never go back and work for someone else again.

You are contemplating embarking on a journey that many people think about but few people do much about. When you start your first business, to paraphrase the prelude to *Star Trek,* you are about to "boldly go where you have not gone before."

This guide is written for the "first-timer," the person who has limited business education and experience. It is intended to provide an entrepreneurial blueprint for starting a successful new venture. This book cannot guarantee success, but it does offer numerous ideas and insights that will increase your chances of beating the odds.

This book is not intended to encourage you to start your own business or to discourage you from doing so. Instead, it is designed to help you size up your own strengths and limitations and to have you look before you leap. Some readers will realize that they are not willing to take the risk or that they lack key skills. It is better to learn this now rather than after the business is started.

Other readers may find that they have the confidence and the competence, but they need to rethink their business idea. Starting a business is like riding a horse: You may be a capable rider, but if your horse is weak, you will not go very far. The same applies to starting a business. New business success requires knowing what you are doing and capitalizing on a good opportunity. You may be ready, but market conditions must also be right. Be patient and don't be discouraged. This book will help you identify emerging opportunities.

A few readers may find that they are ready and that the marketplace is ripe with opportunities to harvest. If you are in this group, I wish you the best and offer you two pieces of advice: Fasten your seat belt and keep your copy of this book close by because you are about to embark on what may be the journey of a lifetime.

Part 1
Prerequisites for Start-Up Survival and Success

1
Creating a New Business

The United States is characterized as a land of opportunity. One particular area of opportunity is the freedom to go into business for yourself. The free enterprise system gives people the freedom to try to succeed. This freedom also involves the risk of failure. This "blueprint" by no means presumes to cover all the material available on the subject or to guarantee success. Instead, it is intended to provide a set of guidelines, insights, and resources that will help you beat the odds.

Profit has been defined as the reward for successfully taking risks. The benefits of having your own business are twofold. First, you can generate considerable personal wealth from a well-managed business—even a one-person business. Second—and this is often the most satisfying aspect of running your own business—you have the feeling of freedom associated with "being your own boss," making your own decisions, and building a business from scratch.

However, by choosing not to be an employee of someone else, you lose the security of a regular paycheck, a predictable work schedule, fringe benefits, paid vacations, and a retirement plan. Having your own business involves risking your property, your health, and your pride. Your family life will also be challenged. Your spouse will have to make sacrifices. You may become a stranger in your own house as you commit whatever time it takes to get the venture up and running. Dinners together, weekend trips, and vacations may have to be put on hold until your business generates positive cash flow and you can hire additional people. Even when you are at home, you won't really be there. Your mind will be jumping from one entrepreneurial challenge to another. Accordingly, if you are considering starting a business so that you can be your own boss, you should remember the old adage, "Nothing ventured, nothing gained, but also nothing lost."

CAN YOU BEAT THE ODDS?

If there is one word that best describes the type of person who starts his or her own business, it has to be *optimistic*. Yet despite this optimism, it is a cold, hard fact that more than half of the 800,000 businesses started this year will not be around 5 years from now. Some will fail, some will be sold to people who think they can beat the odds, and some will be closed by their founders because they are just not worth the time or effort. Only 20 percent of the businesses started this year will be around in 10 years. Half of the survivors will be producing only a marginal profit.

The process of starting a business involves answering numerous questions. The first two questions to be answered are, "Do I have what it takes to be successful?" and "Am I starting a business where a real and lasting opportunity exists?" When the owners of businesses that failed are asked what contributed to their demise, they tend to mention too much competition, high interest rates, government regulations, inflation, recession, and numerous other such factors. Let's set the record straight. These factors may have contributed to their problems, but mismanagement is the primary reason most businesses fail.

Almost all business failures can be attributed to a lack of managerial experience and knowledge. In most cases, the founder

1. Entered a market that was already crowded with competition.
2. Did not offer exactly what prospective customers wanted to buy.
3. Failed to make the appropriate changes in business operations to meet a changing marketplace.
4. Started the business with insufficient funding.
5. Lacked sufficient knowledge about legal, financial, purchasing, accounting, employee relations, or marketing matters for that type of business. This lack of knowledge resulted in the inability to come up with the right answers when faced with pressing business decisions.

This is one of the reasons franchises have become popular. Most franchisors (the people who sell franchise rights) screen prospective franchisees for business knowledge and experience. Some franchisors also offer extensive training programs, ongoing management assistance, and a systematic rather than trial-and-error approach to running a business. For a fee, most franchisors increase the probability that the business will be successful. While success is not guaranteed, franchisees' track record for success is higher than that of first-time independent business start-ups. Most franchisees succeed. Most independent businesses started by first-timers do not.*

Yet despite all the hazards and pitfalls, the dream of having your own business can be realized. Whether it is an independent business or a franchise, if you know *what* to do, *how* to do it, and *when* to do it, you should be able to beat the odds.

DON'T BE ONE OF THE LOSERS

In spite of differences in age, ethnic background, religious beliefs, and gender, most of the people who are successful in business have a lot in common. First, they were prepared to start their businesses. They usually had experience in that business or a similar type of business. Anyone who is thinking of starting a business should get a job in a business of that type first. There is no substitute for experience. Experience provides insight into the nature of products, services, customer needs, employees, suppliers, seasonality, and so on. The high failure rate for new businesses in their first few years indicates that there is little room for mistakes. The average business makes less than 4 cents profit per dollar of sales before taxes.

The competitive world of business shows little mercy for the trial-and-error approach used by novices. Experience reduces some of the surprises first-timers encounter and enables them to anticipate and prevent most problems. Experience as an employee, however, is not the same as experience in managing that type of business. Obviously, managerial experience in that type of business will enhance your chances for success.

Experience may help, but education and formal training are also important. Just because you have done something before is no guarantee that you are doing it right or that the way you are doing it is the best way. Education and formal training in the "technical" fields of business, particularly accounting, finance, marketing, and law, are essential in today's competitive times.

---

*This should not be interpreted as a blanket endorsement of all franchises. Please consult with an attorney and an accountant when considering any franchise—or for that matter, when starting or buying a business. Buying a business will be discussed in Chapter 10. Franchises will be discussed in Chapter 11.

PREREQUISITES FOR START-UP SURVIVAL AND SUCCESS

Your business will be only as good as the decisions you make. If you do not understand the uniqueness of your situation and do not possess state-of-the-art knowledge about how to identify opportunities and solve various types of problems, you are destined to fail. Education and experience will not guarantee success, but they will reduce the trial-and-error approach to managing that is the primary reason so many businesses fail.

You must also guard against adopting the attitude, "I'll just call my accountant or attorney and ask what I should do." At first glance, this seems like a logical attitude. To be successful, however, you need to have a good working knowledge of every aspect of starting and managing a business. This isn't to say that you shouldn't consult professional advisers on matters related to their field. You should seek their advice on technical matters, and you should consult with them early in the decision process rather than after the fact. You will never know all the answers, but it is important that you know the questions that need to be answered and where to get advice.

A business is like a forest. If you do not have a good understanding of each tree (accounting, marketing, employee relations, etc.) and how the trees are interrelated, there is little likelihood that you will have the depth and breadth of knowledge necessary to make the right decisions. For example, owners or managers of troubled businesses frequently cite "working capital" as a problem. In laypeople's terms, this means that their expenses are greater than their sales or that their cash receipts and disbursements are not synchronized. They do not have enough cash to pay their rent, to replace their inventory, to meet their payroll, and so forth. Working capital problems are actually multifaceted. Generally, to turn the situation around, the owner or manager will need to find ways to increase sales, reduce expenses, collect outstanding receivables, lower the amount of money tied up in inventory, and improve in a dozen other areas. Few things exist in a vacuum in operating a business. You need to be a good generalist and have specialists who can supplement your knowledge (possibly a partner or other employees) in the business or available as advisers.

KEY ENTREPRENEURIAL QUALITIES

Some people have what it takes to start a business; others don't. Louis Armstrong, Jr., the great trumpeter, observed, "There are some people who don't know and you just can't tell them." Successful entrepreneurs exhibit nine qualities that separate them from most people.

They Are Opportunity Seekers

Entrepreneurs live by the creed, "Within every problem lies a disguised opportunity." They are always looking for areas where people's needs aren't being met well enough or at all. They know that there are an infinite number of opportunities in the marketplace. They recognize that more people working outside their homes will increase the demand for services and timesaving appliances. They know that professional, two-income couples often prefer to write a check and have someone else paint their houses, cut their lawns, and do their errands. They are aware that in the years ahead, people will be more concerned with their health, will look for ways to keep fit, and will prefer health-related foods. Accordingly, most entrepreneurs are frustrated because they know that their lives are too short to harvest all the opportunities that exist today and those that are destined to emerge in the years ahead.

They Are Future-Oriented

Entrepreneurs have a vision of what is possible and are willing to invest their time and money in transforming their ideas into business ventures. They subscribe to Alan Kay's philosophy, "The best way to predict the future is to invent it." They don't live in the past, nor will you hear them say, "In my day, we used to walk five miles through the snow to get to school." They believe that just because something has not been done before does not mean that it cannot be done. They are in tune with the present and are actively involved in monitoring trends that may reveal opportunities that are just over the horizon. They think at least 3 to 5 years ahead and are prepared to make short-term sacrifices in order to capitalize on long-term opportunities. They resist the temptation to pursue fads and are not seduced by get-rich-quick schemes.

They know that as people live longer and enjoy better health than past generations, they will travel more and seek avenues for using their time more constructively. The "graying" of our population, particularly the baby boomers, will create new opportunities for businesses that tailor their offerings to an aging, yet active, population. The rising standard of living and the increasing diversity of people in the marketplace will also provide numerous opportunities for people who are prepared to create businesses to meet emerging needs. They also recognize that the first firm to enter an emerging market often establishes a formidable competitive position.

They Are Committed to Being the Best.

Entrepreneurs have contempt for the status quo. They know that the last words of a dying business are, "But that's the way we've always done it." They are always looking for new ways to do things and new things to do.

They recognize that in a changing market, what worked well yesterday will not work as well today, will be inappropriate tomorrow, and will be obsolete the day after that. They are good learners and listeners; they know that running a business is a continuous process of learning, experimenting, and changing. They know that excellence does not come from hitting an occasional home run; it comes from hitting singles on a regular basis. They know that people who try to hit home runs frequently strike out. Success comes from doing almost everything well rather than doing just a few things in an exceptional fashion. As Tom Smith, president of Food Lion, put it, "We don't try to be 1000 percent better on a few things, we try to be at least 1 percent better than *our* competition on 1000 things." They also know that you will not succeed by imitating your competitors. You have to be better. And to be better, you must have the courage, ability, and commitment to be different. They are willing to be the first business to have a 24-hour, seven-days-a-week toll-free ordering number, the first to deliver the product or service to customers, the first to install a drive-in window, the first to have the confidence to offer a satisfaction guaranteed, no-questions-asked full refund return policy.

They Are Market-Driven and Customer-Oriented

Entrepreneurs know that you are successful only to the extent that you are able to create and maintain customers for a profit. To paraphrase Stew Leonard, founder of Leonard's Dairy, "Customers don't come into my store and ask, 'What can I do for Stew Leonard today?' We must be constantly asking, 'What can we do for our customers?' " They know that businesses need to modify their approaches to fit the market, rather than trying to change the market to fit what the owner wants to offer. They know that their customers are the lifeblood of their businesses. They frequently ask their customers what they are looking for and how the business can be improved to meet their needs. Everyone in the business recognizes that it is customers that actually provide the payroll, not the owner. They know that they are not in the business of selling goods or services; they are in the business of providing satisfaction. They view themselves as customer problem solvers, and they treat each customer as if the business's future is in his or her hands.

They Value Their Employees

Entrepreneurs recognize that a business will only be as good as its employees. They know that dedicated employees may be one of the business's greatest competitive advantages. They also know that the quality of customer relations is directly related to the quality of employee relations.

Successful entrepreneurs are honest in their dealings with all people, particularly their employees. They set the right example for their employees and try to involve them when making various decisions. They encourage employees to learn various activities so that the business will not be dependent on only one person. Too many businesses fail because the owner or manager made all the decisions and failed to develop a successor. If you are a perfectionist, it is unlikely that you will delegate decisions or develop your people. The desire to be your own boss may be strong, but don't let it hurt your business.

Some business owners actually drive away good employees because they do not offer their employees a promising future or the opportunity to try their ideas. If you want to enjoy the benefits of having your own business, such as having a flexible schedule and having a business that is capable of growing and sustaining good profits, then you will have to learn to delegate key decisions to your employees. If you are the type of person who needs to control everything and make every decision, you are going to run yourself ragged and restrict the growth of your business. If you spend all your time running the business, you will not have the time to keep pace with the changes that are taking place in the marketplace or to develop innovative ways to create and maintain customers for a profit.

If you insist on making all the decisions because you feel that no one else can manage the business while you are gone, you will be reluctant to take vacations or even an occasional day off. You need to recognize that no one has a monopoly on having all the right answers. Mark Shepherd, as chairman of Texas Instruments, once said, "Each employee needs to be viewed as a source of ideas, not just another pair of hands." If you want your business to grow, you must create an environment that encourages your people to contribute and grow. In short, your style of management may be one of the reasons your business is not growing. Another point worth noting is that an employee who is frustrated and/or constrained today may quit and become your most formidable competitor tomorrow.

They Are Realistic

Entrepreneurs know that the business world is not a perfect place and that people don't always play by the rules. They realize that their competitors' ads and salespeople may not be truthful in their promotional claims. They know that employees will not always show up for work, and that when they do, they may help themselves to their employer's inventory and supplies. They have also learned that suppliers will not always honor their promises. They know that when suppliers say it was shipped yesterday, it probably wasn't, and that if it was, it probably wasn't exactly what they ordered. They also know that if you create a better mousetrap, the world may not beat a path to your door. Instead, the few people who slowly trickle into your store may inform you that another business just opened down the street and that it is offering your new product or service at one-half your price! Successful entrepreneurs realize that there are no free lunches and no guarantees of success. There is only one way to make a profit in the game of business. You have to do it the old-fashioned way—you have to earn it.

Entrepreneurs look before they leap. They don't test the depth of a stream by jumping in with both feet. They do their homework, gather the data, plan their work, and then work their plan. They also know that life is full of surprises. They know that there are no time-outs; you can't stop the world so that you can get your act together. They know that in order to succeed in the long haul, you're going to have to be the best. They also know that lasting success comes from good management, not good luck.

Entrepreneurs also know the difference between a dream and a solid business opportunity. They know that wishful thinking will not cut it in the competitive marketplace. A new venture cannot be launched without a solid business plan. As someone once observed, "If you fail to plan, you are planning to fail." They know that there are a lot of similarities between being a parent and starting a business. It is a lot easier to conceive of a business than to keep it going. They know that starting a business is not something to be taken lightly. They know that it is not something that can be turned on and off like a light switch.

They Are Tolerant of the Tedium

Entrepreneurs know that being an entrepreneur is not that glamorous. They know that life is full of compromises. It also involves mundane activities and thankless tasks. Starting a business involves blood, sweat, and tears. Most people believe that starting a business is a labor of love. Most entrepreneurs are quick to acknowledge that the labor often exceeds the love.

The story of the housekeeper being interviewed who said, "I won't do windows" has direct application to starting a business. When you start a business, you must be prepared to do whatever is necessary. You may be excited about going off on buying trips and putting together creative sales promotions, but you'll also have to keep track of all payroll-related expenses, monitor inventory levels, deal with employee problems, and handle anything else that comes up. There will be many days when you feel as if you spent the whole day plugging holes in the dike with your thumbs.

You may want to have your cake and eat it too, but you are going to have to shop for the ingredients, toil in the kitchen making it, and spend time cleaning up. Entrepreneurs know that the excitement associated with opening your own business can quickly become 60- to 80-hour workweeks. They know that unexpected business situations will force you to cancel your personal plans more often than you would like. They know that family and friends may have to be put on hold on a regular basis. As one entrepreneur once observed, "Being your own boss may eventually have its benefits, but in the early years it also means packing your own lunch. You will not be able to go out to lunch until you hire your first employee because until then, no one would be there to answer the phone."

They Are Resilient

Entrepreneurs know that business success is not a 100-meter sprint; it is a marathon run over tall peaks and down through deep valleys. Few new businesses are overnight successes. As someone noted, "It may take 2 years to know if your business is a lemon and 7 years to know if it's a pearl." Success is not just the result of having a great idea or identifying a "gap" in the marketplace; it takes patience and persistence. To succeed, you will have to handle conflicts, compromises, setbacks, and surprises. You will also have to deal with contractors, building inspectors, and competitors. You will have to be driven from within because there will be times when no one is going to be there to pat you on the back and say, "Hang in there; things will get better."

Starting and managing a business is not smooth sailing. It is more like canoeing through rapids. You are never in total control, you cannot foresee everything that is around the bend, and there are going to be times when you have to improvise just to stay afloat. You must have what is called "a tolerance for the turbulence." As Fred Murphy put it, "If sailing on a big and placid lake is your style, go to work for a large corporation, but if white-water canoeing is to your liking, try a small company."

They also know that in business you need to have the strength to hang in there when things get tough. Experience shows that what you do when you are faced with a formidable challenge and how you handle failure may have a lot to do with whether you will succeed. Most entrepreneurs experience one or two failures before they experience their first success. Your ability to take a punch, pick yourself up, dust yourself off, learn from your experiences, and reenergize yourself to do things in a better way will affect your ability to beat the odds.

They Are Focused and Decisive

Entrepreneurs know that decisions must be made even though they don't have all the information they want and that the person who procrastinates will be passed by. They know that they must have the courage of their convictions and that they will also have to listen, to learn, and to be flexible. They know that they will have to make judgment calls and that there is no way to eliminate risk.

They know that there are more losers than winners. They will be the first to admit that creating a viable business is a constant challenge and a perpetual juggling act. To succeed takes more than being street smart; it also takes an almost inexhaustible supply of energy and the ability to make the right things happen the right way at the right time.

CONCLUSION: STARTING A BUSINESS IS SURVIVAL OF THE FITTEST

This chapter has had one simple message: "Starting a business is not a casual undertaking." The deck is stacked against you. If you are going to accept the challenge, you must do everything you can to improve your chances for success. You will need to have (1) identified a solid business opportunity, (2) the necessary skills and abilities, (3) the right approach to doing business, and (4) sufficient funds to start and operate the business until it can stand on its own.

This chapter has helped identify some of the personal qualities that may give you an edge in the competitive arena. Starting a business and keeping it going is not the job for someone who prefers to be a caretaker. Entrepreneurs are people who enjoy the opportunity to change the world around them. If you want to simplify your life and play it safe, then work for someone else—don't consider being an entrepreneur. As André Maurois noted, "Business is a combination of war and sport." You may not have the goal of being in the *Inc.* 500 in the next 5 years and in the *Fortune* 500 within 10 years, but you will need to have certain qualities if you are to succeed in the competitive arena.

If you have not been discouraged, then you may find it worthwhile to take the following Entrepreneurial Qualities Self-Test. You may not have the answers for the first five questions right now, but you need to give these questions serious thought. Also, you may not get the highest ratings on all nine entrepreneurial qualities. Even the most successful entrepreneurs have certain weaknesses. If you have a low score on most of the nine qualities, however, you should think twice about starting a business.

ENTREPRENEURIAL QUALITIES
SELF-TEST: PART 1

1. Why am I going into business (for the money, the freedom, the challenge, for employment for myself and my family)?
   Answer: _____

2. What is the minimum annual salary I would accept in return for quitting my job and starting a business?
   Answer: $ _____ per year.

3. What amount of time am I willing to commit to starting and managing a business?
   Answer: The maximum number of hours per week: _____
   The minimum number of hours per week: _____

4. What is the maximum amount of risk of business failure I am willing to accept? (One chance in 10, or 10 percent; 3 chances in 10, or 30 percent; etc.)
   Answer: I am willing to accept a _____ chance in 10, or a _____ percent chance of failure.

5. How long do you plan to have the business?
   Answer: I expect to be involved in the business as its owner for at least _____ years.

6. How do I rate on the nine entrepreneurial qualities?

                                                     Low Medium High

a. I am an opportunity seeker.   1 2 3 4 5

If you have not already identified at least one opportunity that has merit, then give yourself one point. If you are the type of person who is constantly identifying opportunities in numerous areas, then give yourself five points.

b. I am future-oriented.   1 2 3 4 5

If you are always reading about the past, are committed to maintaining traditions, and frequently reminisce about the "good old days," then give yourself one point. If you are fascinated with technological change and space exploration, are one of the first people to try new products, and monitor global sociopolitical trends, then give yourself five points.

c. I am committed to being the best.   1 2 3 4 5

If you have a habit of doing just enough to get by and are usually late (even if it is only by 5 minutes) for social and professional events, then give yourself one point. If you are the type of person who strives to be the best in everything you pursue, who takes pleasure in going beyond the call of duty, who is willing to learn new things, and who believes that there is always a better way, then give yourself five points.

d. I am market-driven and customer-oriented.   1   2   3   4   5

If you don't like meeting other people and believe that you always know what is best, then give yourself one point. If you enjoy helping other people, even strangers, and are always open to other people's ideas for how things (including yourself) can be improved, then give yourself five points.

e. I value employees.   1   2   3   4   5

If you prefer to work alone; believe that if you want the job done right, you're going to have to do it yourself; have been divorced at least once; and feel that people have to be gluttons for punishment to want to have children today, then give yourself one point. If you believe that work can be a rewarding experience, that people will be responsible if you give them responsibility, and that your best employees should have the opportunity to become partners or buy stock in your business, then give yourself five points.

f. I am realistic.   1   2   3   4   5

If you believe that if you have faith, things will work out for the best, that good intentions will always prevail, and that hard work is all that it takes to succeed, then give yourself one point. If you believe that life is what you make it, that the deck is stacked against a new business, and that most business decisions are judgment calls, then give yourself five points.

g. I am tolerant of the tedium.   1   2   3   4   5

If you won't do your own tax preparation, haven't waxed your car yourself in the last two years, and haven't flossed your teeth since your last dental appointment, then give yourself one point. If you don't put off doing tedious, time-consuming tasks like those mentioned, then give yourself five points.

h. I am resilient.   1   2   3   4   5

If you are hesitant about trying something you have never done before, are not willing to speak in public, and mope around after you have failed at something, then give yourself one point. If you look forward to new challenges and traveling to foreign lands; thrive on unstructured, ambiguous, uncertain situations; and bounce back with renewed vigor after experiencing a setback, then give yourself five points.

i. I am decisive and focused.   1 2 3 4 5

If you have difficulty making even the simplest decisions, like what you are going to eat for breakfast or the clothes you are going to wear to work, then give yourself one point. If you have a clear idea of what you want and what needs to be done, and can make decisions quickly (without analyzing things to death to avoid making mistakes), then give yourself five points.

Self-Test: Part 1 Score Sheet

How do I rate on the nine entrepreneurial qualities?

Quality:	Low	Medium			High
1. Opportunity seeker	1	2	3	4	5
2. Future-oriented	1	2	3	4	5
3. Committed to being the best	1	2	3	4	5
4. Market-driven and customer-oriented	1	2	3	4	5
5. Value employees	1	2	3	4	5
6. Realistic	1	2	3	4	5
7. Tolerant of the tedium	1	2	3	4	5
8. Resilient	1	2	3	4	5
9. Decisive and focused	1	2	3	4	5

Total points = _____

Scoring Breakdown

1. If your total score is *less than 25 points,* then get a job with a company that offers job security or try to win the lottery so that you don't need to work.
2. If your total score is *between 25 and 35 points,* then take a look at your attitudes and see if you can adopt a more entrepreneurial approach to life.
3. If your total score is *more than 35 points,* then you have some of the entrepreneurial qualities. This is no guarantee of success, but it means that you can proceed to the next chapter.

2
Identifying New Business Opportunities

AN OPPORTUNITY CAN BE FOUND WITHIN EVERY PROBLEM

Congratulations! If you are reading this chapter, you feel that you have the personal qualities it takes to start a business. The quiz at the end of this chapter will help you determine whether you have the business skills you need in order to start and run a business. You are now at the point where you need to answer the question, "What type of business should I start?" The greatest mistake people make when they start a new business is to try to sell products that they like. People who like reading want to start bookstores. People who like animals want to start pet shops. People who like to dine out or to cook want to start restaurants. This may be human nature, but it is a backward approach to starting a business.

The first law of entrepreneurship is, "You need to offer what people want to buy, not what you want to sell." Customers do not buy what you like, they buy what they want. The first step in determining what type of business to start is to do market research or to "listen to the market." Too many people start a "business in search of customers." This tends to be an exercise in futility. By listening to the market, you can find "customers in search of a business."

CREATING CUSTOMERS

Customers in search of a business are people who are not having their particular needs and wants met well enough or at all. Think about your own purchasing behavior. If existing businesses do not offer exactly what you want, then either you do not buy at all or you buy the closest alternative available but continue to search for the business that will give you what you are looking for.

Market research tries to identify needs that people have that are not being met, the number of people with those needs, what exactly they are looking for, how much they are willing to pay, how you can get in touch with them, and what is the best way to get what they want to them. There are about 300,000,000 people in the United States. Few of those people are getting exactly what they want. Therefore, there are millions of customers in search of a business.

When customers finally find a business that offers what they want, they tend to thank the manager for taking their money. They also tell their friends, neighbors, and colleagues about that business. How's that for free advertising? The more you offer what people want to buy, the less they are affected by your competitors' advertisements, price cutting, or location. A high degree of customer loyalty is one of the factors that separates the winners from the losers.

Anyone thinking of starting a new business must heed the saying, "The purpose of a business is to create and maintain customers for a profit." Almost every new business starts without the benefit of having any customers. Getting customers is only half the battle. Keeping them is the other half.

Quite a few businesses have failed because their managers saw themselves as selling products and services. Successful entrepreneurs know that a business makes a profit only when it provides satisfaction. Numerous large firms have based their advertising programs on the "marketing concept" of listening to the market and tailoring their offerings to meet the needs of specific groups of customers. Toyota's slogan has been, "You asked for it, you got it!" Penney's slogan at one time was, "At Penney's we know what you're looking for!" Burger King is known for its "Have it your way!" slogan. When the other hamburger franchises were out of tune with a number of people's preferences, Wendy's initiated its "Where's the beef?" ad campaign.

When you offer what people want, at a price that is fair, in a reasonably convenient manner, then you are one step closer to creating a customer. You may be able to sell something you stock to some people, but you have not created customers unless they want to come back and have talked favorably about your business to people they know. When you are trying to decide what to offer, remember the saying, "Successful businesses offer goods and services that don't come back, to people who do!"

MAINTAINING CUSTOMERS

To maintain customers, you need to stay in tune with them and change your business to meet their changing needs and expectations. This is a never-ending process. Even the most successful businesses lose customers on a regular basis. A rule of thumb is that the average business loses one-third of its customers each year. Customers move away, switch to a competitor whose offerings are more consistent with their desires, lose their need for such a product or service, or die. Therefore, even established businesses need to continuously listen to the market to find customers in search of a business and change their operations to stay in tune with their existing customers.

New businesses and businesses that want to grow have to work even harder to establish or expand their customer base. Managers who do not listen to the market or who take their customers for granted are destined to fail. If you conduct market research on an ongoing basis, treat each customer as if that person is your business's only customer, and fine-tune your business to what the market wants, then you will increase your likelihood of being successful. Remember, the marketplace is like the ocean's tide. Instead of trying to change it, concentrate your attention on where it is and where it is heading. If you can sense upcoming changes and offer the market what it wants, the way it wants it, and when it wants it, you may find owning a business to be a mentally and financially rewarding endeavor.

ARE THERE ANY OPPORTUNITIES LEFT FOR NEW BUSINESSES?

Quite a few people are skeptical about whether someone can start a new business in a world that appears to be dominated by large firms. The perennial questions are, "Can a new David compete in a world of Goliaths?" and "Are new businesses relegated to living off big businesses' table scraps?"

The answer to the first question is a resounding, "Yes—they can compete." The answer to the second question is, "No—they don't have to eat table scraps." Nearly every large firm was once a new small business that was able to establish itself in a world of larger competitors.

Yet the most likely way to succeed is not to compete against bigger firms. New businesses should avoid competing head-to-head with larger, established businesses. This is particularly true when it comes to price competition and the breadth and depth of product selection. Most large firms enjoy economies of scale. They can buy their goods in larger quantities and qualify for quantity discounts. If they are manufacturers, they may be able to produce the product at a lower unit cost. Larger firms are usually able to carry a broader selection of products than smaller businesses. For example, large retail stores may carry numerous brands (product breadth) and a number of models (product depth) in their effort to attract a large number and variety of customers. Some "megastores" try to offer one-stop shopping by having something for everyone.

FIND GAPS IN THE MARKET

Your new business may have a better chance of succeeding if you do not try to compete with larger firms on the same basis. Instead, you should try to identify things that consumers want and that larger firms do not offer well enough or at all. In certain cases, being bigger does not guarantee being better. Almost all large businesses have weaknesses; it is impossible to be everything to everybody.

Big businesses are built on compromise. They need to generate a high volume of business to cover the investment associated with the large-scale operations that are needed to serve large markets and provide economies of scale. Economies of scale are possible only when you can serve mass markets or large groups of consumers with similar interests. Wal-Mart, Lowe's, and most other large retailers use this strategy. Ironically, their attempt to keep their costs down so that they can appeal to consumers via lower prices has created opportunities for smaller businesses. As already noted, most attempts by small retail businesses to compete on price alone are likely to be futile. A new venture's probability of success will be much higher if it is willing to compete on other bases, where big businesses may not be able to be as competitive in creating and maintaining customers for a profit. Your business's competitive advantage may rest on your ability to tailor your offering to a small group of consumers' (one market segment's) needs very well rather than to a lot of people's (the overall market's) needs in a lukewarm manner. You have a better chance of succeeding if you strive to *delight* a few people rather than just *satisfy* the masses.

The following example illustrates how a new business may be able to attract customers. Mary Smith graduated from Midwestern State University 10 years ago with a degree in agricultural sciences. Since that time, she has been working for the county agricultural extension service in Middletown, Illinois. The idea of having her own business has been on her mind for the last few years. Mary is considering starting a lawn and garden center because her professional life has revolved around helping people grow plants. A few months ago, Mary realized that it would be worthwhile to ask Susan Williams out to lunch. Susan was one of Mary's sorority sisters at Midwestern State University and is now a business consultant with a regional accounting firm. Mary conveyed her interest in starting a lawn and garden center and her desire to open it in her hometown. Susan informed Mary that she had already violated the first two business commandments: (1) "Thou shall not start a business just because you like the products" and (2) "Thou shall not open a business in a geographic area just because you live there or would like to live there." Susan indicated that there might be better business opportunities and better locations. Mary insisted, however, that her mind was made up and that she was prepared to accept the risk.

Their conversation then shifted to what Mary could do to increase her chances of success. One of Mary's first concerns involved how she would be able to compete against the large discount store in her hometown. Mary had learned that the garden shop at the large discount store offered a 50-pound bag of lime for $1.39. She found this disturbing because the suppliers of that brand of lime had told her that the price to small retailers was $1.40 per bag. Mary would have to pay more for a bag than what the discount store was selling it for!

The suppliers suggested a retail price that would be a 40 percent markup on cost. That meant that Mary would be charging $1.96 for the same 50-pound bag of lime that the discount store was selling for $1.39. Mary would have a significant price disadvantage. To make matters worse, the price differential on many of the products she planned to carry was not that different from the price differential on the bags of lime. Some suppliers even indicated that her business was too small for them to supply. Mary wondered how she would be able to create and maintain customers for a profit if she had this price differential and might not even be able to carry some of the most popular brands. In spite of her frustration, however, Mary believed that there was an opportunity for a really good lawn and garden center. If she could come up with ways to beat the competition, she would continue investigating the possibility of starting a garden center.

Susan used the lime example to illustrate how a small business may be able to establish a competitive advantage. She identified the following possibilities:

1. Identify a target market—a specific group of consumers who will be doing a lot of landscaping and who are not located within a 10-minute drive of the large discount store. Many consumers are not willing to drive all the way across town to save a few cents. This is particularly true for consumers who have high incomes and who value their free time.
2. Offer bags of lime in different sizes. Who says everyone wants a 50-pound bag? Some people won't even be able to lift a 50-pound bag. Other people won't want to store what they don't use. Mary may be able to carry or create her own 10-pound bags—or, better yet, sell lime by the pound. That way she will be able to offer her customers the quantity of lime that they want to buy and use rather than some standard size that is convenient for the firm packaging the lime.
3. Provide a soil analysis service for her customers for free or at a minimal charge. Mary will then be able to determine whether her customers need lime and how much they will need.
4. Offer a delivery service for purchases over $20. Most discount stores either do not deliver or charge a $50 delivery fee.
5. Rent lime spreaders for a nominal rate. After all, how many consumers want to buy a $30 spreader that will be used only once a year?
6. Offer an application service, where one of her employees would spread the lime for a reasonable fee.

There are many other ways in which Mary could offer her customers far more than a bag of lime. The ideal situation would be a service package in which customers would call her garden center and have one of her employees (1) come out to do a soil sample, (2) determine the amount of lime needed, (3) apply the lime periodically, and (4) have it charged to the customer's credit card. This service package would cost between $30 and $50 per half-acre yard. The service could be available on an annual contract basis for individual residences and institutions.

Mary could offer a similar service for applying weed-killing fertilizer in the spring, greening fertilizer in August, and rye grass in October. She could also offer a flower planting service throughout the year.

The more that Mary can give targeted groups of customers exactly what they want (products, services, and information), the less the price differential for the bag of lime will affect her business. By offering her customers a "have it your way" approach to doing business, she may be able to create and maintain customers for a profit. The discount store may have an average lime-related sale of less than $2. Mary may be able to generate an average lime-related sale of $25 by providing the additional services. Some homeowners do not have a clue about what they need to do to keep their yards in good shape. They are not looking for the lowest price. Mary's competitive advantage would be in *providing answers to their questions* and *solutions to their problems* rather than just in selling them 50-pound bags of lime.

It is safe to say that not all of Mary's customers would be interested in these services. This is why large discount stores would not consider offering them. Large discount stores are geared to consumers who tend to be price-sensitive and willing to do the work themselves. Mary believes that a segment of the overall market would be delighted to substitute their money for their time and effort.

Mary will have a better chance of being successful if she adopts the "Swiss cheese" approach. Every marketplace has "holes" of opportunity for small businesses. These holes represent gaps in the market where big businesses cannot go or choose not to go. Big businesses tend to be a bit choosy. They will not locate in every small town, they cannot meet everyone's unique needs, they do not change very quickly, and they are not very flexible. For example, small clothing boutiques exist because large department stores tend to offer products that will appeal to most people. Boutiques are designed to offer people with money and particular tastes a select line of products and services that they cannot find at the larger stores. Discriminating buyers do not want to buy something right off the rack that can be found at most stores; they want things that are unique.

There are at least two other areas of opportunity for new businesses. Opportunities exist for new businesses to serve or supply larger businesses. Most large businesses rely on smaller businesses to supply them with products and services. Larger firms frequently look to employment agencies, maintenance businesses, trucking firms, and numerous other types of businesses as an alternative to performing these functions for themselves.

The service part of the economy is expected to continue growing in the years ahead. This represents a particularly attractive area of opportunity for new businesses. Service businesses usually require less money to start on a small scale. Also, large service businesses may not have a cost advantage because service businesses have limited economies of scale. The relative competitive strength of smaller businesses is evident in the lawn and garden center example. At first glance, it appeared that Mary was selling products, such as lime, fertilizer, and plants. However, a closer look reveals that Mary's strength would be in the services she offered.

YES, THERE ARE OPPORTUNITIES!

The moral of this chapter is that if you can offer products and services that people want but cannot find at existing businesses, then you may be able to create and maintain customers for a profit. If you can provide goods and services in a quicker, more convenient, less expensive, or higher-quality manner, you may have an edge in the competitive arena. The bottom line is that you should start with a real opportunity, not just a personal desire. You should start with the current going in your favor. Mary was reducing her chances for success by selecting her business before she determined whether it was a viable opportunity. The best way to start a business is to spend a considerable amount of time analyzing the market for opportunities.

WHAT KIND OF BUSINESS SHOULD I START?

The following six-step process can be used in deciding what type of business to start:

Step 1: List problems in the marketplace.

Step 2: Identify corresponding business opportunities.

Step 3: Determine the needed capabilities and resources.

Step 4: Project the financial dimensions.

Step 5: Rate the opportunities in terms of personal preferences, financial worthiness, and perceived risk.

Step 6: Select the business opportunity to pursue.

Only after you have identified the opportunities, evaluated your capabilities, and determined the potential profitability of each potential business venture will you be in a position to consider starting your own business.

Step 1: List Problems in the Marketplace
The first step in starting a new venture is to listen to the marketplace. The prospective entrepreneur needs to generate a list of areas where people's needs are not being met well enough or at all. It is particularly important that you do not restrict yourself to one particular type of product, service, or geographic area. You should keep an open mind and a broad perceptual field.

It has been said that a decision will be only as good as the best alternative. This also applies to starting a new venture. Your business will never be any better than the strength of the market need. This situation is similar to a horse race. Someone once observed that no jockey ever carried the horse across the finish line. Regardless of how astute you may be in business (as a rider), if the market (the horse) isn't there to support you, you will not go very far.

You need to direct your attention to generating a sizable list of market problems. The quantity of problems is more important than their respective quality at this time. In subsequent steps, you will look at the relative quality of each problem.

The Market Gap Approach to Identifying Problems

Richard M. White, Jr., offered an interesting approach to identifying problems or "gaps" in the marketplace. According to White, you can find opportunities in almost any aspect of life. He uses the example of looking at problems encountered by adults. Through a sequence of questions, White divides adult life into work versus leisure. He then narrows his focus to the time of day when adults encounter problems. In this example, he concentrates his attention on problems people encounter "after work but before dinner on weekdays." White's list of problems includes fatigue, heavy traffic, feet are tired and hot, clothes are rumpled and cling, the dog must be taken out to do its business, telephone solicitors are irritating, and so on. White indicates that hundreds of problems are common just during the brief "leisure-adult workday postwork-predinner" time interval.[1] The same market gap analysis could be applied to other aspects of life, such as (1) adults traveling with preschool-age children via airlines, (2) owners of powerboats over 20 feet long after the summer is over, or (3) college freshmen moving away from home for the first time.

You need to make an extra effort to avoid judging the relative merit of each problem at this time. In Step 1, you will only list problems in the marketplace. Step 2 is designed to ascertain whether business opportunities may be hidden within the list of problems.

Step 2: Identify Corresponding Business Opportunities

You should now direct your attention to each of the problems or gaps you have identified and determine whether it can be transformed into a business opportunity. One of the interesting things about this step is that each problem or gap may foster numerous different business opportunities. People who have idle time while they are in airports waiting for flights provide a good example.

Opportunities to reduce the idle time could include (1) a 1-hour laundry service for the business traveler who is going from city to city and wants to travel light; (2) a "nap hotel" that provides a Pullman-type berth with an alarm, permitting the traveler to nap in privacy for an hour or more; (3) a business services center providing fax, photocopying, access to computers, secretarial assistance, a message center, and even a private meeting room; or (4) a health club providing massage, hot tub, sauna, and so on, to take the edge off traveling. One enterprising individual started a business to turn idle time into recreational time. He rented a small space and offers a golf driving range that videotapes your swing and provides feedback on your drive.

Each problem area or gap needs to be "exploded" into various possible business opportunities. Step 2 calls for an open mind and mental dexterity. The questions "Which businesses can I do?" and "Which ones will be profitable?" should be avoided at this time. Step 2 deals only with whether there may be ways to address the problems.

In the United States, not to mention other countries, there are millions of customers in search of businesses. Nearly every person in the marketplace has needs that are not being met well enough or at all. The people who started some of this nation's most successful businesses listened to the market. They knew that within every problem, there may be a disguised opportunity. They knew that by identifying problems in the marketplace, they would find customers in search of a business. Big problems mean big opportunities. Businesses that have become household names were started by entrepreneurs who listened to the market. They heard people saying, "I wish there was a business that . . ." Then they created businesses to offer what the market wanted.

Some of Today's Most Popular Businesses Were Yesterday's New Ventures

In the late 1960s, Perry Mendel kept hearing parents of young children express frustration over the lack of day-care facilities. He researched the existing state of day care in the South and found that most day-care operations were run as individual businesses. He also learned that many of these facilities were located in people's homes. Existing day-care facilities were not set up to provide day care for a large number of children. Their locations may have been convenient for the owners of the day-care businesses, but they were not convenient for the parents of the children.

Perry Mendel's research indicated that most existing day-care customers were still in search of a business. His study of trends also revealed that the market for day-care services would experience rapid growth for quite a few years. Existing industry trends suggested that nearly 50 percent of all women would be employed by 1980. He recognized that with more women working, especially women with preschool-age children, there would be a greater need for high-quality day-care services.

Perry Mendel believed a professionally managed day-care business could be set up that would offer first-class service at locations that were on the way to and from work. By providing the latest toys and recreational facilities, including a swimming pool in warmer geographic areas, and offering nutritious meals at a price no higher than that charged by traditional mom-and-pop backyard day-care businesses, these centers could capture a significant part of the market. Mendel's Kinder-Care, Inc., has become the largest day-care business in the free world.

Kinder-Care, Inc., is not the only "find a gap in the market and fill it" success story. Every large business started with a person who listened to the market and had the mental dexterity to identify the opportunities that were disguised as problems. Henry and Richard Bloch (they chose to use the name Block for their business) listened to the market and heard people who were frustrated with having to prepare their tax returns each year. The Blochs recognized that millions of people did not know how to prepare their tax returns, wanted a second opinion so that they could sleep at night, or were looking for ways to reduce their taxes. They found that people would be willing to pay a small fee if reliable tax preparation could be provided at convenient times and locations. The Blochs figured that they would be very successful if they could capture even 1 percent of the market. H & R Block has become the nation's largest tax preparation firm.

In the 1950s, Anthony A. Martino sensed another problem experienced by millions of people at one time or another. He recognized that America had become a society of automobile owners. He also realized that automobiles frequently break down. Anthony Martino analyzed the various auto problems and the extent to which customers were still in search of a business. He knew that he would be better off repairing cars rather than manufacturing them, because service businesses usually take far less capital to start and because he would be facing less formidable competitors.

Anthony Martino listened to the market and found a gap. Sooner or later, most cars need transmission repair or replacement. He heard the market saying that people were unable to have their needs met well enough by the existing businesses. Auto dealers specialized in selling cars, and service stations specialized in selling gasoline. Few businesses specialized in transmission repair or replacement. Anthony Martino carefully analyzed customer needs and the nature and extent of competition. He then developed AAMCO Transmission Services. He chose the name AAMCO because it would appear near the beginning of the Yellow Pages section and because it used his initials, "A. A. M." His franchise became the world's largest transmission specialist.

In 1972, Anthony Martino realized that there must be other problems in the automobile industry that were business opportunities in disguise. Again, he listened to the market. This time he found that cars have a bad habit of hitting other cars. Sooner or later, most people get into an accident that requires bodywork and repainting. Anthony Martino found that few businesses specialized in this side of auto work. As with transmissions, customers were in search of a business. When he had to select a name for his business, he merely reversed his initials and started MAACO for (Martino, Anthony A., Company). Millions of cars have been painted or repaired at MAACO centers. Today, there are more 500 franchise outlets.

Kurt Ziebart was another person who saw the almost unlimited opportunities created by the millions of automobiles. In the 1960s, he recognized people's growing desire to keep their cars longer as a way to beat inflation. He also recognized that car bodies tended to rust out. He found customers in search of a business. He developed Ziebart Rustproofing Centers. For less than 2 percent of the price of a new car and one day's time, his rustproofing process would extend the life of a car by a couple of years. The cost-benefit ratio, convenient locations, and one-day service proved to be a formula for success. There are over 500 Ziebart outlets in 44 countries.

Ray Kroc had been employed as a food service equipment salesperson. However, when the company he worked for refused to consider distribution of a new five-spindle mixer, which Kroc felt would increase his sales of drink cups, he decided that it was time to start his own business. He obtained the national marketing rights to the mixer and started his own company in 1939. While he was traveling in California, he stopped in to see one of his customers to learn why that customer was buying so many mixers. When Ray Kroc saw the drive-in restaurant run by the McDonald brothers, he saw more than a place that sold a lot of hamburgers. He saw a concept that could be franchised from coast to coast. Ray Kroc recognized that California was a good barometer of changing tastes in America and the growing desire for convenience.

In 1947, Burton Baskin and Irv Robbins recognized that the population was interested in variety and that vanilla, strawberry, and chocolate ice cream were no longer sufficient to meet the market's interest in different flavors. They started Baskin-Robbins 31 Flavors. Years later, they recognized that, while fast-food restaurant franchises were growing in popularity, they did not offer much in the way of desserts. Baskin and Robbins used what is called a "parasite" approach and located their franchises as close as possible to fast-food franchises. This marketing decision was beneficial because they did not have to do as much advertising. The need to invest in large parking lots was also reduced. Quite a few of their customers just walked over to Baskin-Robbins from the fast-food franchises. The Baskin-Robbins formula for success still appears to be working. There are over 4500 stores worldwide.

Some of today's most prominent e-commerce businesses grew out of simple observations of gaps in the marketplace. Jeff Bezos started Amazon.com when he saw a statistic about how business on the Internet would grow by 2300 percent. David Filo and Jerry Yang started Yahoo! when they recognized that people needed a better way to search for information. When his girlfriend said, "There must be a better way to buy and sell Pez dispensers," Pierre Omidyar formed eBay. He recognized that the Internet could be a great way to bring buyers and sellers together.

Other businesses, while less well known, also illustrate what happens when someone sees a gap in the market and fills it. Here are just a few examples:

1. *Aqua Vox, Inc.* Michael Benjamin recognized that one of the most frustrating aspects of scuba diving was the inability of scuba divers to communicate with one another while they were underwater. He developed a device that sells for $100 that permits underwater communication. Michael's problem/opportunity/capability/profitability equation was right on target; his firm's first-year sales exceeded $1 million.[2]

2. *My Own Meals, Inc.* Mary Anne Jackson was able to turn a nighttime routine into a new business. She recognized that one of the cumbersome aspects of being a parent was preparing a child's lunch for the next day. Her company was the first to market packaged meals for kids aged 2 to 10 on a large scale. The entrees are pressure-cooked and vacuum-sealed in plastic pouches. Her meals, which can be microwaved, are available in numerous grocery store chains.[3]

3. *Tweedies Optical, Inc.* Tweedy Prager encountered a problem finding appropriate eyeglasses for her 3-year-old twins. She found that most eyeglasses for children were merely downsized versions of adult

frames. She started her business by offering a line of "spiffy specks" eyeglass frames that are attractive and fun to wear. Her line of frames for kids from 4 to 8 years old was so well received that she developed a line of frames for children between 9 and 13 years old.[4]

4. *Abt Enterprises.* Nancy Abt came to the conclusion that there must be a better way to help people cool off in the heat of the summer. She developed and received a patent on her product, The Cool Advantage. Her product is like a collar that wraps around your neck and holds blocks of foam that are soaked in salt water. When the blocks, which are in polyurethane insulating bags, are frozen, they are colder than regular ice. Her product has a cloth cover that is seamed with Velcro strips. The design enables people to wear it while playing tennis or any other sport. Nancy then directed her attention to other target markets as additional potential customers for her product who might benefit from its ability to provide either warmth or cooling. Particular attention was directed to anyone who may need heat or muscle relief, such as chefs or people who suffer from multiple sclerosis.[5]

5. *Pacific Bio Systems, Inc.* Arthur Peterson and Francis Keery demonstrated that if you develop a product that is quicker and better, you may be able to get consumers to switch to it. They recognized a problem experienced by medical personnel in every hospital. Their research revealed that it usually takes doctors 10 minutes to scrub their hands and arms before surgery. They developed an automatic hand-washing machine called Stat Scrub. Doctors place their hands and forearms into "sleeves" that clean them in less than 2 minutes. The machine is also better at eliminating bacteria than manual scrubbing. Like Nancy Abt, Arthur and Francis then looked for additional groups of consumers who might be in search of a better and quicker way to clean their hands and arms. Potential target markets included people who manufacture chemicals, pharmaceuticals, and computer components.[6]

Some of Today's Gaps May Produce Tomorrow's Success Stories

The preceding examples reinforce the point that listening to the market can pay off. Thousands of new businesses will be started this year by people who find gaps in the market. Some of the start-ups are almost destined to succeed. As the following businesses illustrate, that entrepreneurial strategy of starting a business where there are customers in search of a business is still one of the best ways to identify opportunities for a new business.

1. *Ruff Rider LLC.* Carl Goldberg founded Ruff Rider LLC in 1995 to sell canine vehicle restraint harnesses. When Goldberg's dog almost lost its life by taking out his car's front windshield in a car accident, he vowed that he would never put his dog at risk again. With the guidance of his veterinarian, he created the Ruff Rider canine vehicle restraint system. It is available in numerous sizes. He noted, "There are 26 states with laws stating it's illegal to transport a living animal over the road in a moving vehicle in a way that [might] cause tortuous injury or death."[7]

2. *Waterstone Medical Inc.* Dan Tribastone provides a good example of finding an opportunity where you work. He was working as a registered nurse in an orthopedic operating room in 1994 when he observed a serious shortcoming during orthopedic surgery. He noticed that the body part undergoing reconstruction is constantly flushed with water. An operation could use 75 to 100 liters of fluid. Yet the canisters being used were so small that the operation required 25 to 35 canisters. Nurses were constantly having to disconnect and reconnect containers. After experimenting with various containers, he started selling a disposable 3.5-gallon canister that cut the number of connections to a fifth of what it had been.[8]

3. *Fuel Belt Inc.* Vinu Malik provides a good example of how an opportunity can be found through recreational activities. Malik had been competing in triathlons for 8 years. He and other triathletes were frustrated with how large and cumbersome the bottles were that they used to stay hydrated. He decided that he could develop a better water system. He developed a system in which four small, flat bottles are attached to a belt. His product caught on because the weight of the water could be spread out around the runner's waist. Before long, his new belt became the official worldwide Hydration Belt of Ironman.[9]

The preceding examples are only a fraction of the thousands of new product and service opportunities that exist today. They also illustrate two interesting points. First, listening to the market to identify customers in search of a business may be far more fruitful than trying to generate new business ideas from scratch. The sequence market needs first, product or service offering second is what separates the entrepreneur from the inventor. The best entrepreneurs begin by identifying unmet needs rather than product or service ideas. If the entrepreneur can identify an unmet need, in most instances he or she can develop or contract with someone else to develop the product or service to meet the need.

Second, they demonstrate that new business opportunities are not restricted to high-technology products. The most promising new business opportunities involve improving everyday life for regular people. Fred DeLuca demonstrated that you don't need to have an MBA or a high-tech product in order to succeed. After graduating from high school in 1965, Fred used a $1000 loan from a family friend, Pete Buck, to create what is now Subway Restaurants. Fred and Pete wanted to open a submarine sandwich shop that would provide an alternative to the typical fast-food hamburger.

Starbuck's Coffee Company provides another example of how perceptiveness and the ability to fill gaps in the market can foster exceptional growth. Most people considered coffee to be a mature market. However, Howard Schultz was able to take coffee drinking to a whole new level. Some people buy a cup of coffee from a Starbuck's store at least 5 days a week.

Each of these businesses is an example of how an entrepreneur can take a fairly common aspect of human behavior and create a business. Simply putting a bit of a twist on a product or service that makes it more in tune with the market's needs than the products or services offered by existing businesses may put you on the road to having a viable new business venture. The examples also illustrate the point that perceptiveness may be more important than innovative ability. If you can identify a need, you can probably find an innovative way to meet it. If you start with an innovative product, however, you may not be able to find people who want to buy it.

These examples illustrate the value of listening to the market. The "listening for gaps" approach is beneficial when you are trying to identify what types of goods and services have potential. Other approaches are also available.

The Market-Area Saturation Approach May Help Identify Opportunities
The market-area saturation approach involves looking at one or more cities to see if there is room for another business. Industry data may show that it usually takes a certain number of people to support each type of business. The following examples of the average number of inhabitants per store have been provided by the *Census of Retail Trade:*

Bookstores: 26,000 people per store

Nursery and garden supply: 26,000 people per store

Women's clothing: 5000 people per store

Furniture stores: 3000 people per store

Florists: 8600 people per store

If you want to see whether there is an opportunity for a stationery store in a town with a population of 60,000 people, check the data. Census data indicate that there are, on average, 33,000 inhabitants per stationery store. If the area already has three stationery stores, there may be little room or opportunity for another store.

A word of caution needs to be provided here. Many businesses fail because they were started in a town where the owner lived or wanted to live. This restricts your opportunities and may be a fatal mistake for your business. As mentioned earlier, you cannot change the market. If you want to have the highest probability of success, you must be willing to locate your business where there are customers in search of a business—not where you want to live.

The market-area saturation approach is helpful as a quick indicator of a business opportunity, but it has numerous potential drawbacks. It does not take into consideration whether the existing stores are large or small, successful or unsuccessful, or whether they are independent, franchises, or part of a chain. The method also does not take into consideration the exact locations of the businesses, the brands they offer, or their pricing strategy. It also fails to take the nature of the population into account. A town with a large number of retirees may be entirely different from a town that is made up primarily of blue-collar families, is oriented toward tourists, or has a large university.

The Segmentation Approach May Help Identify Gaps

Another way to identify business opportunities is called the *segmentation approach*. With this technique, you start by looking at the overall market for a particular product or service. Next, you try to identify different types (segments) of customers and the extent to which their needs are being met. This approach may incorporate certain aspects of the market-area saturation approach. However, even if the market-area saturation approach indicates that there are already enough businesses of that type in the area, specific opportunities may still exist if the area has a large number of people with high levels of income who are not having their particular needs met. This might be the case with Mary's Lawn and Garden Center. The segmentation approach may also reveal that a certain part of the larger area has been growing rapidly and that there is no business of that type within a 5-minute drive to meet this segment's needs. This approach has been popular for determining the need and location for neighborhood convenience stores, pizza delivery services, car washes, and so on.

This approach is particularly useful in identifying whether opportunities exist for specialty businesses, such as French restaurants, gourmet shops, travel agencies, or yard services. A particular segment of people who are similar in terms of education, age, income, market value of household, type of job, number of children living at home, and other such factors may have a propensity to be customers in search of specific types of businesses.

The segmentation strategy is based on the notion that no business, no matter how large, can be all things to all people at all times. Particular groups of people have particular needs. Even if the number of businesses in a market appears to exceed the saturation level, sizable opportunities may exist. The hotel-motel business illustrates this point. Some motel franchises recently introduced "suites" for people who want to meet with other people while they are traveling. One franchise directed its advertising primarily to female travelers. Even though the number of hotels and motels appeared to be at the saturation level, the executives of this motel franchise found that this segment of business travelers was still in search of a business that would offer facilities more conducive to conducting business.

This strategy is particularly attractive to women traveling alone. The company's market research indicated that many women feel uncomfortable with traditional motel rooms. The traditional motel room with only a bed and a bathroom did not meet some of the changing needs in the marketplace. A couple of other motel and hotel franchisors recognized another segment of the market that was not having its needs met. They found that people who are staying for more than a few days may also want a small kitchen so that they do not have to go to restaurants for every meal.

These businesses recognized the existence of a sizable segment of people who want a motel to be an office and another sizable segment who want it to be a home away from home. Instead of trying to be all things to all people, each franchise wanted to be the "best" for a specific segment of people. Business travelers with particular needs became the target market segment for each motel franchise.

Perceptiveness May Be More Important than Inventiveness

The interesting point about all these examples is that none of these people or businesses that have been so successful "invented" their basic products or services. Ray Kroc (McDonald's) didn't invent the hamburger, Perry Mendel (Kinder-Care) didn't invent day care for kids, Fred DeLuca (Subway) didn't invent the submarine sandwich, and Howard Schultz (Starbuck's) didn't invent coffee. However, these entrepreneurs were perceptive and resourceful. They identified a problem or a gap in the market and turned it into a business opportunity.

Another way to develop a list of product or service ideas is to review issues of popular entrepreneurial magazines such as *Inc.* and *Entrepreneur* for the last few years. These magazines provide numerous examples of new business ideas, discussions of emerging trends, and profiles of successful start-ups. Their Web sites also provide a wealth of information, tools, and resources. *Entrepreneur* magazine offers manuals on how to start various types of businesses, such as a restaurant, a bed and breakfast, a child-care service, a personal concierge service, a home inspection service, a staffing service, and dozens of other businesses.

Step 3: Determine the Needed Capabilities and Resources

Now that you have listed problems in the marketplace and identified the corresponding business opportunities, the time has come to determine the capabilities and resources needed for each of the opportunities that may have merit. People often make the mistake of ruling out various opportunities as they develop and review the list generated in Step 2 because they are not familiar with the business or lack experience in it. They tend to investigate only those areas that they already know as an employee or as a customer, or that they can learn in a short period of time.

At first glance, this appears to be a logical approach. This approach, however, is called "entrepreneurship by Braille." When you use it, you tend to overlook emerging opportunities or get involved in areas where the market could be saturated quickly. If you can get into a business that easily, then other people can also get into that type of business and become your competitors.

As noted in Step 2, you should be willing to investigate opportunities that may be new to you. You might say, "What about the need for experience in that type of business that was emphasized at the beginning of this book?" The interesting thing about the six-step process is that if you do a good job in Step 1, you may be able to spot emerging opportunities before other people even see them.

Prior experience is very important, but with sufficient lead time you may be able to gain the experience and education that you need in order to have a chance to beat the odds. The H & R Block example illustrates this point. Henry and Richard Bloch were not certified public accountants, nor did they need to be tax experts as they started Step 2. Because they identified the growing opportunity for individual tax preparation early, they had enough time while studying the market to learn about tax accounting and to gain the necessary experience before they started H & R Block Tax Service.

This process can be accelerated in two ways. First, if you already have a strong background in starting and managing a business, you can hire specialists to deal with the technical side of the business. This is what the Blochs did. Second, you can bring in a partner with strong technical experience in the field instead of hiring someone. This is one of the principal reasons why many new businesses start as partnerships. A partner may be able to contribute valuable knowledge and experience as well as money to the business venture.

In Step 3, you review the list of potential opportunities generated in Step 2 by asking, "For which of these opportunities do I already have, or can I acquire (via learning, hiring, or partnership), the knowledge and experience necessary to create and maintain customers?" If you already have or can acquire what is needed before anyone else even recognizes the opportunity, you may be able to cultivate and capture a large portion of the market. It is interesting to note that few areas of business take years to learn. Most learning takes place in the first year. In 1 year you may learn 80 percent of what can be learned in 5 years of experience. The last 20 percent is also important. But if you are the first to enter the market, the first 80 percent may be enough to keep your head above water while you try to learn the other 20 percent.

If you sense an emerging opportunity early and commit yourself to learning as much as possible before you open your business, you will increase your ability to beat the odds. When competitors enter the market, they will not have the experience factor that will enable you to make better decisions. Remember, most new businesses fail because of trial-and-error management or the lack of a market opportunity. If you have the knowledge and experience and are prepared to offer the market segment you target what it wants, then you may be able to beat the odds.

In Step 3 you should also address various other factors that may be prerequisites for starting a business. Most new ventures have technological, equipment, legal, investment, and time requirements. Technological requirements, which are closely related to skill requirements, refer to how sophisticated the process for providing goods and services may be. Low- or no-technology businesses usually demand minimal skills and equipment. High-technology businesses usually require larger investments in equipment, take more lead time, present difficulties in attracting qualified employees, and encounter more sophisticated competition.

All of the elements in Step 3 tend to be interrelated. In certain cases, you may be able to substitute automated equipment for labor. In other cases, the technology is covered by a patent, and you will have to secure the rights to use it. This may take additional time and increase the amount of investment needed to start your business.

In Step 3, you are not expected to do an in-depth analysis of the necessary capabilities and resources. Instead, it is intended to have you take a look at whether there may be factors that will keep you from pursuing each opportunity. You may find after reviewing trade data that it usually takes $150,000 to start a particular type of business rather than the $60,000 you thought would be needed. You may find that one firm has exclusive patent rights and will not license the rights to its technology or equipment to anyone else. Conversely, you may also find that certain business opportunities that originally seemed complicated may be rather straightforward because equipment and skilled labor are readily available.

When you review the list of opportunities generated in Step 2, you may find that some of them require considerable education or experience. If you do not have the time to learn the skills and you find that no one with the capabilities you lack is available to hire or bring in as a partner, then you should drop that opportunity from the list. You should also drop the opportunity if you find you cannot secure the essential resources.

Step 4: Project the Financial Dimensions of the Remaining Opportunities

The next step in identifying the right new business opportunity for you involves analyzing the financial side of the remaining opportunities. In Step 4 you determine the expected level of sales, expenses, and profit; the initial capital required; and the projected cash flow for each business. Step 1 revealed that needs are not being met in the marketplace. Step 2 revealed that there may be a way to transform the unmet needs into a business opportunity. Step 3 indicated that you have or can develop the capability to offer one or more segments of the market what they want. Step 4 addresses whether you will be able to create and maintain customers for a sufficient level of profit to justify the effort, investment, and risk.

Step 4 attempts to answer three questions. The first question is, "How much money will it take to start each type of business?" The second question is, "What return (profit) on investment will each opportunity yield?" The third question is, "How soon will the business be able to generate a positive cash flow?" The third question is critical because too many businesses run out of money before they can stand on their own.

Step 4 is intended to screen out the opportunities that do not have profit potential. It brings two particular points to the surface. First, it illustrates the need to have a good understanding of financial accounting. Second, it serves as a "reality check" by stressing the need for your new business to have the potential to make a reasonable profit and generate a positive cash flow soon after it opens its doors.

Some people find this second point controversial. These people say that "being their own boss," "interest in the products," or "helping others" is their primary concern. Making a lot of money is important to them, but it is a secondary concern. You may want to start a business for a lot of reasons, including meeting the challenge and being your own boss, but you should go into it with both eyes open. If you want to be your own boss and enjoy the lifestyle associated with having your own business, your business will need to make a profit.

In some cases, starting your own business is like courtship and marriage. There may be a lot of excitement at first, but in too many businesses and marriages, the honeymoon ends sooner than anyone had expected. The moral of the story is that when you are thinking about starting a business, you may go into it for the fun of it, but before you begin, you should be sure that there will be a sufficient profit to keep you going if the fun ends. The emotions associated with doing something special are an integral part of human nature, but they should not overshadow the need for your business to make a profit. The emotional side and your personal preferences will be addressed in Step 5, after you have projected each opportunity's relative financial merit.

Profit is not a dirty word. If your business is making money, you can handle the daily pressures more easily. Profit permits you to hire additional people to ease your own workload. Profit means that you may have money available to meet life's little surprises. Also, if you reach the point where you want to get out, a profitable business is easier to sell than one that has been shaky from the start. Do not start a business as you would start a hobby; too much is at stake.

You should start a business that has the potential to make a good and lasting profit. Even the Internal Revenue Service makes this distinction. If you do not show a profit on a regular basis, the IRS may rule your business a "hobby" and not permit you to list your expenses as business deductions. You may have numerous reasons for starting a business. Profit does not need to be at the top of the list, but your venture's ability to yield a sufficient return needs to be reasonably high on the list.

Two key considerations for Step 4 involve the associated degree of risk. In Step 4 you have to answer the questions, "How much money am I and others willing to put into a business venture?" and "What is my desired return on investment?" The amount of money or capital required to start a business and what it will yield vary with the different types of businesses. Fortunately, data on the amount of money required can be calculated, and data on the average return on investment may be available from trade associations and other financial sources.

The first step in learning more about the financial side of each type of business is to contact the corresponding trade association. Most large libraries have *The Encyclopedia of Associations* (published by Gale Group), which lists the addresses and phone numbers for various trade associations. Most trade associations collect financial information from their members. In some cases, trade associations may provide you with these data free of charge. You can get additional information about certain types of businesses by looking through the *Business Periodicals Index* and *Bacon's Guide to Periodicals*. These and other sources of information can be found in the reference section of most libraries. These indexes identify articles about various types of businesses that have appeared in the last few years. These articles may provide valuable information about market trends as well as current financial data. Five other sources of financial data are also worth reviewing. *Industry Surveys* (published by Standard & Poor's), *Almanac of Business and Industrial Ratios* (published by Aspen Publishers), and *Financial Studies of the Small Business* (published by Financial Research Association) provide key operating ratios for businesses of numerous types and sizes. *Annual Statement Studies* (published by RMA, the Risk Management Association) is particularly helpful. The *U.S. Industrial Outlook* (published annually by the U.S. Department of Commerce) gives historical data, current estimates, and

5-year projections for nearly 200 industries. Bankers and accountants are also in a position to provide additional financial information on various types of businesses.

After reviewing the various sources of financial information and doing some preliminary projections of possible levels of sales and expenses for each of the business opportunities that made it to Step 4, you should have a better idea of average profit levels, initial capital requirements, returns on investment, and the time it will take each type of business to pay its way. You should also have a rough idea of whether you will need to borrow money, bring in a partner, or seek additional investors.

Step 4 is intended to provide an initial view of each business opportunity's relative financial merit. Doing an in-depth financial analysis of a large number of business opportunities would be an insurmountable task. This is why it is important for you to gather as much information as you can from trade associations and other sources of financial information. The more information you can get from external sources, the sooner you can move on to comparing the alternatives in Step 5.

Two points should be stressed at this time. First, one of the appeals of franchises is that most franchisors are in a position to provide financial information on their franchise units. This reduces the need to start from scratch when making financial projections.

Second, you will need to do a more in-depth financial analysis of the business opportunity in your business plan for the venture that comes out on top in the six-step process. Chapters 7 and 8 are designed to assist you with these more comprehensive financial projections.

At this time, you should be able to eliminate those opportunities that do not appear to have profit potential and those with an initial capital requirement that is beyond the amount you will be able to raise. Hopefully, at least a few opportunities will be left for consideration in Step 5.

Step 5: Rate the Opportunities
Each of the remaining business opportunities will now be rated on three important criteria: (1) personal preference, (2) financial worthiness, and (3) perceived risk. As noted earlier, your personal preferences are an important factor to consider when starting a business. However, your personal preferences have been postponed to this step for two reasons. First, considering your preferences earlier would have limited the opportunities to what you know. Second, you might have been seduced by an opportunity that had limited, if any, profit potential. After all, few people enjoy having a business that

goes into bankruptcy. You are more likely to enjoy having your own business if it is generating a healthy financial return.

You should rate each remaining opportunity on a scale of 1 to 5. Ask yourself, "Which of these business opportunities am I willing to invest the next few years of my life in?" If you are excited about the prospect of spending 60 or more hours a week for the next 5 to 10 years without taking a vacation to pursue a particular business opportunity; then give it 5 points. If you find the opportunity to be moderately interesting and would consider hiring someone else to run the business if you get bored, then give it 3 points. If after reviewing an opportunity you find it to be contrary to your interests and you would not even want to be a limited partner in it, then drop it from your list.

Each opportunity should then be rated in terms of its financial worthiness. This involves establishing a minimal profit or return on investment objective. Even though all the opportunities that remain at this point appear to have profit potential, you may need to eliminate the ventures that will not yield a sufficient level of profit to justify the risk. A good place to begin when trying to establish a minimum return objective is to determine the return you could get on your money if it were put in a safe investment like a 5-year certificate of deposit or a medium- to long-term government bond.

If the current return or yield on these safe investments is 8 percent, why should you risk your money for anything less than 8 percent? A good rule of thumb is that your minimum return on investment objective should be greater than the return associated with a safe investment. If you set your minimum return objective at 3 to 4 percentage points higher than the available return on a safe investment, you would use an 11 to 12 percent return as the threshold for evaluating each business opportunity. If you really want to deal with the risk, then set your threshold at twice the safe investment rate.

If your preliminary financial projections for a business opportunity for the first 5 years reveal the average annual return to be at least 30 percent, then give the opportunity 5 points. If the projected annual return is 2 to 3 percentage points above the threshold rate, then give it 3 points. Any business opportunity that appears to be unable to generate at least a 6 percent return on your investment before taxes should be dropped from the list. Even if you gave that opportunity a 5 on the personal preference scale, you should think twice before considering it any further.

Remember, businesses make money; things that take your time and cost you money are hobbies. Quite a few people consider lowering their minimum return objective because they really like a particular business opportunity. People are great rationalizers when they find business opportunities that look like they will be fun. Exercise some self-discipline from the beginning and make a commitment to yourself not to start a business that will not achieve your minimum return objective.

The final criterion for Step 5 is risk. Risk and financial return tend to be related. Generally speaking, the greater the risk, the greater the financial return you should expect if you succeed. Profit is defined as the reward for taking entrepreneurial risk. Step 5 takes risk into account by raising the question, "Are there aspects to this business that are particularly risky?" You need to identify any areas that could jeopardize each opportunity. Particular attention needs to be directed to what are known as "fatal flaws." These are situations in which there may be a regulation that prohibits such a venture in that community (billboards), the need to get a license (a nursing home), or the need for a substantial start-up loan from a bank (most new businesses). Nearly every business idea is based on a few assumptions. You assume a certain rate of technological change, certain economic conditions, certain legal factors, and so on. The fewer things are susceptible to surprises or major disaster, the lower the level of risk.

If the business opportunity is almost certain (a 0.9 or 90 percent chance) to succeed and you consider your data to be sound, then give the opportunity 5 points. This would be the case if you had a patent on a product, had direct access to all the raw materials, and had customers already lined up with money in their hands to buy it. This set of circumstances is relatively rare; most business opportunities have their fair share of risk. Conversely, if the opportunity seems to have substantial risk associated with it at every turn (like a high probability that Wal-Mart will be locating near it), then give it a rating of 1 or 2.

Step 6: Select the Business Opportunity to Pursue
At this point, you should be in a position to narrow down the list of opportunities to one or two potential ventures. Step 6 involves ranking each remaining opportunity on a 15-point scale. The 15-point scale gives each of the three factors (personal preference, financial worthiness, and perceived risk) equal weight. If you want to place more weight on personal preference, then you can either eliminate all opportunities that score less than 3 points on that dimension or double the number of points allocated to that dimension and rank the opportunities on a 20-point scale.

The ideal situation would be to have at least one opportunity score 5s on all three dimensions. This would be particularly appealing if the opportunity had a small initial capital requirement. Don't expect to find an opportunity this good; if it were that good, someone else would already be doing it, so if it seems that good, you must have overlooked something in your research. The following rating of two potential ventures indicates that Opportunity 5 is superior to Opportunity 3 if the three factors are given equal weight. The rating system indicates that Opportunity 5 has more merit even though it has a lower personal preference rating. In the second example, personal preference is given twice the weight of the other factors. In this case, the additional weight for personal preference results in both opportunities being tied with 15 points.

Example of equal weighting (1) for all three dimensions:

Opportunity #3:

Personal preference of (4×1) + Financial worthiness of (4×1) + perceived risk of $(3 \times 1) = 4 + 4 + 3 = 11$ points out of 15 possible points.

Opportunity #5

Personal preference of (3×1) + Financial worthiness of (5×1) + perceived risk of $(4 \times 1) = 3 + 5 + 4 = 12$ points out of 15 possible points.

Example of a higher (2) weighting for the personal preference dimension:

Opportunity #3:

Personal preference of (4×2) + Financial worthiness of (4×1) + perceived risk of $(3 \times 1) = 8 + 4 + 3 = 15$ points out of 20 possible points.

Opportunity #5

Personal preference of (3×2) + Financial worthiness of (5×1) + perceived risk of $(4 \times 1) = 6 + 5 = 4 = 15$ points out of 20 possible points.

Ranking the opportunities on the 15-point scale will direct your attention to the best opportunity for you at this time. It is hoped that the best opportunity scored at least 10 points on the 15-point scale, with no dimension receiving a score of less than 3 points. If none of the opportunities scored 10 or more points, then you have three courses of action. You can accept the best opportunity, even though it scored less than 10 points. You should avoid this temptation. Don't be one of the people who say, "I've already made up my mind; don't confuse me with the facts." Too many people go into business because they didn't know better. Don't be one of the people who knew better but still went into business based on wishful thinking or blind faith. Exercise self-discipline and avoid the temptation to rationalize away the situation by saying, "I'm sure that if I try hard, it will succeed." In this case, the old saying, "It is better to have loved and lost than to never have loved at all" does not apply. It is far better not to start a business that is destined to fail than to start one and fail.

Your second possible course of action would be to start the whole six-step process all over again. You may have missed some problems or opportunities in your initial analysis, or some new ones may have emerged since you started your analysis.

The third possible course of action would be to view the time you invested in pursuing a business opportunity as a learning experience. To paraphrase a Kenny Rogers song, "knowing when to hold them and when to fold them" is an important part of pursuing a business opportunity. It may turn out that there just isn't a good fit between the present market needs and opportunities, your personal capabilities and preferences, your financial expectations, and your tolerance for risk. If this is the case, then it is natural for you to be frustrated with the time and money you spent on your analysis. It may be advisable for you to invest your next couple of years in learning more about business, either through education or through experience. You can then initiate the six-step process again when conditions may be more favorable.

If the six-step process has identified an attractive opportunity, you are now in a position to go on to the seventh step: conducting additional market research to determine whether the market opportunity is truly worthwhile. The eighth step is then to develop the business plan. The following chapters describe the factors that need to be addressed as part of your "blueprint" for building a business that should give you a reasonable chance for beating the odds. As you will see, the time has come for you to roll up your sleeves, put some new batteries in your calculator, sharpen your pencil again (or boot up your electronic spreadsheet software), and do an in-depth analysis of the opportunity you have selected to pursue.

ENTREPRENEURIAL QUALITIES
SELF-TEST: PART 2

1. What length of time am I willing to commit to the venture (3 to 5 years or a career)?

   _____ years

2. 2. What is the maximum amount of money I am willing to invest in the business?

   $_____

3. What is the desired target return on my investment?

   _____ percent

4. What is the minimum rate of return that I will accept on my investment?

   _____ percent

5. What are my strengths (education, training, experience, or personal qualities) for starting and managing a new business?

   a.

   b.

   c.

   d.

   e.

6. What are my weaknesses (education, training, experience, or personal qualities) for starting and managing a new business?

   a.

   b.

   c.

   d.

7. For each weakness, what do I plan to do to reduce it (get more education, get more experience, bring in a partner, hire an employee, etc.)?

   Weakness: Plan to reduce it:

   a.

   b.

   c.

   d.

8. In terms of business skills, I rate my understanding or experience of:

	None		Some		High
a. How the economy works, economic factors	1	2	3	4	5
b. Legal factors	1	2	3	4	5
c. Budgeting and profit planning	1	2	3	4	5
d. Financial management and control	1	2	3	4	5
e. Employee relations and personnel management	1	2	3	4	5
f. Managing day-to-day business operations	1	2	3	4	5
g. Buying and inventory control	1	2	3	4	5
h. Analyzing the marketplace	1	2	3	4	5
i. Determining which goods and services to offer	1	2	3	4	5
j. Promoting and advertising products or services	1	2	3	4	5
k. Location analysis	1	2	3	4	5
l. Pricing products or services	1	2	3	4	5
m. Personal selling and/or customer relations	1	2	3	4	5

Total Points = _____

SCORING BREAKDOWN FOR QUESTION 8

1. If you have *more than 58 points,* you have a very strong background. However, this will not guarantee you success. If you are entering a highly competitive marketplace, you will be competing against people who already know what does and does not work. A strong background is important, but it will still take time to learn all the ins and outs of the marketplace.
2. If you have *between 46 and 58 points,* then you may have a sufficient understanding of business to proceed to Chapter 3. If you have one or more areas that received a 1 or 2 rating, get additional training or experience. The marketplace does not reward trial-and-error learning on the job once you start your business.
3. If you have *less than 46 points* (an average of less than 3.5 points per area), then you have only a moderate understanding or an unbalanced understanding of the basic business concepts. You may not have sufficient depth or breadth of knowledge and experience to start and

manage a new business. Consider additional training, work experience, bringing in a partner or manager with the needed skills, or buying a franchise that offers extensive training and assistance. In any event, you are not ready to start a business on your own at this time. .

NOTES

[1] Richard M. White, Jr., *The Entrepreneur's Manual* (Radnor, Pa.: Clifton Book Company, 1977), p. 57.

[2] Joan Delaney, "100 Ideas for New Businesses," *Venture,* November 1988, p. 36.

[3] Ibid., p. 42.

[4] Ibid., p. 49.

[5] Ibid., p. 64.

[6] Ibid., p. 54.

[7] Gisela M. Pedroza, "Road Dogs," *Entrepreneur,* May 2002, p. 112.

[8] Don Debelak, "I Needed That," *Entrepreneur,* May 2002, pp. 127–128.

[9] Ibid.

Part 2
Preparing Your Business Plan

3

The General Overview and Legal Structure

Now that you have identified the type of business opportunity you want to pursue, it is time for you to begin preparing your business plan. While you now have a general idea of the kind of business you want to start, numerous questions remain unanswered. Once people have completed the six-step process described in Chapter 2, they often feel that they do not need to prepare a formal business plan because they know what goods or services they want to offer to the one or more market segments they plan to serve. Getting to this point may have taken a lot of time and thought, but a lot of decisions still need to be made. Preparing a business plan helps you identify the questions you still need to answer. The plan then provides a framework and timetable for its implementation.

Your probability of being successful when you start a new business is directly related to the degree to which your business plan is accurate and complete and reflects various realities. Therefore, preparing a useful business plan will take considerable time and effort. It may take at least 4 months to prepare a business plan for even the simplest new business. A note of caution also needs to be introduced at this time. Some people believe that they do not need to prepare a business plan if they do not need to borrow money, bring in a partner, or issue stock. This is a mistake. A business plan is not the same thing as a request for funding; it is your blueprint for building a successful business. You need to have a plan even if you don't need financing because you are the primary audience for your business plan.

While people who are planning to start a business usually say that they have a business plan, in most cases all they really have is a loosely defined concept in their mind of what they plan to do. Your plan needs to be the product of deliberate effort, and it needs to be in writing.

Anyone who tries to build anything, especially something as complicated as a business, without having a blueprint is courting disaster. It is true
that a business plan may help you get financing for your business, but it is
important for two other reasons as well. First, your plan allows you to take
the mental journey before you commit resources and take the physical journey. It identifies specifically the *who, what, when, where, how much, why,* and
how of your proposed venture. The plan may indicate that your venture will
require much more money than you had anticipated, that its break-even
point is much higher, or that there is too much competition. Second, your
business plan is a reflection of your ability to manage. If you do not have the
patience, perseverance, skill, and information to prepare a business plan,
you probably do not have the ability to start and manage a new business.

Most business plans have three basic components. They start with a
general overview of the business, they then discuss how the business will
create and maintain customers, and they conclude with a set of financial projections that indicate the level of profit the business is expected to make in
its first few years of operation. The following business plan outline identifies
most of the items that should be addressed in a business start-up:

I. Executive Summary
II. Table of Contents
III. Overview of the Business Concept
    A. Identification of the market opportunity
    B. Growth and financial objectives for the business
    C. Discussion of the legal form of organization and ownership
    D. Profile of the management team and organization chart
    E. Description of the market(s) to be served and the location of the
       business
    F. Basis for financing the business
    G. Timetable for establishing the business
    H. Exit strategy
IV. The Marketing Part of the Business Plan
    A. Description of the industry: an overview of its history, trends,
       and influential factors
    B. Analysis of immediate and potential competitors
    C. Profile of the target market(s) and geographic area to be served
    D. Presentation of the marketing mix for creating a competitive
       advantage and maintaining customers
       1. Product-service strategy
       2. Price strategy

       3. Promotional strategy

       4. Physical distribution and location strategy

   E. Projected sales and market share

   F. Identification of any proprietary position, including patents, licenses, copyrights, franchise rights, exclusive agreements, etc.

V. The Financial Part of the Business Plan

   A. Projected initial capital requirement

   B. Projected opening-day balance sheet

   C. Projected first-year income statement

   D. Projected first year-end balance sheet

   E. Projected cash flow for the first year

   F. Projected income statements for the second through fifth years

   G. Projected balance sheets for the second through fifth years

   H. Key operating ratios

   I. Description of the sources of debt and equity financing for start-up and growth

   J. Projected return for the owners-investors

VI. Supplemental Factors

   A. Operational issues

   B. Identification of risks and insurance coverage

   C. Identification of employee-related regulations and tax reporting requirements

   D. Identification of all legal factors, including licenses, taxes, zoning, and other reporting requirements

THE EXECUTIVE SUMMARY

A business plan begins with an executive summary. The executive summary is one or two pages in length and captures the essence of the proposed business venture. Even though it appears at the beginning of the plan, it is usually written after the rest of the plan has been completed.

The executive summary serves a very important purpose: It forces you to articulate the basic components of your business venture. The executive summary is often called the "elevator pitch." It can be viewed as what you would say if you had less than 1 minute to tell someone about your business. First-timers find this to be a challenge. Too often, they say something general like "I plan to start a family-oriented restaurant serving home-cooked food."

It is not unusual for bankers, potential partners or investors, suppliers, or friends to ask you about your proposed venture. The executive summary provides a very concise description of your business. It profiles the proposed business in terms of its legal form, the specific market(s) to be served, the business's competitive advantage(s), its projected rate of growth, how it will be financed, and the projected return to its owner(s). It goes beyond generalities. The executive summary contains the vital facts about your business and reflects the research that went into preparing your business plan. If it is done well and reflects a solid business proposal, anyone who reads it will want to read the entire business plan.

OVERVIEW OF THE BUSINESS CONCEPT

This part of the business plan is devoted to identifying why the business is being started and what you expect it to become in 5 or more years. The overview of the business concept forces you to state what your objectives are, when you plan to achieve them, what risks you expect to encounter, and who will be involved in the venture.

Most successful businesses were formed in order to capitalize on a specific market opportunity. The first part of the business plan should identify that market opportunity. The opportunity could be something as specific as "to provide computer-controlled lawn sprinkler systems for a targeted market segment of upper-income homeowners in Landfall, a planned retirement community in Wilmington, North Carolina," or as general as Fred Smith's concept, "to provide overnight delivery throughout the United States," which served as the basis for creating Federal Express. The description of the market opportunity will be fairly brief at this stage because it will be addressed in detail in the marketing part of the business plan.

THE OBJECTIVES FOR THE NEW BUSINESS

The next section of the business plan identifies your objectives for the business. As noted earlier, one of the benefits of starting your own business is that you can start it for any reason you want. Your objectives could range from "making a 20 percent annual return after taxes on owner's equity, to be sustained over 10 years" to "providing jobs for all six members of my family until I retire."

In any event, it is important that you state your objective(s) in specific terms. If you want to create a business that will have sales of $30 million and a net worth of $2 million in 10 years and be recognized as the leading firm in its field, this needs to be stated in writing. If you plan to start a new type of venture, franchise it within 6 years, and have at least 100 franchisees in 10 years, this needs to be stated. The same applies if you have the objective of creating a business with patents that will be bought out by a *Fortune* 500 company for at least $5 million within 5 years. It does not make any difference whether your objective is to be on the cover of *Inc.* magazine or just to have your business provide you with an after-tax income of $30,000 per year; your objective needs to be put in writing and stated as specifically as possible.

Objectives can be viewed as dreams with a deadline. They should be stated as desired destinations with a targeted date of arrival. You must avoid the temptation to say things like, "I want to make money" or "I want to have a growing business." These aren't objectives; they are merely directions. Objectives serve as the basis for all your business decisions. If your objectives are vague, then you will have difficulty deciding how much your operations will need to expand and how to finance that growth.

THE LEGAL FORM OF ORGANIZATION

You will need to decide early in the planning process which legal form of organization will be the most appropriate for your business. This turns out to be a multiple-choice question. Most businesses operate as one of the following three legal forms: the sole proprietorship, the partnership, or the corporation. You should understand the characteristics of each form so that you can select the most appropriate form for your particular type of business. You should contact an attorney for assistance in determining the appropriate legal form. If you do not know an attorney who specializes in commercial law, then ask respected business owners whom they would recommend. This is not the time to get an attorney who is a generalist.

The Sole Proprietorship Form of Organization

The sole proprietor is his or her own boss and therefore usually makes or breaks the business. The legal implication of a sole proprietorship is that because the proprietor has sole control of the business, she or he also has sole responsibility for the business. Accordingly, legal and financial liabilities arising out of the operation of the business extend directly to the owner and are not limited to the business enterprise. This is the major disadvantage or risk associated with a noncorporate form of business. In a corporation, business liabilities usually stop with the business enterprise and do not extend to the owners of the business. Compared to corporations, proprietorships are easier to initiate, have less government regulation, and may be subject to lower taxes.

In a sole proprietorship, all business income is treated and therefore taxed as the personal income of the owner. In a sense, you are not creating a business when you start a sole proprietorship—the business is merely an extension of you. Therefore, you file a Schedule C with your 1040 that shows the revenues and expenses for your sole proprietorship. The net income or loss is added to or subtracted from any other personal and investment income that you, the sole proprietor, report on your tax return. As a sole proprietor, you will also need to pay social security (FICA) and Medicare for yourself and the employer's share of social security and Medicare for any employees you have. The relative simplicity of forming and operating this form of business may explain why nearly 75 percent of all businesses in the United States are sole proprietorships.

If you choose to start your business as a sole proprietorship, you should remember to do three things. First, you should check to see whether you need to register your business in the state and county in which you plan to locate your business. In most cases, you will also need to file a "fictitious-name" or "DBA" (doing business as) form. In some states, this is called a "certificate of assumed name." This form indicates who is the proprietor of the business if someone wants to initiate legal action against the business. You will be expected to file this form unless the name of your business is identical to the name that appears on your official personal records. If your name is Susan Reeves Smith and you plan to call your business "Susan Smith's Auto Repair," you will still have to file a DBA form, just as you would if the business were to be called "The All American Auto Repair Shoppe." You should also check with your state's department of commerce, county office, or city hall to see if you will need to secure a "privilege license."

Second, attorneys usually recommend that you prepare a "right of survivorship" document. In some states, if you die, your business must be liquidated because technically you were the business, and therefore the business can no longer exist. The right of survivorship gives you a vehicle for indicating what should be done with the business. Certain states will permit you to include the disposition of the business's assets in your will. The beneficiaries are then free to continue the business, sell it, or liquidate the assets as they see fit. This may keep probate proceedings from freezing the assets you have tied up in your business.

Third, being a sole proprietorship does not mean that you have to run the business. The word *sole* indicates that you are *solely liable* for the business. You can still hire someone to run the business for you. In any event, you may consider designating someone, possibly an employee or your spouse, as your agent. If you expect to be away from the business for extended periods of time, it may be worthwhile to give someone you trust the legal right to act on your behalf. This is similar to granting someone a durable power of attorney to act on your behalf. Job descriptions for your employees are another way of authorizing certain people to do certain things. In some states, if your spouse is involved in the business, it may be considered to be a partnership rather than a sole proprietorship.

The agency relationship may be particularly worthwhile if you are hospitalized or become mentally impaired. The agency agreement can be drafted in such a way that it permits someone to carry on any or all aspects of the business until you get better or until the business can be concluded in a constructive manner. The right of survivorship and the agency relationship are very important. If you plan to use them, don't put them off until later. Life is full of surprises, and it would be a shame if your business were to be liquidated because something bad happened to you. If you are going to put a significant part of your life into your business, then take a few legal precautions to make sure that it can withstand your misfortune.

The Partnership Form of Organization

A partnership is a noncorporate form of business with two or more owners. Partnerships exist when at least two people formally combine their ideas, talents, or capital for business purposes. A partnership is in many ways similar to a proprietorship. Legal and financial liabilities extend beyond the business enterprise to include the owners. If the business defaults on any of its obligations, creditors can generally look to any of the partners individually to satisfy the obligations of the business. Accordingly, if a creditor of a partnership seeks to collect what is due from the partnership and is unsuccessful, the creditor may then seek to collect the entire amount from any of the partners without regard to what share of the business that particular partner owns. It would then be up to that partner to seek restitution from the other partner(s).

From a tax point of view, partnerships are taxed like proprietorships. Partners include Form 1065 with their 1040. They are taxed on their share of the partnership's profit at their personal income tax rate. Partners are expected to pay social security and Medicare on their share of the partnership's income.

Because of the need to divide profits, losses, responsibilities, and liabilities, it is strongly recommended that prospective partners use the services of an attorney to draw up a written partnership agreement. You should have a formal partnership agreement even if the state you will be operating in does not require a formal written agreement. Such a contract should spell out each partner's respective rights and responsibilities.

Two other legal factors need to be noted. The death, withdrawal, or addition of a partner automatically and legally terminates the original partnership agreement; however, the agreement can stipulate what will happen when such an event occurs. Therefore, expansion, dissolution, and buyout arrangements should be agreed to in advance. The agreement should indicate how the assets and liabilities will be evaluated and distributed when the partnership is terminated. It should also indicate how disputes among the partners will be resolved.

A partnership will be expected to register in the county in which the business will be located. It may also be required to file a DBA or assumed-name form. Partnerships may also be required to secure a "privilege license" from the state or county. The right of survivorship and agency relationship documents are usually of little value because of the nature of a partnership. The reluctance of people to be held liable for the actions of the other partners and the difficulty of adding or deleting partners may explain why less than 10 percent of the businesses in the United States are partnerships.

The partnership just described is considered a *general* partnership. Each partner has unlimited liability. A *limited* partnership may be formed in which one or more of the partners are limited partners. A person can be a limited partner if the partnership agreement indicates his or her involvement in the business is purely financial. Under no circumstances can a limited partner be involved in any of the business's decisions. The limited partner's liability is thus limited to the amount of money that he or she invests in the business.

A limited partner may have limited liability, but she or he also has a limited opportunity to express her or his thoughts on how to improve the business. This can be particularly frustrating if the business gets into financial trouble. If a limited partner becomes involved in business decisions, the courts may declare that person to be a general partner with unlimited liability.

The major advantage of the limited-partnership arrangement is that it may provide a means by which other people can invest in the business without the need to form a corporation. As someone once said, "The best partner is a silent partner!" If all your partners are limited partners, you get the benefit of their money without having to consult them as you would general partners when decisions need to be made. For this to happen, however, your partners will have to believe in your business concept and trust your business judgment.

The limited partnership has merit from a legal and financial perspective. Unlike the general partnership, if appropriate provisions are made in the limited partnership agreement, it may continue after the withdrawal or death of a limited partner. That person's share of the partnership is usually purchased by the remaining partners according to some prearranged formula. It may also be possible for limited partners to transfer their ownership interests without dissolving the partnership.

The limited partnership does not relieve every partner of unlimited personal liability. At least one of the partners must be a *general* partner. If you are going to be making business decisions, then you will be a general partner. You will have the same unlimited liability as if the business were a general partnership or a sole proprietorship.

It should be clear by now that if you go the partnership route, you should choose your partner(s) carefully. An irresponsible or incompetent partner could cost you everything. You should also use caution when considering friends as potential partners. Just because you are friends does not mean that you will be good business partners. The same applies to family members. If you want to start a business, start it with the right people. There are enough challenges; do not add to them by reducing your ability to make objective business decisions.

Limited Liability Companies

Before moving on to the corporate form of organization, it may be worthwhile to discuss limited liability companies, or LLCs. This legal form of organization is a hybrid that has some of the features of a partnership and some of the features of a corporation. While there are a number of differences between LLCs and the other forms, the most important thing about them is that they provide limited liability for their owners. Unlike the case with sole proprietorships and partnerships, no one has unlimited personal liability.

LLCs do not have partners or stockholders; their owners are called members. LLCs do not issue stock or have partnership shares; they have ownership "interests" that are identified in the LLC's articles of organization. The limited liability does not come without drawbacks. Members cannot freely transfer their ownership interest. Transfer of ownership usually requires the unanimous written consent of the other members. The duration of the venture may also limited. In most cases, LLCs cannot operate for more than 30 years. There may also be a restriction on whether one or more of the members may own a larger or smaller percentage of the business than other members. The relative newness of this legal form and the variation from state to state in the statutes controlling it means that you will need to seek the advice of an attorney who has extensive experience with LLCs in that state. You should also consult with a CPA about taxation and how social security and Medicare obligations should be reported.

The Corporate Form of Organization

Corporations represent about 20 percent of all businesses in the United States. Corporations differ from proprietorships and partnerships in many ways. First of all, a corporation is considered a legal entity. It is treated as something separate from its owners. If a corporation is sued, defaults on its loans, or goes bankrupt, the shareholders' losses are limited to the amount that they invested in the business. This means that the stockholders have limited liability.

If you choose the corporate form for your business venture, you may nonetheless find that you are still personally liable. Banks and other creditors may require you to personally cosign any loans or other business agreements. Most new corporations start and operate without an abundant supply of cash. For this reason, the power company, the phone company, and some of your suppliers may ask the major stockholders to personally guarantee the corporation's obligations if the corporation should become insolvent.

The stockholders can become personally liable for the actions of the corporation for at least two other reasons. First, if the firm fails to conduct its affairs as a corporation, then it may be treated as if it were a proprietorship or partnership. The stockholders, through the firm's board of directors, must adopt bylaws, conduct regular meetings, and elect officers. The board must also keep records of its meetings. If the corporation is not conducted accordingly, the Internal Revenue Service or other creditors may request that the courts declare that the owners of the business are personally liable for claims. The other instance in which the stockholders have unlimited personal liability is when they are involved in any type of criminal activity when conducting the corporation's affairs. This type of situation is rare, but it is quite clear that the owners' personal liability is limited only when they behave in an appropriate and legal manner.

The corporate form is appealing because it limits the stockholders' legal and financial liabilities. Yet this form has three major drawbacks. First, it takes more money to start a business as a corporation. The incorporation process tends to cost hundreds or thousands of dollars. Second, it takes more time and paperwork. You must file your articles of incorporation with the secretary of state in the state in which you plan to conduct your business, register the firm in the state or country where its principal office is to be located or its real estate is to be held, elect directors, establish bylaws, issue stock, conduct meetings, and keep formal records of corporate decisions. In some states, certain types of businesses (law firms, accounting firms, or medical practices, for example) cannot be formed as corporations, so the owners retain a higher level of personal liability. In these cases, the businesses are formed as professional services partnerships.

The major drawback of the corporate form is in the area of taxes. Corporate profits are subject to double taxation because corporations are legal entities. The corporation will pay a federal tax on each year's profits to the Internal Revenue Service. Most firms are also required to pay a state income tax on their profits. The corporate income tax is the first wave of tax imposed on a corporation's profits. The second wave occurs if the corporation's board of directors decides to distribute as dividends any of the firm's profits that are left after state and federal taxes. Stockholders are obligated to pay federal and state personal income taxes on dividends they receive from the firm. Corporate profits are thus taxed twice: once at the corporate level, and then again as dividends at the stockholder level. As you can see, the benefits of limited personal liability come at the cost of double taxation.* A major advantage of the corporate form over partnerships and sole proprietorships also derives from the fact that a corporation is a legal entity. When a partner or sole proprietor dies, the business also ceases. Similarly, whenever a new partner is added or a partner wants to leave, a new partnership may have to be formed. This is not the case with the corporate form. If someone wants to become an owner of a corporation, that person buys the corporation's stock. The sale of stock transfers ownership from seller to buyer. Stockholders can come and go without affecting the legal status or operations of the firm. Moreover, if the corporation needs money to expand its operations or pay off debt, it may be able to raise funds by selling additional stock.

The laws pertaining to the formation and conduct of a corporation— including the minimum number of directors, officers, and stockholders— vary from state to state. It should be noted that in most states one person can own all the stock in a corporation. However, if you plan to be the sole owner, make sure that every aspect of the business's operations (checking accounts, for example) are separate from the personal side of your life.

The "Subchapter S" or "S" corporation is a special type of corporation that may appeal to people who plan to start a small business. The S corporation is frequently referred to as "the corporation that is taxed like a partnership or proprietorship." This is not exactly the case, but there are some similarities. Your accountant should be in a good position to assess the merits of your forming your business as an S corporation.

---

*As this book goes to press, Congress is considering eliminating or reducing the tax on stockholder dividends.

The first thing that needs to be recognized about an S corporation is the tax distinction. An S corporation does not pay federal income tax. Instead, the stockholders report their share (percentage of ownership in the firm) of the corporation's profit for that year on their personal tax returns. The stockholders pay a tax on the firm's profit rather than on the dividends they receive. In a sense, S corporation stockholders pay the corporate federal tax (and the corresponding state corporate income tax) at their personal tax rate on their federal (and state) returns. If you own one-half of the shares of stock in an S corporation that made $80,000 in a given year, you would report S corporation income of $40,000 on Schedule K-1 of your personal federal tax return. In a regular corporation, the firm pays a federal tax on its profits and the stockholders pay tax only on the dividends they receive. Some states treat S corporations as regular corporations and therefore tax the stockholders on the dividends they receive. Many states also charge a corporate income tax.

Check with your CPA on whether your state recognizes Subchapter S status. Your CPA should also be in a position to analyze the difference in tax rates between a regular corporation and an S corporation. Corporate tax rates and personal tax rates are not the same.

S corporation status has certain benefits, but it also has restrictions. The IRS limits the number of people who can own stock in an S corporation. The "S" indicates that only a "small" number of people can own stock in the corporation. The IRS allows no more than 75 stockholders for an S corporation. Moreover, an S corporation may be able to issue only one type of stock. A general corporation can have common stock and preferred stock, voting and nonvoting, and cumulative and noncumulative stock.

There are many things to consider when you select the legal form for your business. Fortunately, you may be able to change the legal form after you start your business, if you meet certain requirements. Nevertheless, you should give this decision the time and attention it deserves from the very beginning. You should also seek the advice of an attorney who specializes in business law to determine what may be the most appropriate legal form. The attorney should also advise you on other aspects of forming and operating your business. The legal form you choose for your business will affect your initial capital requirement, your ability to raise money, your personal liability, how profits or losses will be reported and treated, the tax obligations you will incur, the corresponding cash flow for your business, and how you conduct your business.

You may find it helpful to ask yourself, "Which legal form will be most appropriate in 3 to 5 years?" This will give you a good idea of which legal form you should select when you start your business. Businesses that are expected to grow and to need additional funds are usually formed as corporations. Most medium-sized businesses and nearly all large businesses are corporations.

PROFILE OF THE MANAGEMENT TEAM AND ORGANIZATION CHART

This part of the business plan will indicate whether the business has a good chance of beating the odds. A viable business plan demonstrates that a market opportunity exists and that the people who will be involved in the business will be able to capitalize on that opportunity.

One of the facts of business life is that a business cannot be better than the people in it. Since the primary reason for business failure is mismanagement, you will need to show that you have stacked the deck in your favor. This section of the business plan should identify who will be involved in the business, what role each person will play in its operations, and how these people's skills and experience will increase the business's chances for success.

Take a close look at the people you plan to have as part of your business. If their previous experience will reduce trial-and-error processes and if they will be bringing skills that will supplement your own strengths and minimize your weaknesses, then you should be in good shape. If you plan to hire friends and relatives just because they are friends and relatives, then you should step back and ask yourself whether you are trying to start a viable business or a social club.

Businesses succeed because they are run by people whose decisions are better than their competitors' decisions. Be sure that you put together a team that will give you a competitive advantage. When you bring capable and experienced people into your business, it will be able to hit the ground running. One of the advantages of buying a successful business is that its people have already demonstrated their ability to make the right decisions. Part of the price you pay when you buy an existing business is for goodwill. Good people are a significant part of this goodwill. If you start your business with experienced people, you will be starting with goodwill. This increases your chances of beating the odds.

This section of the business plan should include an organization chart that shows which positions need to be filled, who will be in each position, and how many people will be employed in the first year of operation (see Figure 3-1). The salary and fringe benefits for each position should also be indicated. Job descriptions should reflect how the work will be divided. The organization chart should indicate how the jobs will be coordinated.

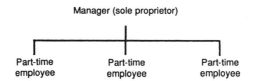

Figure 3-1. Organization Chart for the First Year

The business plan should also include brief profiles of the people who will play an influential role in the business. Each person's biographical sketch should indicate why this person was selected and any relevant background. Particular attention should be given to past experience and education. Each person's résumé should be included in the appendix to the business plan.

The need for having a management team has grown over the years. There are so many different dimensions to starting and managing a business that no one person can learn or do all of them. When one person tries to wear all the hats and be a Jack-of-all-trades, things quickly fall through the cracks. Most "one-man shows" either remain one-person businesses or cease being businesses altogether.

If you want your business to grow and prosper, you will need to have a team of people who know what needs to be done and who will do their jobs well. Pricing decisions will have to be made by people who understand the market and your business's costs. Budgets will have to be prepared by people who understand cost-volume-profit relationships. As the business grows, your job will be to coordinate the people who make the technical decisions.

If you are the sole proprietor, you will need to indicate in your business plan whether other people will be employed and, if so, what their responsibilities will be. If you plan to start your business as a partnership, you will need to indicate the division of work between the partners. Your partnership agreement should state specifically which partner will be responsible for selling, ordering inventory, hiring personnel, writing checks, and so on. A survey by the Smaller Business Association of New England indicated that of the partnerships entered into by its members, two-thirds had broken up. The primary reason for the breakups was changing interests or interpersonal conflict among the team members. It is important that each person's duties and responsibilities be determined in advance. This part of the business plan helps to clarify the division of work and the division of management as well as to identify potential areas of overlap, duplication, or weakness. Each partner's right to increase, decrease, or even sell his or her part of the business needs to be stated in this part of the business plan.

If you will be using the corporate form of organization, the business plan should also profile the people who will be serving on the firm's board of directors. Some states may require the board to have at least three directors. Since the board is elected by the stockholders, it is not uncommon to find the major stockholders on the board. Nevertheless, the board should provide additional strength to your management team. It is advisable to have people on the board who will provide a sense of direction, who will be candid in their review of operations, and who will contribute valuable advice to the management team. People who can open doors with suppliers and distributors, help find key people, and provide additional funding should be sought for the board. Your board should have at least one person on it who has started a business from scratch and guided its growth for at least 5 years. This person may keep you from committing many of the classic mistakes made by first-timers. Most directors will insist on directors' and officers' liability insurance coverage before they come on the board.

If you do not go the corporate route, you should consider setting up an advisory committee (sometimes referred to as an advisory board) to provide you with advice on key decisions. Your advisory committee should be composed of businesspeople from your community whom you respect. It may be easier to find people to serve on your advisory committee than on your board of directors because advisory committees do not make decisions. This means that they are less vulnerable to litigation and personal liability. You will probably have to pay them for their time, but you may find that they welcome the opportunity to serve as a sounding board for a modest honorarium. In any event, the résumés of the people who will serve on your board and/or advisory committee should be included in the appendix to the business plan. This part of the business plan may also identify who will serve as legal counsel and who will be the accountant for the business.

If you plan to grow, your plan should reflect how the business will grow in terms of the number and nature of positions and jobs (see Figure 3-2). It may be worthwhile to include a projected organization chart in your plan that reflects the way you expect the business to look in 5 years. Your objectives and financial projections should be set in a 5-year time frame. You should be able to show the type and size of organization needed to achieve those goals and the basis for the employment expenses included in your projected income statements. If you plan to outsource any operations, the plan should indicate this. It should also indicate whether the business will achieve any significant economies of scale.

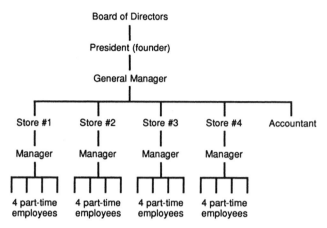

Figure 3-2. Organization Chart for the Fifth Year

DESCRIPTION OF THE MARKET(S) TO BE SERVED AND THE LOCATION OF THE BUSINESS

This part of the general overview describes the basic thrust of your marketing efforts. The general overview identifies (1) the goods that you will be offering, (2) the type of customers you will be trying to attract, (3) the geographic territory you will be trying to serve, (4) whether you will be operating out of more than one facility, (5) whether you will be a franchise, (6) whether you will have the exclusive rights to a brand, and (7) what you plan to have as your competitive advantage(s). This section can be viewed as a preview of the marketing plan.

The marketing plan will discuss each area in more detail. The following example profiles a new venture's marketing effort:

> Early Childhood Development Center (ECDC) is designed to meet the needs of parents who want their pre-kindergarten-age children to experience various aspects of learning that are not available in "typical" day-care facilities. Many parents want their children to be enrolled in an ongoing program that will enhance each child's personal development. Industry data reveal that a substantial opportunity exists for a "developmental learning center." Traditional preschools are expected to grow 3 to 4 percent per year, whereas developmental centers are expected to grow between 10 to 20 percent per year for the next decade.

Most preschools are merely day-care centers. They have grown because they have offered working mothers an alternative to hiring a babysitter while they are at work. ECDC is not intended to compete with the traditional day-care business. Instead, it is designed to provide experiences that will permit children to grow as individuals and be "ahead of the game" when they start regular school.

ECDC's developmental experiences will include computers, foreign languages, and performing arts. Field trips will also be offered on a regular basis. ECDC's staff will be selected for their background, education, and experience. Each staff member will have a degree in early childhood development.

Enrollment in ECDC will be limited to 110 children per facility. The limited enrollment will assure parents that their children will receive individual attention. There will be three classes each for the infant and 1-year-old age groups, and two classes for the 2-year, 3-year, and 4-year-old groups. Each of the infant and 1-year-old classes will be limited to six children. The other age groups will have a limit of nine children per class. Tuition for the infant and 1-year old classes will be $900 per month for each child. Tuition for the 2-, 3-, and 4-year old classes will be $1000 per month for each child. This is higher than the typical preschool rate, but ECDC is not the typical preschool, nor is it directed to the typical parents. ECDC is targeted to children whose parents have a combined household income of at least $100,000 per year and who want their children to attend a developmental program even if the wife does not have a full-time job.

The Norfolk, Virginia, metropolitan area has been selected for ECDC's first facility. A market study indicated that a growing number of young professionals are moving to the Norfolk metropolitan area because of its diversified economic base and proximity to the Atlantic Ocean. The market study also revealed that few preschools that offer the developmental approach exist.

ECDC plans to build a 6000-square-foot facility on a 3½-acre site in a suburban location. Three acres will be used for the development center's building, outdoor area, and parking. The other half-acre will become ECDC's headquarters as it expands its operations. The site was selected because it is within a 5-minute drive of two of the most popular high-end residential neighborhoods for young professionals in the Norfolk area.

ECDC plans to expand its operations to other cities with populations of at least a quarter-million people in the mid-Atlantic area. The 5-year plan calls for building two additional facilities in the Tidewater area of Norfolk, Hampton Roads, and Newport News, in the second year. ECDC is expected to have 15 facilities by the end of the fifth year. Expansion plans include at least two facilities each in Charlotte, Greensboro, Raleigh, Baltimore, and the suburbs of Washington, D.C.

ECDC's marketing goal is to generate annual sales of $13,129,200 with a pretax profit of $1,050,336 in uninflated dollars in its fifth year, when it will have 15 facilities in operation. This projection assumes that each facility will have three infant and three 1-year old classes as well as two 2-, 3-, and 4-year old classes. It also assumes that each facility will be operating at 85 percent of capacity.

If ECDC's management believes that the market will continue to be strong for at least another decade, then ECDC will continue adding an average of four new facilities per year. ECDC's long-range plans may include expanding its facilities to include kindergarten through eighth grade. ECDC's overall plan is to maintain ownership and management of its facilities rather than to franchise its operations. This strategy may slow ECDC's growth, but it should enable management to maintain the quality of its development programs and facilities. This will be essential if ECDC is to fulfill its 10-year goal of being recognized as the leader in offering experientially based, individualized development programs for preschool-age children.

BASIS FOR FINANCING THE BUSINESS

The general overview should identify how much money will be needed to start the business and how it will be financed. Chapter 7 provides a basis for estimating your business's initial capital requirement. Chapter 8 indicates the basic configuration of your business's assets, liabilities, and owner's equity. The general overview summarizes the financial projections from Chapters 7 and 8. If you plan to start your business as a sole proprietorship and finance it with your own money, then this section of the general overview will be a statement such as

Johnson's Landscaping Service will have an initial capital requirement of $26,500. It will be funded by Suzie Johnson, the sole proprietor, with money currently held in a 6-month certificate of deposit.

If your business will be formed as a partnership, then the overview should reflect the partnership agreement, which states who is putting in how much money; who, if anyone, will be a limited partner; and how much money, if any, will be borrowed to start the business. The following statement reflects such an agreement:

> S.J.T. Specialty Products will have an initial capital requirement of $46,000. It will be funded in the following manner:
>
>> $10,000 from John Smith, a general partner
>>
>> $10,000 from Paula Jones, a general partner
>>
>> $10,000 from Allison Taylor, a limited partner
>>
>> $16,000 through a 5-year secured note from John Smith's mother with monthly principal and interest payments with a 13 percent APR

If the business will be started as a corporation, then the overview should indicate how much of the firm will be financed through debt. The basis for funding may be reflected in the following:

> Amalgamated Enterprises, Inc., will have an initial capital requirement of $120,000. Initial funding will be provided by issuing 80,000 shares of common stock at $1 per share. The following people will serve as the initial stockholders:
>
>> $25,000 for 25,000 shares from Irving Stevens
>>
>> $25,000 for 25,000 shares from Helen Brown
>>
>> $15,000 for 15,000 shares from Steve Johnson
>>
>> $15,000 for 15,000 shares from Bill Cohen
>
> A $40,000 collateralized loan with 12.75 percent APR from Irving's father, John Stevens, will also be used to finance the business. The note calls for interest payments on a monthly basis and a balloon payment for the principal of the note at the end of the 5-year term.
>
> All four shareholders have provided personal guarantees for the loan.

As you can see, the way the business is financed depends on the legal form of the business, the amount of money to be raised, and whether the business will be funded by its owners/investors and/or by a loan. The funding could also include short-term trade credit from one or more of the suppliers of inventory or equipment. This type of financing should also be noted in the general overview. The general overview should also indicate whether the business will need additional funding at a later date and, if so, how this funding will be secured. If the business plans to expand its operations, retire a short-term note, or buy back stock from its stockholders, then the overview should indicate when this is likely to occur, the amount of money involved, and how it will be funded.

TIMETABLE FOR ESTABLISHING THE BUSINESS

A considerable amount of time goes into starting a business. You will need to identify all the activities that will have to be completed, estimate how long each will take, and determine which of them must occur sequentially.

The general overview should include the date you plan to open your business and the schedule of activities that must be completed by that target date. The timetable usually starts with a period for identifying market problems. This will be followed by a period for the analysis of each problem to determine whether the problem represents an opportunity. Another block of time will have to be allocated to select the opportunity that will serve as the core of your new business venture. These three steps could take from 3 months to a couple of years.

Your timetable will need to reflect numerous other activities as well. Some of them will take only a couple of days. Others may take weeks or months. Your timetable will include (1) finding the right target market and geographic area to serve, (2) determining the optimal type and size for your facility, (3) identifying potential locations, (4) selecting the appropriate site, and (5) negotiating the terms of the lease or building the facility, as well as (6) moving in and preparing the facility.

The timetable should distinguish between when you plan to start your business and when you will be open for business. If you will be making your own product, you will need to contact machinery vendors and allow sufficient time for delivery and installation. The same applies if you will be a retail business. You will need to determine which brands to carry, contact the suppliers to see if they will do business with you, place your orders, and allow enough time for the orders to be delivered before you open your doors.

You will also need to advertise for any employees you need, interview people, check their backgrounds, and train them before they come into contact with your customers. The timetable also needs to reflect the time it takes to have your sign, letterhead, business cards, and so on, made and shipped. Your Web site will also need to be prepared, and your grand opening advertising will need to be planned and scheduled. If your promotion plan includes any "teaser" advertising that lets customers know about your business months before it opens, your timetable will have to include this, too. Teaser advertising can make a big difference in your first few months' sales and cash flow.

Almost everyone underestimates the amount of time it will take to start and open a business. It takes a lot more time and work than managing an existing business. Every decision has to be made for the first time. You will have to identify what needs to be done, how long it will take, how much money you will need, and when you will pay for each facet of the business. It will seem as if every question leads to five more questions.

Anyone who is thinking about starting a business should keep Murphy's Law in mind at all times. According to Captain Ed Murphy, "If anything can go wrong, it will . . . and at the most inopportune time." Suppliers may not ship items on time. If they do, they may send the wrong type or number. Employees may quit after you have trained them but before you open for business. Construction of the "perfect" new building you leased may be delayed 3 weeks, thereby allowing you only 1 week to move in before you open.

Your business should be based on good ideas, yet ideas alone do not assure success. Timing is important, too. You need to be sure that you open your business at the right time of year. You also need more than a one-page "to do" list to orchestrate the various activities. A timetable increases the probability that the right things will happen at the right time. Life is full of surprises. A timetable will also indicate when you have to initiate a contingency plan so that you do not get derailed. A modest investment in a user-friendly project management software package may be worth every dollar you spend on it. Having a few dollars in reserve will also be helpful. When things do not work out as expected, having a few uncommitted dollars may enable you to deal with the unexpected things that are destined to occur.

Many new businesses start off on the wrong foot because their founders forget to do something or miss a deadline. For example, many first-timers miss having their businesses listed in the phone book and the Yellow Pages. The phone book may be distributed each summer, but the deadline for finalizing your contract and providing your ad layout may be in January or February. You may not plan to open your business until August, but you will need to have the answers to numerous questions in January if you want to have your business in the Yellow Pages when it opens its doors. By January or February you will need to have (1) selected the name for your business, (2) made sure that it and its Web site address are registered, (3) signed a letter of agreement or lease, (4) gained approval from your venders to supply the brands you want to offer, (5) received authorization to handle various credit cards, and (6) decided on the hours you will be open if you want this information to be given in the phone book and the Yellow Pages.

The actual process of finalizing your phone number and your Yellow Pages ad may take only a small amount of time, but if you don't have the necessary information before the deadline, you may miss out on what may be an essential part of your marketing plan. Quite a few of your prospective customers "let their fingers do the walking." It is difficult enough for a new business to attract customers; if you miss the phone listing deadline, you will be stacking the deck against your business before you even open its doors. Business visibility and business viability go hand in hand. The phone listing will not guarantee success, but not having it when you open your doors will almost certainly result in failure. The same thing may apply to various other activities that will need to be identified, planned, and scheduled.

Mismanagement is the primary reason that new businesses fail. If you plan ahead, you may be able to identify potential problems and prevent them before they can jeopardize your business. Life is full of surprises, and few things will go as planned. Nevertheless, if you have a plan with a timetable and if you are a flexible and resourceful individual, you may still be able to get a few hours of sleep each night in the period before you open your business.

EXIT STRATEGY

While your business plan is designed to help you start your business, you should not start this journey without a clear idea about your final destination. Most people are so caught up in the challenges of starting a business that they do not think about how they will exit from it. You need to think about how long you want to own the business. If you are in your fifties and you hope to retire within 5 to 10 years, then you need to think about whether you will want to sell the business at that time or whether you will hire someone to run it for you so that it can provide you with a stream of income. If you have numerous ideas for businesses, you may start your business with the intention of growing it quickly so that you can sell it within a few years and start what could be the next in a series of businesses. If you want your sons or daughters to have the opportunity to own the business, then the transition should be part of your plan. Your exit strategy should address the questions of *to whom, by when,* and *for how much.* For example, your exit strategy may be "to grow my business to the point where it can be sold for at least $400,000 within 5 years."

THE GENERAL OVERVIEW HELPS YOU THINK THINGS THROUGH

It should be apparent from the preceding discussion of the general overview that preparing a business plan is not something that can be done overnight. The plan forces you to put your business concept into specific terms. To paraphrase George Odiorne, a noted management professor, consultant, and author, "If you can't put your ideas into words, dates, and dollars, then you don't know what you are talking about, and you should forget it rather than wasting any more of your time." The general overview is valuable because it helps you clarify what you have in mind. It is also helpful because it gives other interested parties, including critical suppliers, prospective employees, potential customers, and leasing agents, a good idea of what will be involved in your proposed business venture.

This chapter has noted the importance of consulting with a CPA who has extensive experience with start-ups and an attorney who understands the nuances of the various legal forms and regulations. Your CPA should also be in a position to assist you in filing for an employer identification number, identifying the various accounting reports that need to be filed, and making sure that all employee-related records (federal income tax, state income tax, FICA, Medicare, unemployment insurance, workers' compensation, and so on) are kept and contributions are made on time. Your CPA can also help you set up your accounting system.

Your attorney will help you with the various forms (partnership agreement, articles of organization, or articles of incorporation, and so on) and make sure that proper legal procedures (drafting corporate bylaws, reviewing your lease, establishing credit arrangements, and so on) are followed. Your attorney can help you check with your state's department of commerce, county clerk, and city hall to find out what permits and licenses you will need to have in order to start your business. Your attorney and your accountant can also help you make sure that your business needs are properly handled from an estate planning perspective.

One final point needs to be made when it comes to selecting and using professional advisers. You get what you pay for, so it pays to seek the advice of qualified advisers.

4

Selecting the Right
Target Market

Our free-enterprise system encourages competition. This means that it is a buyer's market rather than a seller's market. If you do not offer what the market desires and you are no better than your competition, then you are destined to fail. Simply stated, if you don't have enough customers, you don't have a business.

In order to succeed, you must give prospective customers a compelling reason to go out of their way, to ignore your competition, and to give you their money. If your business activities are simply going to be a lukewarm rehash of what the business down the street is doing, then you had better reserve some space in the obituary section of the newspaper for your business.

If your business is no better than its competitors on the things your target market truly values, it will not succeed. There is simply too much competition for consumers' dollars—and the consumers know it. Your business must provide consumers with a compelling reason to try your business, to tell their friends about it, and to keep coming back. If you are not in a position to offer consumers exactly what they want, when, how, and where they want it, at a price they feel is fair, and still make a profit, then you should forget the whole thing.

The marketing part of the business plan begins with the identification of consumer wants that are not being met well enough or at all. The process of listening to the market in general terms was discussed earlier. Now you need to get down to the specifics.

The marketing part of your business plan describes how you will attempt to create and maintain customers for a profit. At this time, you need to describe your industry, your market, your territory, your competition, your prospective customers, and your marketing mix. This is important because no business operates in a vacuum. Your business plan must reflect the unique environment you will be operating in as well as what you plan to have as your competitive advantage(s).

STUDYING THE INDUSTRY

Before you start any kind of business, you need to have an in-depth understanding of the industry you will be in. You should join the trade association for your type of business. A trade association is made up of people who are in that type of business and people who are suppliers to businesses in that trade. The trade association and its members have a wealth of information that they have gained through extensive experience in that type of business. By tapping their knowledge and insights, you will definitely increase your chances of being a success. Most trade associations offer magazines or newsletters. They also schedule exhibits and speakers on a variety of topics to assist their members. Check the *Encyclopedia of Associations* (published by Gale Group) for a listing of trade associations for your type of business.

You should also gather information about trends in your industry, in areas such as products, services, expenses, advertising, credit policies, rate of growth, foreign factors, current laws, pending regulations, technological changes, and so on. *Industry Surveys* (published by Standard & Poor's) profile 45 major industries. *U.S. Industry and Trade Outlook* (published by the U.S. Department of Commerce) has a section on emerging industries. The *Business Periodicals Index* may identify articles about trends in your type of business. The *Complete Small Business Sourcebook* (published by Times Books) and the *Encyclopedia of Business Information Sources* (published by Gale Group) may also be helpful. A number of Internet search engines and Web sites can also provide useful information. It may be worth the time to visit similar businesses in other cities to learn what works.

It is important for you to know (1) whether you are about to enter an industry that is experiencing growth and increasing profitability rather than one that is mature and saturated, (2) whether the industry is sensitive to inflation or interest rates, (3) whether chains and franchises dominate the market, (4) whether the industry is susceptible to foreign competition, (5) whether it is subject to major technological change, (6) who the major suppliers and customers are, and (7) what the future may hold. If you understand the nature of your industry, you will be in a better position to analyze the specific market you plan to enter. You will also be in a better position to identify ways to develop your competitive advantage(s).

ANALYZING THE MARKET

At this time you need to study the specific geographic area in which you plan to start your business. You need to learn about the unique nature of your area. You need to know about the population, the overall rate of growth of business activity, whether people move frequently and to what neighborhoods, whether the downtown area is the center of business activity, whether new suburban malls are planned, who the employers are and whether they have a promising future, whether new roads are planned, and various other factors that may affect business conditions in general and the business you plan to start in particular. Census data, the *Survey of Buying Power,* and the local chamber of commerce can be helpful here. You will be looking for the level of disposable income and whether the population has exhibited a willingness to try new products, services, and businesses.

One of the most important parts of your market analysis involves identifying the people (or businesses) who may have a desire to purchase your type of product or service. Your overall geographic market may include hundreds or even thousands of people who may have an interest in your product or service. You are trying to identify the number of potential customers, who they are, how often they buy, whom they are currently buying from, how much they spend, and if they are brand or store loyal.

You want to learn which people are satisfied customers and which are still in search of a business. It will also be beneficial to know how much money is spent on the type of goods and services offered in your geographic area. The *Economic Census,* which is conducted every 5 years in the years ending in 2 or 7, provides information on various businesses. The *Economic Census* information is available on the Bureau of the Census's Web site.

From these data, you will be able to learn who buys what, how often, and from whom, and what these customers may be looking for. No business can be all things to all people. Even though each customer is unique, in most markets there are a number of people who have some common interests. Just as a jigsaw puzzle is made up of different pieces, markets are made up of different segments. Each segment represents a group of people who have similar features or interests (see Figure 4-1). By analyzing the market, you will be in a position to (1) identify the people who consume your type of

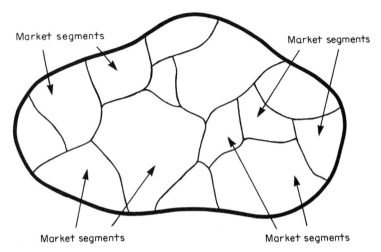

Market segments

Market segments

Market segments

Market segments

Figure 4-1. Market Segmentation: Each Market Consists of Numerous Segments

goods, (2) classify the market into various segments, (3) ascertain which segments are still in search of a business, and (4) determine which segments should be the target market(s) for your business.

COMPETITIVE ANALYSIS

The next step in analyzing your market involves doing a complete analysis of the businesses that are already offering your type of goods and services in the geographic area under consideration. You want to learn how many businesses are already in the marketplace, what they offer, and where they are located. Once you have gathered these data, you will be able to develop a competitive matrix (see Figures 4-2 and 4-3) that reflects the strengths and weaknesses of the businesses in the market.

The competitive matrix is constructed by listing all the businesses vying for customers in a particular geographic area; identifying all the dimensions of their market offerings, known as the marketing mix; and then rating each business on a scale of 1 to 5 in terms of its relative strength on each dimension. The competitive matrix in Figure 4-2 provides a rating of the businesses that are already in that overall market.

The next step is to construct a competitive matrix for each of the market segments within the overall market that is large enough to warrant your attention. This will take some time, but it will help clarify specific market

Competitive factor	Business #1	Business #2	Business #3	Business #4	Business #5
Price	3	1	2	4	3
Quality	3	3	2	3	2
Selection	4	4	3	3	4
Promotion	3	4	2	4	2
Services	4	5	2	3	4
Customer service/ sales personnel	3	3	1	3	3
Facilities/ atmosphere	3	5	2	2	3
Location	3	4	2	2	3

Rating of the business
on this factor

Figure 4-2. Competitive Matrix Reflecting the Rating of Existing Businesses

gaps. A competitive matrix is developed for each segment because consumers in different segments may place a different value or priority on the various dimensions of the marketing mix. A segment made up of lower-income families operating on a limited budget may place a premium on low prices, access to public transportation, in-house credit, and the offer of a warranty. A market segment comprising upper-income, double-wage-earning couples without children may be interested in exclusive brands, knowledgeable salespeople, delivery service, evening hours, and the opportunity to place phone or Internet orders.

You should rate the relative importance of each dimension of the marketing mix on a 1 to 5 scale for each segment in its individual matrix. These matrices can be used to identify whether there are gaps between what consumers desire and what the existing businesses offer in each segment. These gaps represent opportunities because they represent customers in search of a business. For example, if you were investigating the relative merit of starting a retail seafood market, you might find a segment that places a premium (a rating of 4 or 5 on each dimension) on being able to place phone orders, charge their purchase on their VISA card, have their fish filleted, and have it delivered. This segment may not be very price-sensitive (a rating on price of 1 or 2). You would then use the matrix to see if any existing business offers the people in this segment what they are looking for.

If no business in the matrix offers these services, this indicates a possible opportunity to start a business with competitive advantages for that particular segment. It should be noted here that not all gaps represent opportunities. You are looking for gaps where the segment values something to a greater degree than existing businesses are supplying it. Gaps where existing businesses are providing more than the consumers want do not reflect opportunities for new ventures. In your analysis of the competitive matrices, you will be looking for rows that indicate significant gaps in high-valued dimensions for all the existing businesses. Figure 4-3 indicates that none of the existing businesses offer the level of quality or the level of customer service desired by consumers in that market segment.

Particular attention should be directed to dimensions that the segment highly values, but where existing businesses are not within one rating point of the value that segment places on it. You want to find gaps of at least two points because it may be easy for an existing business to change what it is doing if its gap is only one point. For example, if a business in Figure 4-3 already had a score of 4 on customer service, it might be able to improve its score by hiring a better staff, providing incentives, and/or improving its

Selecting the Right Target Market 81

Competitive factor	Business #1	Business #2	Business #3	Business #4	Business #5
Price	[3] 3 x 3 = 9	★ [3] 1 x 3 = 3	★ [3] 2 x 3 = 6	[3] 4 x 3 = 12	[3] 3 x 3 = 9
Quality	★ [5] 3 x 5 = 15	★ [5] 3 x 5 = 15	★ [5] 2 x 5 = 10	★ [5] 3 x 5 = 15	★ [5] 2 x 5 = 10
Selection	[3] 4 x 3 = 12	[3] 4 x 3 = 12	[3] 3 x 3 = 9	[3] 3 x 3 = 9	[3] 4 x 3 = 12
Promotion	[2] 3 x 2 = 6	[2] 4 x 2 = 8	[2] 2 x 2 = 4	[2] 4 x 2 = 8	[2] 2 x 2 = 4
Services	★ [5] 4 x 5 = 20	[5] 5 x 5 = 25	★ [5] 2 x 5 = 10	★ [5] 3 x 5 = 15	★ [5] 4 x 5 = 20
Customer service/ sales personnel	★ [5] 3 x 5 = 15	★ [5] 3 x 5 = 15	★ [5] 1 x 5 = 5	★ [5] 3 x 5 = 15	★ [5] 3 x 5 = 15
Facilities/ atmosphere	★ [4] 3 x 4 = 12	[4] 5 x 4 = 20	★ [4] 2 x 4 = 8	★ [4] 2 x 4 = 8	★ [4] 3 x 4 = 12
Location	[2] 3 x 2 = 6	[2] 4 x 2 = 8	[2] 2 x 2 = 4	[2] 2 x 2 = 4	[2] 3 x 2 = 6
Relative strength for this segment	95	106	56	86	88

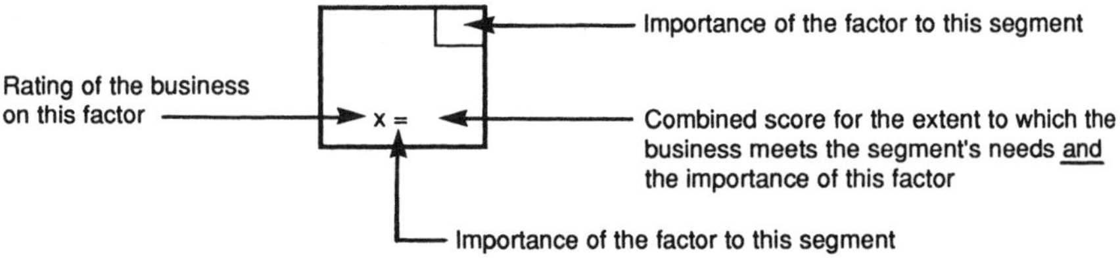

Rating of the business on this factor ———▶ x = ◀——— Combined score for the extent to which the business meets the segment's needs <u>and</u> the importance of this factor

◀——— Importance of the factor to this segment

——— Importance of the factor to this segment

★ Indicates that a "gap" exists between what this business offers and what this segment wants.

Figure 4-3. Competitive Matrix Reflecting Gaps in the Marketplace

information system. Gaps of at least one point are indicated with asterisks in Figure 4-3. A whole row of asterisks indicates that customers in that segment are not satisfied and that they are searching for a business that will give them what they want on that dimension. Competitive matrices that have numerous rows of asterisks may be what the military calls "target-rich environments" for new businesses.

The development and analysis of the competitive matrices are similar to Step 1 (identifying problems/gaps in the marketplace) and Step 2 (identifying corresponding business opportunities) in Chapter 2. The development and analysis of the competitive matrices need to be followed by Step 3 (determining whether you can develop the capability to be better than your competitors and meet the segment's needs) and Step 4 (estimating the profitability and the return on investment before you select the segment you are going to use as the target for your business). If (1) a sufficiently large need is evident and the competition does not appear to serve it, (2) you believe you can provide the segment what it wants, and (3) in doing so, you can generate a level of profit that meets your return-on-investment objective, then this is where you should focus your attention.

IDENTIFYING YOUR PROSPECTIVE CUSTOMERS

At this point, you should be able to develop a customer profile that describes specifically the nature of the people in your target market. The overall market is like a target. Your target market is the bull's-eye. Remember, no business can be all things to all people. You should concentrate your attention on being the best to the people in your target market.

If you cannot provide a customer profile of your target market in terms of who they are, where they live, whether they have white-collar or blue-collar jobs, what they do with their time and money, and their preferences for products, services, and brands, you will not be able to tailor your marketing mix to their specific needs, interests, wants, desires, and behavioral patterns.

Big businesses and a number of small businesses try the "shotgun" approach to creating customers. They try to be or do too many different things for too many different people. They are not very successful because their marketing mixes are compromises. They try to have something for everyone rather than offering the best for a few. When a business treats the market in general terms as if everyone is alike, few people get exactly what they want. The rest of the people remain customers in search of a business.

This is also true when a business tries to serve a combination of segments with a single marketing mix.

You need to use the "rifle" approach, in which you select a specific market segment (bull's-eye) and offer the customers in that segment exactly what they are looking for. This is a crucial component in the formula for creating and maintaining customers for a profit. This process is similar to the way hunters go after big game. Successful hunters identify a certain type of animal to go after, study its unique behavior patterns, and develop an approach to shooting it. Businesses try to appeal to a group of people by offering a marketing mix that is tailored to that group's unique interests.

A distinction should be made between businesses and hunters. Businesses want their customers to come back time and time again. They also want their customers to encourage their friends and associates to try their businesses. In fact, many hunters have replaced their rifles with cameras. They have realized that their hunting will continue only as long as they have animals to "shoot" with their cameras.

Let's stay with the business-hunter-photographer analogy a little longer. The similarities provide additional insight into how a new business can create and maintain customers for a profit. Your new business will be successful to the extent that you are able to identify a group of customers in search of a business, know the group's unique characteristics, and tailor your marketing mix to those characteristics. The most successful hunters/photographers try to learn as much as possible about their target before they initiate the hunt. They try to learn how big it is, how it moves, whether it lives alone or in groups, and whether it has a keen sense of smell, sight, or hearing. The more the hunter/photographer knows about the target, the higher the probability of a successful expedition. The same applies to a new business's ability to create and maintain customers for a profit.

Unfortunately, it may be more difficult for you to learn about the nature of your target market(s) than it is for hunters to learn about their prey. A significant part of animal behavior is the result of instinct. Consumers can be more elusive because most of their behavior is learned. People are also more complex. Their attitudes are the product of many factors, and numerous forces influence their behavior. The fact that their expectations may also change over a period of time adds to the challenge of attracting and keeping customers. This means that you will be shooting at a moving target.

There are six useful sets of factors that can help you identify the nature of the people who constitute your target market. People may be described using demographic, geographic, psychographic, benefit, usage, and consumer loyalty factors. These characterizations will help you formulate a customer profile, which is discussed later in this chapter.

Demographic Factors

This set of factors is fairly easy to measure. Demographic factors include age, gender, level of income, occupation, nationality, education level, race, religion, and stage of family life cycle (single, married, married with preschool children, retired, and so on). This type of information is readily available for most cities and counties in the United States. If you are trying to determine which geographic areas may offer the best opportunities, demographic analysis may be beneficial. This approach uses census data.

The census of population is done every 10 years by the U.S. Census Bureau. The Census Bureau also publishes the *Statistical Abstract of the United States,* which provides an annual summary of population, prices, income, housing, and other such data. The *Statistical Abstract* is accessible via the home page on the Census Bureau's Web site. The *Statistical Abstract* provides population data and population projections for cities. It also provides valuable demographic (age, gender, income, education, and so on) information for cities. The *Statistical Abstract*'s "Income, Wealth, and Expenditures" section profiles expenditures for various product categories by various demographic groups. The information available ranges from the number of people who own pets or play golf to the percentage of people in a particular market who access the Internet. The *Statistical Abstract*'s "Communications" section provides information about newspaper, television, and radio usage. The *Statistical Abstract*'s "Factfinder" home page allows you to access information quickly and to compare demographic factors for various geographic areas.

Census data are analyzed and profiled in various helpful ways in the Census Bureau's *State and Metropolitan Data Book.* The *Editors and Publishers Market Guide* also provides census data in a useful format.

Marketers frequently use these databases when they are trying to locate new markets. Ray Kroc referred to the *Editors and Publishers Market Guide* so often when he was looking for additional locations for McDonald's restaurants that he kept a copy of it in his personal jet. Your local library may have these sources. If not, check with the reference librarian at the nearest university.

These databases will enable you to put together a multidimensional profile of the area you want to research. Once you have developed a profile for each area, you will be able to compare the areas under consideration to determine which ones have the most potential.

The *County and City Data Book,* published by the U.S. Department of Commerce, contains the following types of information on each city:

- Number of people employed in manufacturing, wholesale and retail jobs, professional services, and government, and number who are self-employed
- Average value of a household
- Average age of a household
- Percentage of female householders with husband present
- Number of children enrolled in elementary schools
- Number of children enrolled in high schools
- Number of people with a high school education
- Number of people with a college education
- Percentage of the population that has moved within the area, within the state, and out-of-state or to another country
- Percentage of population of each race

The September issue of *Sales and Marketing Management* magazine each year provides the Survey of Buying Power, which offers the following information for regions, states, counties, and cities:

- Population and projected population growth in the next 5 years
- Median age of the population and the percentage of the population in each age group
- Number of households and the average number of people in a household unit
- Total retail sales and sales volume for various businesses, including food stores, eating places, general merchandise stores, furniture and appliance stores, and drugstores.
- Percentage of households with incomes of less than $20,000, $20,000 to $34,999, $35,000 to $49,999, and over $50,000

The September issue also lists each area's *effective buying index* and its *buying power index.* The effective buying index reflects the amount of disposable income available in that area. It is based on the number of people in the area, the median household income, and the effective buying index. This index is very helpful in comparing geographic markets in terms of each market's ability to buy certain products and services. *Demographics USA—Survey of Buying Power,* published by *Sales and Marketing Management* magazine, provides more detailed information and data that are not available in the September issue.

The *Editors and Publishers Market Guide* provides a profile on more than 1500 cities and communities in the United States and Canada in which a daily newspaper is published. The following information is included in each profile:

- Principal industries
- Largest shopping centers
- Number of retail stores by category, including chain stores
- Sales by category of store
- Disposable personal income
- Population estimates
- Number of passenger autos
- Newspaper circulation

Numerous other sources of demographic information for a market may also be available from each city's planning department, the respective state's department of commerce, the local chamber of commerce, area banks, business schools at neighboring universities, and the U.S. Small Business Administration. Local newspapers often have a wealth of information about their communities.

Geographic Factors
People can also be described in terms of where they live. Geographic factors include whether people live in (1) the north or the south, (2) an urban, suburban, or rural area, (3) a small town or a large city, (4) a warm or a cold climate, or (5) tropical or arid conditions.

Psychographic Factors
These factors pertain to people's lifestyles—and include such things as whether people are (1) outgoing or withdrawn, (2) confident and willing to try new things or risk-averse and satisfied with the status quo, or (3) energetic and athletic or reserved and homebodies. Psychographic factors provide insights into people's interests, attitudes, and propensities to behave in a particular manner.

Benefit Factors
People buy products and services for various reasons. Restaurants provide a good example. People may go to a restaurant because they like the food it

offers, but they may also go there because they like the cocktails, the bartenders, the atmosphere, the waiters and waitresses, the free food and lower prices for drinks at happy hour, or the opportunity to meet people and to be seen. In some cases, they go out to eat because they do not have anything at home to eat, because they just want to get out of the house, or because they don't want to prepare the food and wash the dishes.

Benefit analysis applies to movie theaters as well. Most teenagers do not go to a theater to see a movie. They go to meet their friends and to check out the other teenagers. Adults go to health clubs for numerous reasons, not just to be more fit. Many people join health clubs or spas because these offer a socially acceptable way to check out people of the opposite sex who are wearing next to nothing.

Benefit analysis is important to the development of the marketing mix. If you are not in tune with what people in your target market are looking for, you will not be in a position to satisfy their needs. Remember, you are not in business to sell products and services; you are in business to provide satisfaction. Revlon and Disney exemplify this concept. Revlon's approach to the market can be paraphrased, "We may make cosmetics, but we offer customers hope!" Disney management constantly reminds its employees that Disney is not in the amusement park business. It is in the business of "making people happy."

Usage Factors

People who are involved in marketing have a saying, "If you can't sell all the people something, then sell a lot to some of the people." People can be classified into (1) nonusers, (2) light users, (3) medium users, and (4) heavy users.

If you have a sales goal of $200,000 for your first year of operation and your average product sells for $50, there are various ways for you to reach that goal. You can try to sell one product each to 4000 people. Conversely, you could try to find one person who would buy 4000 items. The last scenario is fairly unlikely, but it does illustrate the value of usage-rate analysis. Some businesses benefit from the 80/20 rule. In these businesses, 80 percent of total sales come from 20 percent of the customers. Businesses obviously need to pay particular attention to that 20 percent. They also want to know where they can find more people like the people in that 20 percent.

Usage-rate analysis has yielded some interesting information. Years ago, a major brewery studied beer consumption. Its research classified people according to how many "12-ounce equivalents" (the size of a beer can) people consumed on a daily basis. People were classified as nonconsumers, light consumers, medium consumers, or heavy consumers. However, the brewery found that it needed to create a fifth category: the "super-heavies." The market study revealed that the number of people who consumed at least twenty-four 12-ounce equivalents a day was large enough for the group to be considered a separate segment.

People in the auto business also pay attention to usage rates. Auto dealers are particularly interested in how often people trade in their cars and whether they lease them or buy them. Tire dealers are interested in how many miles people drive each year and how often they replace their tires. Car washes, muffler shops, and gas stations also want to know about the different usage categories of customers.

Restaurants illustrate the value of the usage-rate classification system as a way of identifying customers. As a restaurateur, you would use one marketing mix if you were going after people who live in one particular neighborhood, dine out three times a week, and are loyal to one restaurant. You would use a different marketing mix if the target market you were trying to attract consisted of tourists or conventioneers who might be in that town only once in their lifetimes. Your marketing mix would again be very different if you were targeting college students. The same principle would apply if you were targeting retirees.

Consumer Loyalty Factors

Consumers vary in their loyalty to particular businesses and specific brands. Some people will not even try a competing brand or business. Other people are willing to shop around and compare product and service offerings. Consumers can be classified as having low, medium, or high levels of loyalty. Anyone who is considering starting a business should investigate the extent to which consumers are loyal to businesses that are already in the market. Highly loyal customers tend not to pay attention to the competitions' advertisements and usually are unwilling to try new stores or new brands. If your market analysis reveals that a large percentage of the people in the market have a low level of loyalty to existing businesses, this means that there are customers who may be willing to try a new business.

PUTTING TOGETHER THE CUSTOMER PROFILE

The preceding discussion of ways in which consumers can be classified or described indicates the multidimensional nature of people in the marketplace. People who are contemplating starting a business frequently say,

"Wouldn't it be a lot easier if all consumers were alike?" It would certainly be easier to tailor your offering to the market if John Smith's interests were the same as Susan Jones's interests. However, if everyone wanted the same thing, then a few large businesses would dominate the marketplace. Their economies of scale would give them a cost advantage that would enable them to offer lower prices than most small businesses.

The beauty of our marketplace is that consumers are multidimensional. Instead of one tremendous homogeneous market, we have numerous distinct segments. Within each segment, there are enough similarities of interests among consumers to enable a business to tailor its offerings to meet a particular group's needs. The differences among people may make it more difficult to identify and understand them, but these differences are the reason why so many opportunities for new businesses exist today. As people's needs change and their desire to express their individuality increases, opportunities for new ventures also increase.

A new business must direct its market offering to one or more segments of the population in which customers are in search of a business. As noted earlier, the rifle approach will be effective only if you can clearly identify the specific target market you will be trying to satisfy. Market analysis and market segment selection require that you be able to compile a customer profile that describes the unique nature of your target market.

The customer profile plays an essential role in your marketing effort. If you can describe the people you are trying to satisfy, you will be in a better position to develop a marketing mix that is tailored to their particular needs. The customer profile can be viewed as a tapestry woven with numerous strands of thread. You need to attempt to identify the key dimensions (threads) and how they are interrelated (woven) to constitute the unique nature of that target market (tapestry)

The customer profile describes the bull's-eye of your target market. The more you understand what the people in your target market value in life, how they spend their time, how they spend their money, and what they want but don't have enough of, the more likely it is that you will be able to meet their needs. If you understand their lifestyles, you will have an idea about what goods and services they need, how often they use certain products and services, and whether they are loyal to a particular store or brand. You will also gain insight into how much disposable income they have and whether they are price-sensitive. If you know their interests, you may be able to advertise on the network or cable shows they watch on television. If you know when they drive to work and what radio stations they listen to, you will be in a better position to design radio spots that are in tune with their interests and that will be aired at times when they are listening. This information may also indicate the best places for you to locate billboard ads if these ads are appropriate for your type of business. Your marketing effort will have the greatest impact when its components are in sync with one another and properly choreographed.

The same logic also applies to locating your business and finding ways to distribute your products or services. If you are going after one particular segment of parents, as was the case with Early Childhood Development Centers, described in Chapter 3, you will want to know where they live so that you can select a location that is within a 5-minute drive of your target market. However, if you plan to manufacture a line of items for people throughout the United States, you may choose a location that is close to distribution facilities.

The customer profile should be as specific as possible. When someone asks you to whom you will be targeting your marketing efforts, you will need to have something more specific than, "Anyone who will buy my products and services." The following customer profile for a clothing boutique may serve as an example of an attempt to identify a specific target market.

> Cachet Fashions International is targeted to professional women between the ages of 35 and 55 who earn at least $70,000 per year; who pay at least $300 for a dress and $150 for shoes for everyday use and $600 or more for an outfit for special occasions; who spend at least $10,000 per year on clothes; who are style-conscious yet maintain traditional values; who are moderately loyal to certain brands yet willing to try a new brand; who want their clothes to be tailored to flatter their figures; who entertain regularly; who drive a car less than 3 years old that costs at least $33,000; who live in a house or condominium valued in excess of $450,000; who take at least three vacations per year, with one or more being outside the continental United States; who have their own personal credit cards with at least a $5000 limit per card; who have at least $15,000 in jewelry; who subscribe to magazines such as *Harper's Bazaar, Town & Country, Architectural Digest,* and *Forbes;* and who live or work within a 60-mile radius of Manhattan.

This customer profile includes many of the factors described earlier. It illustrates that knowing the specifics of its target market will enable a business to tailor its marketing mix to the unique needs, interests, and behavioral patterns of that target market. The same framework can be applied if your business will be selling products and/or services to other businesses.

A business may have more than one target market. Cachet's customer profile was of women in a certain age range with a certain income who lived in a certain area. This isn't to say that Cachet would not be willing to sell its products to someone less than 35 who is on vacation or on a business trip in Manhattan or who doesn't have a full-time job. Most successful businesses also have secondary target markets. Each of these target markets will have a corresponding customer profile.

A secondary target market may also affect the business's marketing mix. If Cachet's secondary target market consists of women who are traveling to Manhattan on a business trip or on a weekend vacation to catch the latest Broadway show, Cachet will have to expand its advertising to include the magazines these people read. Cachet will also need to have a location that is highly visible and convenient to its secondary target market.

Two notes of caution need to be provided here. First, it is usually better for a new business to concentrate on serving one market well rather than trying to have something for everybody. In Cachet's case, it would be better for it to concentrate 80 percent of its sales effort on its primary target market and 20 percent on tourists than to try to split its mix right down the middle. The greater the differences between your primary and your secondary target market, the more you should consider having two separate businesses, each catering to the unique needs of one of your target markets. The rifle approach works best if you are shooting at a target with only one bull's-eye.

Second, being able to identify your target bull's-eye and being able to hit it with your marketing mix do not guarantee success. Remember, if your new business is to succeed, it must be able to create and maintain customers *for a profit*. The bottom line is that you have to make enough profit to justify the time and money you invest in your new business. As you read the next two chapters, on marketing, also make sure to read the chapters on developing financial projections.

5

Product and Price Strategy

Now that you have analyzed the overall market, determined the strengths and weaknesses of the existing businesses in that market, and identified your specific target market, you are in a position to develop your marketing mix. The marketing mix for your business should reflect the sustainable competitive advantages that you plan to have and how you will be able to offer greater satisfaction to your target market than any other business offers.

One of the basic principles of business success is, "To succeed, you must be better than your competition, and to be better, you must be different." Being different does not automatically mean that you will be better. Your marketing mix must be better in areas that your target market values.

Your market offering is better only if your target market considers it to be better. Your target market must value the difference and must be willing to pay for it. For example, the owners of La Tour Eiffel may claim that it is the best French restaurant in Chicago. They may base their claim on the head chef's credentials and her commitment to using only the finest ingredients. Professional accomplishments and expensive ingredients may affect the taste of the food, but it will be the expectations and preferences of the people in the target market that will determine whether they consider it to be the best. This is why it is so important that you be in tune with the people in your target market and that you try to see the world through their eyes.

New businesses must be tailored to the needs, desires, interests, preferences, and behaviors of their target markets. Your target market is the judge and the jury when your business goes on trial in the marketplace. You may believe that you have the lowest prices in town, but if your target market is price-sensitive and believes that your prices are not the lowest, it will go somewhere else. The same applies to your location and the other components of your market offering. If you believe that your business is conveniently located, but your target market considers it to be out of the way, it will take its business elsewhere.

The marketing mix is made up of four components, which are known as the "four Ps." These components are the product-service strategy, the price strategy, the promotional strategy, and the physical distribution strategy. Your marketing mix represents the rifle bullet that your business fires at its target market.

PRODUCT-SERVICE STRATEGY

Each component of the marketing mix plays an integral role in your effort to create and maintain customers. Among the four Ps, product-service strategy may play the most significant role. Businesses are usually described in terms of the products and services they offer the marketplace. Pricing, promotion, and physical distribution are also important. However, if the goods and services you offer are not what people in your target market desire and are willing to buy, it will not matter how low your prices are, how catchy your advertising is, or whether you have a convenient location.

The development of your product-service strategy begins with identifying the products and services to offer. The competitive matrix will be helpful here. Market analysis may indicate that customers in your target market are still searching for colors, sizes, or types of that particular product. The matrix may also indicate that your target market is looking for a specific brand that is not available in your geographic territory.

The product-service mix can be described in terms of its breadth and its depth. Breadth refers to how many different brands you offer. A business with a broad product mix offers a variety of brands. The depth of the product line refers to the number of models offered for each brand. The broader and deeper your product mix, the greater the selection for your target market. A note of caution may be appropriate here. If you offer the wrong brands, it may not matter how many models you carry. This is why it is important to determine whether your target market is brand-conscious and brand-loyal.

Retail sporting goods stores are an example of a type of business that has a broad and deep product mix. Most sporting goods stores carry at least six different brands of shoes and at least five models for each brand. A few decades ago, this was not the case. Everyone wore "regular" white tennis shoes. Now there are low-cut, high-cut, pastel-colored, zebra-patterned, cross-training, yoga, exercise, jogging, and aerobic shoes.

If market analysis indicates a trend toward people wanting to have a different athletic shoe for each sport, then sporting goods stores will need to have this breadth and depth of product mix. Henry Ford's product strategy for his Model T was based on the premise, "You can have your car in any color as long as it is black." This strategy no longer applies to automobiles, and it doesn't apply to most other products in today's Baskin-Robbins, 31-flavors marketplace. In many markets we have gone from a one-size-fits-all product or service to having to offer customized products or services that enable customers to have their individual needs met.

The product-service strategy also involves the services you plan to offer your target market. The United States has become a service economy. Even though service businesses sell labor and/or information, the process of developing a service strategy is not very different from the process of developing a product strategy. The primary difference between products and services is that, in many cases, potential customers may be able to perform the services for themselves. Businesses engaged in selling residential real estate, moving household furnishings, landscaping, hairstyling, preparing taxes, offering exercise opportunities, and painting houses do not just compete against other businesses; consumers of these services may choose to bypass these businesses and perform the services for themselves if they find it worthwhile.

Service businesses succeed to the extent that they are able to provide their services better, quicker, in a more convenient way, or in a less expensive manner than their competition or their customers can. If a service business does not have a competitive advantage, why should consumers give it their money?

Most businesses that sell products also provide various services. The competitive matrix may indicate that customers are in search of a business that will (1) provide a delivery service, (2) take phone orders, (3) have knowledgeable salespeople, (4) accept special orders, (5) provide a warranty or money-back refund, (6) accept credit cards, or (7) provide advice on how to use the products. Amazon.com's success cannot be attributed merely to its offering books at competitive rates. Its ability to provide information about books and to suggest books that may interest the customer makes a real difference. The ability to order books on a 24/7 basis in an almost effortless manner and have them delivered to your door gave Amazon.com a formidable competitive advantage when it opened its electronic doors to the public.

When you are trying to decide which products to carry, keep in mind the saying, "You want to offer products that don't come back to people who do." The more that you offer what the people in your target market want, the higher the probability that those people will be loyal to your business. This is important because the higher your level of customer satisfaction and loyalty, the less likely your customers will be to try other businesses or to be influenced by your competitors' advertisements.

People who are contemplating going into business need to remember that they are not in the business of selling products or services. They need to be in the business of providing satisfaction. If you plan to open a business that sells products, you may find that your greatest competitive advantage comes from the services you offer with your products. Most existing businesses do a poor job when it comes to providing customer service. Their salespeople resemble the living dead. They know little about the products they stock. More often than not, customers feel like calling in the Civil Air Patrol to help find someone to take their money.

If you will be offering the same products as everyone else, at comparable prices, and in a location that is no better than your competitors', you will have to provide your target market some reason to do business with you. The service part of your product-service strategy may make the difference. It could be your competitive advantage—especially if the competitive matrix indicates that there is a significant gap for customer service.

Even if you offer the best products, prices, and location, you need to guard against the tendency to become complacent. If you do, when the next person analyzes the market to identify an area of business opportunity, your business may be rated low on the customer service dimension of the competitive matrix. You will be putting out the welcome mat for additional competition.

It should be apparent that a business's product-service strategy cannot be viewed in isolation or in a stagnant fashion. It is an integral part of the marketing mix. Your product-service strategy needs to be consistent with the other three Ps of the marketing mix. In some situations, your product-service offering may be your competitive advantage; in other cases, it may be less significant. Most businesses can be classified according to the extent to which their target market(s) place(s) a premium on the product-service offering. Accordingly, businesses can be classified into the following categories: specialty, shopping, convenience, and impulse.

Product-Service Classifications

Specialty Items

A specialty business offers a brand that is valued by the target market. This type of business may have exclusive rights to distribute a brand in a particular geographic area. The customers of a specialty business generally are (1) not very price-sensitive, (2) less likely to be influenced by advertisements from competitors, and (3) willing to go out of their way to buy that particular brand, product, or service. This situation was portrayed in two advertisements years ago. Camel cigarettes had an ad that had a picture of a man's shoe with a hole in the bottom. The caption read, "I'd walk a mile for a Camel." The other ad was by Schlitz Brewery. Schlitz had the slogan, "When you're out of Schlitz, you're out of beer!" Both of these companies tried to project the image that they offered specialty items. If your market analysis indicates that the target market has a strong preference for a specific brand, product, or service that is not available in your geographic area, this may represent your best opportunity to develop a competitive advantage.

Having a specialty business often involves customizing your product-service offering to the needs of your potential customers. Years ago, an individual who was an avid pizza consumer was standing at the order counter of his favorite pizza restaurant. When he noticed one of his colleagues at the pickup counter, he asked him if bought pizza from any other restaurant in the area. His friend indicated that he went to Guido's Pizzeria when he was across town because Guido's served "white" pizza. The friend said that he occasionally preferred white pizza because it did not have as much tomato paste and did not upset his stomach as much as traditional red pizza. The first person then said that he would have to give Guido's white pizza a try. The chef must have overheard the conversation, because he came out and said, "If you want white pizza, I'll make you white pizza!"

The chef's reaction illustrated several points: (1) The customer is always right; (2) you need to offer what the customer wants to buy, not what you want to sell; and (3) you are in the business of providing satisfaction, not of selling products and services. You must be willing and able to tailor your products and services to your target market. You should not expect your target market to change its wants and behavior to what you want to sell.

Shopping Items

Numerous types of goods and services are considered shopping items by certain segments of the market. Something is considered a shopping item if consumers deliberately compare price and quality when purchasing it. Consumers of shopping items check out numerous businesses so that they can do comparison shopping. They compare the prices and attributes of numerous brands and businesses. While they may prefer one brand to another, they look at the value of the item, or the combination of price and quality. People who are comparing shopping items are looking for a good deal. They may prefer the General Electric brand to the Panasonic brand, but if the Panasonic item is priced lower than the GE item, the consumer may buy the Panasonic product. Brands may still be a factor in shopping items, but brand loyalty is not as strong as it is with specialty items.

Quite a few products and services are shopping items. A large percentage of Americans do comparison shopping. They are willing to check three or more stores in order to find the best value. This is why furniture stores are located near other furniture stores: Most people want to see what is available before they buy the product. The same principle applies to car dealerships and clothing stores. Some restaurants that are located in "restaurant rows" display their menus at their entrances to permit potential customers to check them out. Electronic commerce has made it possible to do comparison shopping with an almost unlimited number of product or service providers. Manufacturers, distributors, and the general public can now compete for the customer's attention through their Web sites and auction sites. The ability to order products and services over the Internet has turned the traditional retail store with its "just around the corner" location upside down for some types of businesses.

If your market analysis indicates that existing businesses offer a fairly wide selection of products or services, but that their prices are higher than they should be, you may have an opportunity to create a competitive advantage by matching their product-service offerings but charging lower prices. This strategy may be effective if you have a reasonable location and if your competitors don't retaliate by lowering their prices. This is why it is advisable that you have numerous competitive advantages when you develop your marketing mix.

You want your business to be the preferred brand with a competitive price. The quality of your people will also affect the quality of the products and services offered by your business. Your people, your location, and other factors that are valued by your target market may provide your business with an additional edge in the marketplace. Your business needs to give its target market a compelling reason to buy its products and services. Salespeople use the term *unique selling proposition* to describe what separates your business from all the other businesses. If you are in the shopping item type of business, you should make sure that your marketing mix gives customers what they are looking for—or, better yet (if it will be more profitable), see if you can transform your business into a specialty business.

Convenience Items

The brand of a product went from being very important in the specialty-type business to being moderately important in the shopping-type business, where selection and value were the key elements. With convenience items, consumers have even less concern for a particular brand, a particular size, or even a particular price. Some consumers place a premium on how easy it is to purchase certain items.

In the last few decades, the United States has experienced a convenience revolution. People prefer not to go out of their way. Either they do not want to go out of their homes or they do not want to get out of their cars. There used to be a gas station on every corner. Now there is a convenience store on every corner. Banks, restaurants, laundries, drugstores, and liquor stores have selected locations near their target markets. They have also built drive-in windows to make it easier for their customers to do business. Other businesses offer delivery service so that the customer doesn't even have to get into the car.

Malls are a kind of large-scale convenience store. Like their predecessors, the large department stores, they try to offer one-stop shopping. It was not that long ago that catalogs and infomercials came on the scene to challenge conventional retail stores. Most recently, Internet sites have made it possible for people to shop from the convenience of their homes, offices, cars, or almost anywhere.

The key ingredient for a convenience item is just what the name implies: It must be convenient to the target market. Most convenience businesses are run on the premise that consumers frequently place convenience ahead of brand loyalty and price consciousness. The typical neighborhood convenience store will not carry all the top brands, nor will it offer a broad and deep product selection. Instead, it will stock one or two brands in one or two sizes. Convenience stores try to carry basic items that people are likely to run out of, such as bread, milk, gasoline, beer, cigarettes, and film. In a sense, convenience stores can be viewed as emergency stores. When people run out of something before they expected to, they want to get it in a hurry. This is why the location and the hours may be the most important parts of a convenience business. The emergency or "I want it right now" nature of convenience items explains why convenience stores can get away with charging higher prices.

The lack of product selection and higher prices are the trade-off for convenience. People are less particular about the brand and price when they are in a hurry or when they just do not want the bother of going some distance to buy the product or service. Convenience businesses tailor their marketing mixes to certain target markets. People who are brand-loyal tend to drive farther to get their favorite brand. People who are price-conscious are willing to shop where they can get lower prices, even if it takes them more time. Convenience items are suited to people in target markets who have disposable income and who place a premium on the value of their time.

Impulse Items

The best way to describe an impulse item is that it is something that the consumer did not plan to buy. Impulse items do not appear on people's shopping lists. They tend to be spur-of-the-moment purchases. Food is the best example of an impulse item. Small food booths at shopping malls make most of their money from people who did not go to the mall to buy food. The same applies to the sale of candy in drugstores and grocery stores. Most people did not go there to buy candy. A large portion of the sales at ice cream and yogurt shops located on major thoroughfares can also be attributed to impulse purchases.

Most impulse purchases are driven by emotion rather than by necessity. Most of the products and services that can be classified as impulse items must be located and displayed in such a way that it is easy for the potential consumer to see them and purchase them. In a sense, people in the impulse-item business make their living by getting customers of other businesses who are looking for other products and services to spend a moment of their time and some of their money on these impulse items. This is why a number of businesses want to have links on popular Web sites. It may be a lot easier to get potential customers to hit their link than it would be to get them to seek out their Web site. These businesses have an almost parasitic relationship with the host sites.

Amazon.com is very effective in getting its customers to buy more items than they might have planned to buy. Not only does its Web site suggest additional books that are tailored to that individual customer, but its "add it to my shopping cart" feature makes buying more books almost effortless. Product-service strategy is important, but the location, visibility, and display of impulse items may be just as important.

Matching Your Product-Service Strategy to Your Target Market

Your business's success will be directly related to the extent to which your product-service offering is tailored to the target market's unique interests. The four categories of product-service offering provide a means for describing how particular your target market may be about products and services.

You need to recognize that something that is a shopping item to one person may be a convenience item to another person and an impulse item to a third person. Automobiles are shopping items to most people. People tend to compare models, prices, financing, and warranties before they make a decision. This process may involve all members of the family, and it may take months before the final decision is made. However, some people will buy only one particular brand, at one particular dealer, and from one particular salesperson. A few people approach buying an automobile as if it were a convenience or even an impulse item. They do not want to wait, and they want to take it with them. The differences in what people look for in products and services represent opportunities for new businesses.

PRICING STRATEGY

Your pricing strategy will depend on numerous factors. Your prices will need to reflect the target market you select, the nature and extent of competition, the strength of your location, your cost structure, the type of goods and services you will offer, and your target market's price sensitivity. There may be as many approaches to pricing as there are factors that affect a business's pricing strategy.

The Standard Markup Approach

Quite a few businesses use the standard markup or cost-based approach for setting their prices. With the standard markup approach, a retailer will base its price for an item on what it paid for that item plus a percentage of that cost. The percentage of cost that is added to the cost is what is referred to as the markup. The standard markup formula is

$$\text{Retail price} = \text{cost} + \text{markup}$$

The markup percentage may be suggested by your suppliers, or it could be based on other cost-related factors. Many retailers use a customary markup of 100 percent of cost. The 100 percent markup is easy to figure. If the owner of a wine and cheese shop buys a bottle of imported French wine for $6, then the bottle would be priced at $12.

Service businesses frequently use the standard markup approach. One CPA firm's hourly rate is three times what it pays the accountants who will be doing the work. The logic behind this pricing strategy is that the price for the firm's services has to cover three important components. The first component is what the CPA firm has to pay the accountants for the work they actually do. The second component is the fringe benefits, social security payments, training time, and the time the accountants are in their offices between clients. The second component also includes training, office rent, insurance, clerical assistance, and the depreciation of equipment. This component represents the "overhead" of the business. The third component is the salaries of the senior managers who coordinate the firm's operations, along with a reasonable profit.

The standard markup approach is fairly common in certain types of businesses. If you are starting such a business and you want to have an idea of what the average markup is, you can check trade data or *Annual Statement Studies* (published by RMA) to get the average markup figure. Trade data frequently report the gross margin as a percentage of sales. The gross margin is the result of subtracting the cost of goods sold from sales. If trade data indicate that the gross margin is 40 percent of sales, then you know that the cost of goods sold must be 60 percent of sales. If an item sells for $10, then the business had to pay $6 for it. The gross margin represents the markup of $4 on a cost of $6 per unit. If the gross margin is 40 percent of sales, then the markup on cost is 66 percent of cost.

The standard markup method has two major shortcomings: It fails to take into consideration either the unique nature of the market or competition, or both. The standard markup approach is based on costs rather than market conditions. It also assumes that your competition uses the same approach and that your customers are willing to buy your products or services at those prices.

If you use the standard markup approach, make sure you use the proper base. Some industries state markup as a percentage of cost; others state it as a percentage of selling price. There is a big difference between a 60 percent markup on cost and a 60 percent markup on selling price.

The Match-the-Market Approach

This approach often resembles the standard markup approach. Businesses that compete against one another may offer their products or services at comparable prices. If they use a standard markup and have comparable products or services, then their prices will be fairly close to one another.

The situation may arise in which one or two businesses in a given market decide to lower their markup percentage in order to attract additional customers. Other businesses may then lower their prices to avoid losing customers. The same situation may arise if a business decides to raise its prices. If one business owner thinks that customers are not price-sensitive, that owner may raise prices in order to increase profits. Some or all of that business's competitors may then "match" the new prices. After a period of time and a number of such changes, prices may reflect what one or two businesses think prices should be rather than the standard markup percentage.

New businesses frequently choose the matching strategy because consumers have already demonstrated their willingness to buy goods and services at these prices. This approach has numerous drawbacks. The primary drawback is that if you have a competitive advantage that your target market values, you should be able to charge higher prices. The match-the-market approach is a "play it safe" approach that fails to consider your unique strengths. Many businesses adopt this approach because they do not want to rock the boat. The match-the-market approach can also be risky. If one business lowers its prices, there is always the risk that a price war will develop in which customers benefit from the lower prices but each business sees its profits vanish. Lemmings will follow other lemmings off a ledge; don't put yourself in a position where you have to match lower prices.

The Market-Based Approach to Pricing

Numerous factors are taken into account with this approach. You begin by analyzing the nature of your target market and determining whether your potential customers prefer a certain brand, whether they have disposable income, whether they are price-sensitive, how often they buy your type of products or services, and whether they consider your products or services to be in the specialty, shopping, convenience, or impulse category.

Using this approach, you pay particular attention to the competitive matrix for your target market. The number of businesses in the market and the extent to which those businesses meet your target market's needs will affect your pricing strategy. The degree to which customers are loyal to existing businesses will also affect your pricing strategy. If the matrix indicates that numerous businesses already offer a good selection of products, brands, or services; have reasonable prices; and are conveniently located, then it may not be advisable for you to set your prices higher than your competitors'. You may be better off matching your competitors' prices or offering lower prices to entice their customers to try your business.

The Market-Penetration Approach to Pricing

If the target market is price-sensitive, then you may consider a market-penetration pricing strategy. This strategy gets its name because you are trying to enter the market by diverting customers to your business or getting people who have not bought the product or service before to buy it because the lower prices have greater appeal. The market-penetration approach works best when existing businesses have been taking advantage of the market by charging higher-than-appropriate prices. If you enter the market and try to divert your competitors' customers to your business, do not be surprised if they lower their prices to match or beat your prices.

Most established businesses prefer not to compete on the basis of price. They want to avoid price wars if at all possible. After all, if prices go up, new competitors may enter the market. If prices go too low, there may not be enough gross margin to cover operating expenses and generate profits. Penetration may be a viable pricing strategy for a new business if its cost structure is considerably lower than the existing businesses' cost structures. Wal-Mart used this strategy when it entered the retail market. It was able to offer lower prices than Sears because it located its stores on the outskirts of cities, where rents were much lower. Wal-Mart's management believed that if it offered brand names at lower prices, consumers would be willing to drive a little farther in order to save money.

You may be able to attract other businesses' customers with lower prices if the other three Ps of the marketing mix are comparable. If your location is too far out of the way, you will probably have to lower your prices even more to make it worthwhile for people to travel farther to buy your goods and services. If your prices are just a few cents lower than those of more conveniently located businesses, you had better not hold your breath while you wait for customers to switch to your business. If you want to attract customers, it may be better to have special sales or to offer time-dated discount coupons than to have lower prices on all the time.

The Skimming Approach to Pricing

If your review of the competitive matrix indicates that customers are still in search of a business, you may have an opportunity to set higher prices. If you have the exclusive distribution rights for a revolutionary new product or a popular brand that the market has been anxiously waiting for, you may have some latitude in setting prices. In such a case, you may consider a skimming strategy. This strategy gets its name from the practice of skimming the cream off the top of milk.

When people really want something, they are usually willing to pay more for it. By charging higher prices, you are going after the group of people in your target market who are willing to pay for something that is new or prestigious. The same applies to your location. If you offer a convenience type of product or service and you are located much closer to your target market than any other business, your price may reflect your competitive advantage.

Most business owners would love to be in a position to use the skimming strategy. It allows them to charge the highest price the market is willing to pay. The skimming approach, however, has four possible drawbacks. First, it assumes that your business is better than any other. Second, it assumes that your market is willing to pay more. The concept of elasticity has considerable bearing on whether the skimming strategy will be effective. The elasticity concept is based on the question, "Will the percentage increase in price be greater than the percentage decrease in the number of units demanded?" If the answer is yes, then you should charge a higher price. Third, higher prices mean that fewer people will be able to buy the items. Fourth, the higher the prices, the greater the likelihood that other businesses will enter the market and lure your customers by offering lower prices.

If you have a competitive advantage, you should be able to set higher prices. Your review of the target market and the probability of competitive retaliation will give you an idea about how much higher your prices can be and how long they can be higher.

Both the penetration strategy and the skimming strategy require judgment. Neither strategy will assure success. Nevertheless, these strategies may be more appropriate than strategies that ignore the nature of the market. Your new business may even use a combination of the two strategies. If there is considerable pent-up demand for your type of product or service and your target market has considerable disposable income, you may start with a skimming strategy. You may then slowly shift to a penetration strategy to keep competitors away and to attract customers who may be more price-sensitive. There may also be situations in which you would do the exact opposite. If there is a lot of competition, you may want to start with a penetration strategy to get customers' interest and then slowly raise prices as customers show that they prefer your business.

Additional Pricing Guidelines

Each of the preceding approaches provides a general basis for pricing products and services. Your pricing strategy also needs to address sales discounts and seasonality. You will need to decide whether you will discount your prices in various situations. The most common type of discount is to put your products or services "on sale." You may lower your prices for certain items temporarily in order to attract new customers, to get your existing customers to buy more, to sell inventory that has been building up, or to raise cash to meet pressing financial obligations.

Before you put anything on sale, you need to answer three questions: (1) Which items will attract customer interest? (2) How much of a discount will I need to offer to attract customers? and (3) How long should the items be on sale? The answers to these questions will depend on your particular situation. You will need to know how much each item costs. Rarely should you discount an item below what you paid for it. You may offer certain products as "loss leaders" to attract customers, but if your prices are below your cost, you may be violating the law. Also, your price discount will need to be enough to influence potential customers. If the item sells for $100, a 5 percent discount probably will not change consumer behavior. You may need to offer a discount of at least 20 percent to attract customers' interest. The discount needs to be large enough to get consumers to buy the product or service.

If the item is seasonal in nature and the season is over, then a larger discount may be needed to get customers to justify buying it and storing it for 6 months before they can use it. Remember, if they do not buy it at a discount, why should you believe that they will buy it next year? Any time you have to discount your prices, it is an indication that you misread the market. Either you bought too many items or your price was too high. Years ago, when the other car companies were offering major rebates, Volvo ran an ad that went something like, "When you offer what people want, you don't have to pay them to buy it."

Some retailers do special discount promotions. They reduce the price by an additional 5 percent per day or per week until the inventory is sold. This is known as a gambler's sale. The longer customers wait, the more they run the risk that the item will be sold out before they decide to buy it. You may also consider offering a quantity discount. Some businesses provide a discount if the customer buys a certain number of items. Tire retailers frequently run the sale, "Buy three tires and get the fourth free!" This comes out to a 25 percent discount on a set of four tires. Quantity discounts are an avenue for reducing your inventory by encouraging your customers to buy more at one time.

Credit cards, charge accounts, and delayed payments also have a bearing on pricing strategy. The primary reason for discounting is to make an item more affordable to potential customers. Some businesses have found that when customers charge purchases on their credit cards, they actually buy more items. The same applies to charge accounts. Furniture stores often let their customers charge items and postpone payments for 6 months or a year. They have learned that this strategy attracts more customer interest than a 10 percent off sale. A note of caution may be appropriate here. Extending credit to your customers is a major decision, and most businesses should avoid it. If you are considering extending credit, be sure you think it through. Extending credit will increase your record-keeping expenses, you will need to have more money on hand to pay your bills, and you run the risk that your customers will not pay their bills. Everything you do in your business should create customer goodwill; extending credit may create ill will.

Odd-even pricing practices may also be worth considering. If your business is in a very price-competitive market, you might consider using odd-number pricing. Retailers have found that when they offer a product at $9.97 instead of $10.00, sales often increase. Research has shown that people frequently perceive a $9.97 item to be in the $9.00 category rather than in the $10.00 category, even though it is only 3 cents away from being a $10.00 item. The 3-cent difference may produce a psychological difference in some consumers' minds.

Odd-number pricing is not appropriate for all businesses. Wal-Mart may offer a man's shirt for $14.97, but Saks Fifth Avenue rarely has an item end with anything other than zeros. Its shirts will be offered at prices of $80.00, $120.00, and $180.00, reflecting different levels of quality. Saks Fifth Avenue wants to emphasize the quality of its products and its exclusiveness. It feels that price competition is for businesses that offer products and services to people who have limited disposable income. Some prestigious businesses do not openly list prices. They feel that price is never an issue with certain target markets.

Two other forms of pricing have gained popularity among some businesses. A number of businesses have found frequent-buyer incentives to be worthwhile. If the product or service is one that is purchased on a fairly regular basis, then offering the sixth or eleventh time free or half off may keep customers coming back to your business. Time-based pricing has also been worthwhile for some businesses. If your research indicates that there are lower levels of demand at certain times of day, you might consider offering special prices at those times. Some restaurants offer early-bird prices. Movie theaters offer matinee prices. Some retail stores offer midnight madness sales. The idea is to get people to buy who would not otherwise buy and to get people to buy during lulls rather than when the business is crowded and you have to pay for more staff. Some businesses offer senior citizen discounts on the slowest day of the week in order to generate customer traffic.

The pricing of products and services is not a simple matter. Prices say something about your business and your target market. Consumers rely on prices to give them an indication of the quality of the item. This is particularly true with service businesses. With a product, consumers can look at it and possibly return it for a refund. It is also easier to do comparison shopping with tangible products. Services provide an interesting challenge because they are not as tangible. If you set a high price for your services, consumers may perceive your business as being a high-quality business. If you set too low a price, they may wonder whether your services will be any good.

Ultimately, the market will determine whether your prices are too high, too low, or just right. If you do not offer the people in your target market what they want for the price you charge, they will consider your products and services to be expensive, possibly too expensive. If you give them more than they expected for the price you charge, they will consider doing business with you to be a good deal. Your pricing strategy therefore plays a major role in whether you will be able to create and maintain customers for a profit.

It should be clear that pricing is multifaceted. Cost factors, psychological factors, and competitive factors have to be incorporated into your pricing strategy. Pricing strategy also has to reflect the dynamics of an ever-changing marketplace. Just a decade ago, who would have thought that both large and small businesses would be selling so much over the Internet? And who would have thought that online auction sites would be selling everything from sophisticated computers to used maternity clothes? The world is truly becoming a smaller place. The availability of alternative sources of products and services will make offering exactly what your customers want at a price that reflects competitive realities even more important in the years ahead.

6

Promotional Strategy and Physical Distribution Strategy

Once you have determined the products and services you will offer and the most appropriate price range for these products and services, you can shift your attention to developing your promotional strategy and your physical distribution strategy. Promotional strategy can be viewed as the way you communicate with your target market. Physical distribution strategy refers to how you make your products or services available to your customers.

PROMOTIONAL STRATEGY

There are various ways that you can communicate with potential customers. Promotional strategy includes advertising, publicity, sales promotions, personal selling, and public relations. Each component of the promotional mix plays a role in your efforts to have potential customers learn about your business and buy your goods or services. Your promotional strategy needs to address the *who, what, when, where,* and *how much* money to spend issues that will affect your business's ability to create and maintain customers for a profit.

The "Who" of Your Promotional Strategy

Your promotional strategy must use the rifle approach discussed in Chapter 4. No business can be all things to all people, and no business has an unlimited amount of money to spend on its promotions. You need to be sure that you are directing your effort and money toward your target market, or it will be wasted.

The better you can identify who the people in your target market are, where they live, where they shop, where they work, what magazines and newspapers they read, what television stations they watch, and what radio stations they listen to, the higher the probability that you will be able to get their attention and influence their behavior. This is why the customer profile is so important.

If you can identify your target market's demographics, then you can check the listenership, viewership, and readership profiles for various media outlets, including local radio stations, newspapers, magazines, and television stations. For example, if you are opening a clothing store and your primary target market is teenage girls, you should review the Arbitron ratings of radio listenership in your geographic area. Most radio stations have a copy of these ratings. You will be able to determine which radio station has the highest listenership in that age category. The A.C. Nielsen rating service does the same for television viewership. Of course, it wouldn't hurt to actually go out and ask potential customers what stations they listen to or watch.

The "What" of Your Promotional Strategy

The "what" involves determining the message that you want to communicate to your target market. Your promotional strategy is intended to take people who may have varying degrees of interest in your type of goods and services and get them to become your customers. This is why it is so important that you be able to identify your target market. When you open your business, your target market will be composed of people who have never been your customers. You will need to know who they are, whom they are currently buying from, why they are buying particular products and services, and to what extent they are still customers in search of a business.

Your promotional strategy is intended to get the people in your target market to modify their behavior. The message you send to them must be tailored to their mental frameworks. Your message must also provide them with an incentive to do business with you. Your promotional strategy should be based on (1) whom you want to influence, (2) what you have to offer them that is better than the competition, and (3) what you need to communicate to them to get them to become your customers.

Remember, a business venture will be successful only if it has a competitive advantage. Your target market needs to know that you exist and how you are better than your competitors. Your promotional strategy should emphasize your competitive advantage(s). Successful promotional strategies are based on the concept, "If everyone is offering a steak, then you must sell your sizzle!" You must know what your target market values. Your promotional strategy should highlight your business's unique selling points.

For example, if your target market is made up of elderly people who live in rural areas and your grocery store is the only one that offers a delivery service, then your promotional strategy should emphasize your competitive advantage.

Promotional strategy can be viewed as a step-by-step process. You want to get the attention of the people in your target market, to have them develop an interest in what you have to offer, and to have them check out your business. The "who" and the "what" must be synchronized. When you are about to open your business, your message should be institutional in nature. You want people to learn about your business: what it offers, where it is located, and when it is open. Your grand opening advertising is then followed with reminder advertising. You will need to stay in your target market's mind and keep it informed when you add new brands, offer new services, or have a special sale.

The "When" of Your Promotional Strategy

There are four major occasions when you should be promoting your business. The first is before you open. It is very important that your new business generate customer interest before it opens its doors. You want your target market to be anxious for your business to open.

Some businesses do "teaser" advertising. A teaser ad might say, "The countdown has begun; there are only 60 days until Johnson's Home Furnishings' grand opening!" The ad could include "Visit our Web site at www._____.com." This business could also do teaser advertising by erecting a sign at the site where the business will be located saying, "Johnson's Home Furnishings, an innovative approach to retail merchandising, will be opening here on June 2." You may be able to get the builder or leasing agent to put up the sign at no cost to you if it also includes the name of that business. The teaser ad and/or sign may pay big dividends. The pre-opening announcement lets prospective customers know about you. This could prompt them to postpone their purchases from existing businesses until they can check your business out.

Second, your business should have a grand opening promotion to attract customers' attention and get free publicity from the media. Newspapers and television stations frequently do stories on new businesses that are opening in town. They may be particularly interested in doing a feature on your business if it has some notoriety. Grand opening promotions and publicity are very important because you will need to generate sales quickly when you open your business. The sooner you sell your products and services, the greater your ability to meet your financial obligations and produce a positive cash flow.

Third, your business will also need to provide ongoing promotions. Your existing customers will need to be kept informed about developments in your business. You will also need to let potential customers know about your business and its sizzle. Most new businesses tend to have a token grand opening promotion and do little after that. You need to develop an ongoing promotional program that will keep your business in your target market's mind. The old adage, "If you build a better mousetrap, the world will beat a path to your door," does not apply in today's marketplace. If the world doesn't know about your mousetrap's advantages and/or if it doesn't know where your door is, you will not sell a single mousetrap. Remember, "If you build it, they will come" works only if your target market knows about it and wants it!

Fourth, there may be occasions when you should have special promotions to boost sales during slow periods. If you plan to have a two-for-one sale or a midnight madness sale or to add a new product or service, you need to have a special promotion to inform your target market of this.

Your promotional strategy must include a timetable for your various promotional events. Your schedule will help you identify when you will need to generate sales with special promotions to offset slow periods. The schedule will also provide a basis for projecting the timing of promotion-related expenses.

The "Where" of Your Promotional Strategy

We live in a world in which people are constantly being bombarded with advertisements. People have become very selective in what they will pay attention to. Your promotional strategy will be effective only if its message gets to your target audience at the appropriate time. The "where" of promotional strategy involves the media you use to communicate with your target market. There are numerous avenues or media available for promoting your business. The key is to know which media will produce the best results. The media to be used will depend on to whom you want to direct your message, the nature of the message, and when it needs to be presented.

Each type of medium has advantages and disadvantages. Television offers color, movement, sound, and broad geographic coverage. Radio offers a means to get to a large number of people at various times of the day and night. Newspapers offer daily coverage to a large percentage of an area's households. Direct mail permits you to send your message to a specific group of people. Billboards take advantage of a captive audience while people are in their automobiles.

There is no one medium that is best for all businesses. There is no one medium that is best for every type of message. If the message is very technical or complicated, you need to use written media. If the message is intended to appeal to people on an emotional level, you need to use media that can convey emotions. Web sites can be very effective in providing both emotional appeal and technical information. They can be designed to provide a wealth of information in a user-friendly format.

If you plan to open a retail sailboat outlet, it may be worth your while to do television advertising. After all, you are not selling sailboats; you are offering excitement, freedom, and fun. Television can capture the sizzle of your product or service. If your Web site is set up to stream video, it may also be an effective avenue for capturing the excitement of boating. You may want to use occasional newspaper ads that provide pictures of your products and feature special promotions. You should also consider using direct mail to people who live in neighborhoods with homes valued above $200,000. These people may fit your customer profile and probably have enough disposable income to afford your brand of sailboat.

Other businesses may find radio, billboard, and newspaper advertising to be more beneficial. Restaurants air radio ads during the morning rush hour to encourage drivers to try their businessperson's lunch special that day. Billboards on major thoroughfares may also promote a restaurant's steak and seafood menu. That restaurant may also run an ad in Friday's newspaper that includes a coupon for a 20 percent discount or a free dessert. One real estate development capitalized on the frustration felt by people caught in long commutes by putting up a billboard with the message, "If you lived here, you'd be home by now."

To the question of which medium is the best, the answer can only be, "The one that does the best job of attracting customers per dollar of cost." Your promotion budget also influences your media selection. You want to get the best return on each dollar invested in promotion. One medium may cost less than another, but you need to determine which one will do the most effective job of getting your message to your target market. Businesses frequently evaluate media in terms of the cost of reaching each 1000 potential customers. This process serves as a good basis for comparing media and for choosing the right radio station, television channel, and so on.

The "How Much to Spend" Part of Your Promotional Strategy

The question of how much money to spend on promoting your business is very difficult to answer. Some businesses spend a certain percentage of projected sales on promotion-related activities. If, for example, you are trying to generate sales of $400,000 for the first year, you may want to review trade data on your type of business to learn what percentage of sales other businesses of your type spend on advertising. Trade data may indicate that the average advertising expense for apparel stores is 3 percent of sales; for bookstores, 2 percent of sales; and for gift stores, 2.5 percent of sales. These figures reflect annual budgets for existing businesses. Your first year's promotional budget will need to be a larger percentage of sales because your business will be unknown and you will be trying to attract customers from other businesses. The percentage-of-sales method may give you a general idea of how much to spend, but spending a certain percentage of sales on promotion does not guarantee that you will generate that level of sales.

The best way to determine your promotion budget is to identify what you want to accomplish. This is known as the target approach. If you want to have 400 people come into your store each week, you need to determine what type and amount of promotion you will need to do in order to achieve that goal. You may find that it will take three prime-time radio spots per day on two different radio stations; a two-column, 3-inch ad in the local newspaper on Mondays, Wednesdays, and Fridays; two billboards located on two major thoroughfares; and 1000 direct-mail promotions per month to achieve your goal. The target approach recognizes that you must reach a critical mass before your promotions will have an effect on the market.

The percentage-of-sales approach indicates what other businesses spend. The target approach determines what you think it will take to achieve your sales goal. The target approach is particularly appropriate for a new venture. There are two other approaches that businesses may also use to determine their promotion budgets. Some businesses simply try to match their competition. They monitor the number of radio spots their competitors air and the amount of ad space in the newspaper that their competitors purchase. They then match their major competitors' promotional programs. This approach has two flaws. First, it assumes that your competitors are doing the right type and amount of advertising. Second, if you don't do a better job of promoting your business than your competitors do, why should your target market do business with you?

Unfortunately, too many new ventures adopt the "how much money do I have left to spend on promoting my business?" approach. This may be the least effective approach. It assumes that after you have allocated money to all of the other aspects of your business, any money that is left is what you can spend on promoting your business. The problem is that few businesses will have enough money left over to do a good job. This is not a "Which came first, the chicken or the egg?" question. If you hope to have enough sales to leave you with enough money to do promotions, you have things backwards. You have to put the horse before the cart. Your promotional strategy needs to be developed as an integral part of your marketing mix and receive its fair share of your overall budget.

Cooperative advertising is one of the reasons you need to think about your promotional strategy when you are developing your product-service strategy. Some manufacturers offer cooperative advertising allowances to businesses that carry and promote their brands. The availability of cooperative advertising may provide the basis for selecting one brand over another if the brands are fairly comparable in quality, price, and image.

Manufacturers that offer cooperative advertising reimburse retailers who promote their brands for from 10 to 100 percent of the retailers' advertising expenses for those ads. If the manufacturer offers a 50 percent allowance, this means that the retailer can either do twice as much advertising or reduce the amount of money it needs to put in the advertising budget. Cooperative advertising also has another benefit: Manufacturers frequently provide camera-ready artwork for promotions. This will make your ads appear more professional and enhance your business's image.

Most people are reluctant to spend a lot of money to promote their business. Their reluctance is quite natural. There is no assurance that money spent on promotions will bring in enough customers to justify the expense. One of the sayings about advertising is, "Only one-half of advertising works. The problem is that you don't know in advance which half it will be!"

If you view promotion as an expense, you will probably shortchange your promotion budget. However, if you view promotion as an investment that is necessary to generate the level of sales needed to produce your targeted level of profit, you may be more willing to allocate the money it deserves.

Selecting the Right Name for Your Business

This may be a good time to address the name for your business. If a picture is worth a thousand words, the name of your new business should be considered part of the mental picture. The name should follow at least three guidelines. First, it should create the image of your business that you want people to have. Cachet Fashions International conveys a level of sophistication that is consistent with its target market.

Second, it needs to be a name that can be remembered easily by your target market. If the name projects an image that people can relate to, they will remember it. Keep in mind that the more difficult it is for people to remember the name of your business, the more you will have to spend on advertising to get them to know it. The key is to be informative but not too cute. Avoid tongue twisters and names with too many words. Cachet Fashions International is almost too long.

Third, the name must be available for use. You or your attorney needs to make sure that the name you are considering is not already registered in your state. The secretary of state's office in your state keeps a record of the names of businesses that are already registered to do business in that state. If the name you want is not already registered, you should check to make sure that it is not being used by another business that has not registered it in that state. The secretary of state's office's list may include only names used by corporations. You should also check with the U.S. Patent and Trademark Office to make sure that the name is not already registered as a trademark.

It is amazing how many new businesses each year have an injunction placed on them that prohibits them from using the particular name they have chosen. Some of the businesses that receive such an injunction have been operating for quite some time before they find out that they are in violation. If it turns out that you are in violation, unless you can reach an agreement with the true owner of the name that enables you to keep using it, you must immediately change the name of your business. This means that you have to change your sign and your ads and start an advertising effort to let the market know your new name. The moral of this story is that you should check the availability of the name you choose and register it as soon as possible.

Two more points need to be made about the legal side of choosing a name for your business. First, you should make sure that the name is not very similar to the name of another business. If it appears that you are trying to steal another business's customers by using a similar-sounding name, that business may seek an injunction to keep you from using that name. You also need to be sure that no part of your proposed name violates any other form of registration. For example, the use of a reversed R in the name may not be possible because it has already been registered by a well-known business.

Many people have trouble coming up with a name for their business that captures the image they want to project. One particular technique may be very helpful here. Go to the library or phone company and look at the advertising sections for your type of product or service in the phone books for a handful of the larger cities in the United States. You may be able to create a unique name for your business that is a hybrid of other names.

If you find in one of those cities a great name that is not registered in your state and that you really want to use, make sure that you do the proper legal work so that you are not vulnerable to legal action. If you come up with a name that is really great, you should protect it by registering it as a trademark. Then, if another business in a different part of the country wants to use that name, it will have to get your permission and pay you for the right to use it.

Finally, you may want to avoid having a name that starts with a letter that is near the end of the alphabet. If you expect potential customers to use the advertising part of the phone book to choose a business, you do not want to be near the end of the listings in that product or service section. This is one of the reasons that the names of many businesses start with the letter *A*.

Your Promotion Mix

Most of the discussion of promotional strategy has been focused on advertising. Promotion also includes the size and layout of your business's sign, its letterhead and business cards, personal selling techniques, point-of-purchase displays, special sales promotions, public relations, and publicity.

A final point needs to be made about your promotional strategy. The most effective form of promotion has not been mentioned. Undoubtedly, the best advertising is having a large number of satisfied customers. When you give people what they are looking for at a price that is reasonable and in a convenient manner, you are creating a group of ambassadors for your business. Satisfied customers can be viewed as free salespeople.

The more you provide satisfaction, the more your customers will recommend your business to other people. The more word-of-mouth recommendations you get, the less advertising you will need to pay for. The less money you need to spend on advertising, the lower your expenses. If you have lower expenses, you can lower your prices. This will give you a price advantage over competitors who do not offer the same level of satisfaction. As you can see, product-service strategy, price strategy, promotional strategy, and physical distribution strategy need to go hand in hand.

PHYSICAL DISTRIBUTION STRATEGY

Physical distribution represents the way in which businesses provide goods and services to their customers. The location of your business usually affects its ability to provide its products or services to your target market. Location is important in two particular situations. First, if the customers normally come to the business, then convenience becomes more of a factor. This is why some people believe that the three most important things for a retail business are location, location, and location. The same may apply to service businesses where the customers come to the business. Hairstyling, dry cleaning, shoe repair, and accounting businesses usually have customers come to their locations.

Second, if your business goes to the customer, your location will affect the speed with which you can provide the service and the costs associated with providing it. Many service businesses go to their customers' locations. The actual location of your business is not that important if you are going into the landscaping, painting, pool cleaning, or parking lot striping business.

Some businesses never come into direct contact with their customers. More businesses are being started that promote their products via Web sites and catalogs, take phone orders, and ship via the mail or commercial delivery services.

There is a trend toward retail businesses delivering their products to their customers. Domino's grew at a phenomenal rate because its founder, Thomas Monaghan, realized that physical distribution could be its competitive advantage. If Domino's could deliver a warm pizza within 30 minutes at a reasonable price, it would attract customers who were in search of a pizza but preferred not to leave their residences to get one. Amazon.com was created when Jeff Bezos recognized that some people might prefer not to have to drive across town to buy a book.

Physical distribution strategy needs to be an integral part of the marketing mix. Too often, people go out and lease the first vacant facility they find. The location of your business may be the least flexible part of your marketing mix. You may be able to add or delete products or brands on a monthly basis. You can change your radio or newspaper ads almost overnight. Most businesses cannot change their locations with the same ease and speed.

You will have to do your homework before you select a location for your business. The location decision is like going fishing—you should find out where the fish are and fish there. Numerous new businesses fail each year because they were convenient for their owners rather than close to their target markets.

Trading-Area Analysis

If you are willing to relocate, then the first step in determining the optimal location for your business is to identify your target market and your trading area. To use the fishing analogy again, you want to identify the *type of fish* that are in search of bait. Then you need to determine *where* they can be found.

Elbert Hubbard observed, "Too many people place a stool in the middle of a field in hopes a cow will back up to them." You cannot create a market—all you can do is locate it and serve it. If you are not willing to relocate to where the best fishing may be, you should at least check out where you are to learn about the fish there.

If you want to determine which city may offer the best opportunity for your type of business, your trading-area analysis should include a review of demographic information for each metropolitan area. Trading-area analysis lets you compare one city with another. The *State and Metropolitan Area Data Book* (published by the Census Bureau) and the *Survey of Buying Power* profile the populations of most cities with a population in excess of 50,000 people. The *County and City Data Book* includes information about cities with more than 25,000 people and townships with more than 2500 people. The *Editors and Publishers Market Guide* and the other references listed in Chapter 4 will also be helpful.

You need to direct your attention to the nature of the population, not just the number of people in that geographic area. In most cases, you will be interested in how many people fit your customer profile rather than in the overall population. It is possible for a city with 70,000 people to have more potential than a city twice its size. Staying with the fishing example, the largest lakes don't necessarily have the largest fish. You will need to learn as much as possible about each trading area before you can determine the best one for your business.

Trading-area analysis helps you determine the number of people who fit your customer profile in each geographic area under consideration (the number of large fish in each lake that may want your type of bait). When you construct a competitive matrix for each area under consideration, you will learn the extent to which customers in each area are still in search of a business (which lakes have the hungriest large fish). This will let you rank the cities under consideration according to which ones offer the greatest opportunity for a new venture. The competitive matrix will also indicate where potential customers live, where the competition is located, and the extent to which you may be able to use physical distribution strategy to develop a competitive advantage.

Your trading area can be defined as the geographic area you plan to serve. It can be divided into three zones. Your primary zone should provide at least 66 percent of your expected sales volume. That is, you expect two-thirds of your sales to come from customers who live or work in this zone. Your secondary zone represents 15 to 25 percent of your sales volume. These customers may be located beyond your primary zone. They will do business with you less often. Your tertiary zone represents customers who will only occasionally do business with you. They represent anywhere from 5 to 20 percent of your sales volume. The secondary and tertiary zones warrant your attention because they can make the difference between profit and loss.

If you are a retail business, your primary zone may be the customers who live or work within a 10-minute drive of your location. Your secondary zone may be the area that is more than a 10-minute drive but less than a 1-hour drive away. Your tertiary zone may be the area beyond the secondary zone, with the customers from this zone being people who make a special trip to your business or who stop by when they are in town. The radius of the zone may be defined in either miles or minutes. In any event, the size of each zone will vary with the type of business, the location of your competition, accessibility, traffic congestion, and your target market. If you plan to set up a specialty business, each zone may be larger because people will be willing to drive farther for your product or service. If you are going to open a convenience business, your primary zone may be less than a 3-minute drive. If you plan to have an impulse business, your primary market may be the people who drive or walk by your business.

The same guidelines may apply for a service business that calls on its customers. In this case, your prices may vary from one zone to another because of the difference in driving time and the cost of providing service calls.

If you plan to offer specialty winter clothing, then your trading area might be the upper Midwest and the northeastern part of the United States. Your secondary market might be the Plains states, the lower Midwest, and the mid-Atlantic region. Your tertiary zone might be foreign markets with cold climates. If you plan to start a food-related business that provides a catalog, your trading area might be the whole country. If you set up a Web site that can take orders electronically, your trading area may be the whole world. If you plan to do any business outside the United States, you should use the services of businesses that specialize in doing business in other countries.

Choosing the Right Location

The process of locating your business can be viewed as traveling through a set of concentric circles. You start by selecting your overall trading area. Next, you try to identify the best general location or neighborhood. Then you try to find the optimal site. It is usually helpful to take out a map and color in your target market. You then indicate your competitors' locations. If your business is a specialty business, the exact location may not be that important. If your business needs to be close to its customers, however, you should look for areas where your target market is not served well enough or at all by your competitors. Areas that are underserved or not being served at all may represent opportunities for developing a competitive advantage by having a better location.

Study each of the more promising neighborhoods to determine which one will provide the best opportunity for your new venture. You will be looking at the overall traffic flow, the nature of zoning requirements, the accessibility for your target market, and the nature of the other businesses in that area. You should also talk to people in the city's planning department to learn about future developments and other changes that could affect your business. Certain neighborhoods offer greater opportunities than others. Once you identify the best area in which to locate your business, you are in a position to look for the best facility and site.

Numerous factors need to be considered when you select the specific location for your business. One of the first things you will need to do is determine the nature and size of the facility needed for your business. If you determine that you need a drive-in window, at least 20 parking spaces, high visibility from the street, large windows, a rear door with a loading dock, at least 3000 square feet, and room to expand if your business is successful, you will be in a position to compare various sites within the area. You may ask a commercial realtor to help you find a location to lease that fits your needs. If no suitable facility is available, the commercial realtor may be able to find someone who owns a favorable site who may be willing to build and lease a facility that will meet your particular needs.

The nature of your business will influence the type of facility you need and how important the exact site may be to your success. Again, if customers are going to come to your business, your location could be very important.

Potential customers often judge the quality of a business by the quality of its facility and its location. If you offer high-quality products and want to attract well-to-do customers, your facility and your location should be consistent with the image you want to project. You will also be judged by the businesses that are located next to your business and by the surrounding neighborhood.

You should try to locate near businesses that are already serving your target market but that will not be competing against you. For example, suppose you are opening a gourmet food shop. You might locate near a high-fashion clothing boutique, a dry cleaner, a bookstore, and a French restaurant. The people that these other businesses will be spending their promotion budgets to attract may also be in your target market. This could reduce your promotion budget and increase your profits.

Most shopping malls try to create symbiotic relationships among their tenants. When stores appeal to similar segments, they help one another. This is particularly true with shopping items. Some of the tenants in malls are called "parasite" businesses. They live off other businesses' customers. Impulse businesses frequently locate next to certain other businesses. They do little advertising. Instead, their locations serve as their promotional strategy. Cookie stands, flower stands, and popcorn stands use a parasite physical distribution strategy. They locate their kiosks in large regional shopping malls that offer high levels of pedestrian traffic. They are willing to pay high rental rates per square foot for their small spaces because they know that their location may be just as important as the sight, smell, and taste of their products.

The key to location analysis is finding a location that enhances your business's chances for success. A day-care facility should be located near where the people in its target market live or work. A massage business will have a greater chance for success if it is located in an elderly community or in a place where people may get sore muscles, like a ski resort. An awning business should locate in an area where people want shade for their homes or where it is windy and awnings will need to be replaced often.

When someone asks, "How important is location to a new business?" the answer is, "It depends on the nature of the business, its target market, and its competition." Physical distribution strategy must be an integral part of your marketing mix. If your physical distribution strategy is not consistent with your product strategy, price strategy, and promotional strategy, your business may fail. Conversely, if your physical distribution strategy is properly researched and planned, it could be one of your business's competitive advantages.

A few final points about locating your business and distributing your products and services need to be stated. First, make sure you or your attorney does a thorough job of investigating the zoning for your business. Second, make sure you consult with an attorney before signing a lease. Third, do not try to do business in foreign markets until you have your act together in the United States.

BE PREPARED TO CHANGE YOUR MARKETING MIX

Make sure your facility can accommodate your business as it grows. If you sign a lease, make sure that it is for the appropriate amount of time and that you have the right to renew it if the location works out.

One of the facts of business life is that the marketplace is in a constant state of change. Your customers' interests may change, new competitors may enter the market, new shopping malls may be built, and manufacturers of the brands you offer may go out of business. Almost everything may change in a relatively short period of time.

You must constantly monitor the market to detect changes and trends while they are occurring rather than after it is too late to change your marketing mix. If you are in tune with the changes and are able to modify your marketing mix to meet them, you may be able to transform the changes into lucrative business opportunities.

7

Determining Your Initial Capital Requirement

If the marketing part of your business plan indicates that an opportunity for creating and maintaining customers exists, then it is time to determine whether you can make a sufficient profit to make the investment of your time and money worthwhile. To do this, you *run the numbers* in the financial part of your business plan. Financial analysis will enable you to estimate the amount of money you will need in order to start your business and the profit that will be generated at different levels of sales.

The financial part of the business plan gives you a chance to look before you leap. Poor management is the number one cause of new business failure, but insufficient capital comes in second. Business success requires having the right amount of funds, the right allocation of funds, and the right timing of funds. Financial planning facilitates business growth and enables financial control. The lack of financial planning, especially when coupled with poor financial practices, can destroy a business even if a good market opportunity exists.

DETERMINING YOUR INITIAL CAPITAL REQUIREMENT

Most people either do not prepare an estimate of how much money they will need to start their business or underestimate the amount of money needed. As business specialist Maury Delmon noted, "The belief that a few thousand dollars and very hard work will buy success has held very little validity since the 1930s." Most first-timers have only a very hazy notion of the amount of cash, stock, or credit required to get their business up and running and to keep it going until it can carry itself.

123

There are numerous ways to estimate the amount of money needed to start a business. Two techniques are particularly helpful. The first technique (which will be labeled the MBA approach) is fairly sophisticated. The MBA approach involves projecting the level of sales for the first year. It then works backward from the end of the year to come up with the monthly cash flow that would be associated with that level of sales and expenses. The initial capital requirement is the amount of money needed at the very beginning of the cash flow schedule to support the business through its cash surpluses and deficits for at least the first year. The MBA approach to projecting the amount of cash needed to start a business is very useful, but it also requires an understanding of accounting that most people do not have. This approach is incorporated into the discussion in Chapter 8, which synchronizes sales, expenses, and cash flow. It is more accurate and should be used with the aid of a CPA if the preliminary estimate reached through the SBA worksheet approach indicates that the initial capital requirement is within your reach.

The SBA worksheet approach is useful because it provides a quicker and less complicated method of estimating your initial capital requirement. The worksheet is included in the U.S. Small Business Administration's (SBA) *Checklist for Going into Business*. It should be noted that the worksheet is not designed to determine profitability. It is designed to provide a rough estimate of the amount of cash needed to start a business.

The SBA worksheet (see Table 7-1) focuses primarily on the amount of money needed to get your business through its first few months. The first few months are critical. If you do not have enough cash to meet your financial obligations while you are waiting for sales to get to the point where the business is self-sustaining, you will have to either find a way to put more money into the business or close it down. This approach forces you to take the mental journey before you actually start the business. It is particularly helpful because most first-timers tend to overestimate sales and underestimate expenses.

Numerous businesses with profit potential never make it because they run out of money. Their cash disbursements exceed the amount of cash that was available when the business was started and the cash it receives via sales. Two things happen in most start-ups that jeopardize their viability. First, cash disbursements are larger and are due earlier (occur quicker or earlier) than expected. Second, cash receipts come in more slowly and are lower than expected. If you don't have enough money to meet your obligations to your landlord, your suppliers, your employees, and all the other people who are an integral part of your business, then your business may fail, just as grapes may die on the vine from lack of sun or rain.

Table 7-1. U.S. Small Business Administration's Initial Capital Requirement Worksheet

Estimated Monthly Outlays	Your Estimate of Monthly Outlays Based on Sales of $_____ for the First Year	Your Estimate of How Much Cash You Need to Start Your Business (See Column 3)	What to Put in Column 2
Item	Column 1	Column 2	Column 3
Owner's/manager's salary	$	$	2 or 3 times column 1
Other salaries/wages			3 times column 1
Payroll-related taxes			3 times column 1
Advertising			3 times column 1
Rent			3 times column 1
Delivery expense			3 times column 1
Supplies			3 times column 1
Telephone			3 times column 1
Utilities			3 times column 1
Insurance			Payment required by insurance company
Loan payments			3 times column 1
Equipment lease/ service contracts			3 times column 1
Legal and other professional fees			3 times column 1
Maintenance			3 times column 1
Miscellaneous			3 times column 1
Starting Costs You Have to Pay Only Once			Leave column 1 blank
Fixtures and equipment			Talk to suppliers
Decorating and remodeling			Talk with a contractor
Installation of fixtures and equipment			Talk to suppliers
Starting inventory			Talk to suppliers
Delivery of inventory			Talk to suppliers
Deposits with utilities			Talk to utility companies
Legal and other professional fees			Talk to accountant and attorney
Licenses and permits			Talk to state, county, and city offices
Advertising and promotion for opening			Estimate what you need
Accounts receivable			Estimate what you need to replenish inventory or cover payroll (service)
Cash			For special purchases and unexpected outlays
Other			Make a separate list
Total Cash You Need to Start Your Business		$	Add up all the estimates in column 2

Modified for this book and used with permission of the SBA.

The SBA worksheet encourages you to have a sufficient amount of cash to meet the numerous contingencies that will arise in your first few months of operation. If you have enough money up front, you should be able to make ends meet until you are able to generate a sufficient level of sales to cover cash outlays. Some businesses are able to have sales cover cash outlays in a few months. In most cases, however, it will take at least a year for cash receipts to exceed cash disbursements.

STEP ONE: ESTIMATING THE FIRST YEAR'S SALES

The first step in using the SBA worksheet involves estimating your sales for your first year. This estimate is crucial to the whole worksheet because it serves as a basis for projecting various cash outlays. Unfortunately, estimating sales is probably the most difficult thing to do when starting a new venture.

There are numerous ways to estimate your first year's sales level. The process of estimating the first year's sales for a new retail business begins with the use of economic data and trade data. A good place to begin is to review the *Census of Retail Trade* data, which may report total sales for your type of product or service in the geographic area you are planning to serve. The census data may indicate, for example, that $3,888,000 was spent on that type of product or service in that geographic area last year.

The census data may indicate both total sales and the number of establishments for the various types of businesses serving that market. If there are currently 10 businesses of approximately equal size in terms of facilities and inventory, then the average sales per business will be around $388,800. It would be unusual, of course, for all the businesses to be the same size. Nevertheless, this process will give you a starting point for estimating the level of sales generated by the average business.

If you plan to focus your attention on a particular segment of the market, you need to determine the percentage of sales to the overall market that sales to that segment represents. If your target market is made up of customers who live in certain neighborhoods, have a certain level of income, and are within a certain age range, you can review census data to determine what percentage of the overall market your target market represents.

Trade data may also provide statistics on what portion of overall sales comes from each segment of the market. If the data indicate that 60 percent of all purchases of that type of product or service are made by people between the ages of 30 and 50 who have household incomes greater than

$100,000 and who live in homes valued at more than $250,000, you can use these data to estimate the portion of the overall market that your target market represents. Given these numbers, you would project your target market's sales for the past year to be $2,332,800:

Overall market sales = $3,888,000

Your target market's share of the overall market = <u>60%</u>

Your target market's level of sales = $2,332,800

If census data are not available, you can get a rough estimate of the area's overall level of sales by figuring the level of sales for the "average" business in that area that is vying for your target market. You would start by figuring the average sales per day for the average business by multiplying the average purchase per customer by the number of customers. The daily sales would then be multiplied by the number of business days in the year to get the average business's annual sales. This number would then be multiplied by the number of businesses competing for your target market.

This approach is rough for at least four reasons. First, it does not take seasonality into consideration. Second, it is difficult to observe certain types of businesses. Third, there may not be an average business. Fourth, the business you observe may also sell other products or services. This will blur your estimate even more. You can see now why census data can be so useful.

Estimating Target Market Potential

Estimating first-year sales involves estimating total sales for the market for the coming year. The census data may be a bit dated, so you need to forecast what you think total sales will be during your first year of business. The overall level of sales in the marketplace could go up or down for various reasons. If the number of people who are likely to buy your type of product or service is expected to increase or if the disposable income of the existing customers is expected to increase, enabling them to buy more goods and services, then you would need to use a number larger than $2,332,800 as your overall estimate of sales for that market.

By reviewing census data trends for the last 3 or 4 years, you may be able to plot the direction and size of the changes that serve as the basis for these trends. Economic and trade data may also be helpful here. You may learn that each household tends to spend $200 per year on your type of product or service. If the number of households in your area is expected to increase by 800 in the coming year, then sales should increase by at least $160,000.

If trade data reveal that for every $1000 increase in disposable income per household, sales of your type of product increase by $20, then estimating the increase in disposable income will also serve as a basis for estimating how much overall sales will increase. Obviously, if both the number of households and the amount of disposable income are expected to increase for your target market, then the overall sales could be quite a bit higher than $2,332,800. A note of caution should be introduced here if your type of business is susceptible to economic or inflationary pressures. Your economic trend analysis may indicate that sales have increased by 3 percent per year for the last few years. If inflation has also been 3 percent per year, the market may not actually be growing at all. Check to see if the number of units being sold is actually increasing. This may be a better indication of a growing market.

The child-care business profiled in Chapter 3 may serve as a good example. Census data provide statistics on the number of households in a particular geographic area and the number of households with both parents (or a single parent) employed who have preschool-age children. These people could be primary customers of child-care services. The National Association of Child Care Professionals may provide an estimate of the expected annual rate of growth in the day-care industry and other helpful information. If the economic census data do not indicate the overall amount of money spent on day-care services in your area, you may have to generate your own estimate. To do so, you could review the listing of day-care centers in the Yellow Pages. You could then call each of these facilities and ask how many children it has enrolled and the weekly rate for child care. Basic math will then give you a rough estimate of both the total amount of money being spent on child care and the average level of sales for child-care businesses in your area.

This approach may not be very scientific, but in the absence of any other data, it will give you an idea about the level of business in the area. You could then look at the expected increase in the number of households, the expected increase in disposable income, and the rate of inflation to estimate what the overall level of sales may be for the coming year. You may need to incorporate an estimate for the number of births in each of the next few years and whether there has been an increase in the number of single parents who work in that area in your overall estimate.

Estimating Your Market Share

The following example will serve as the foundation for the remainder of this chapter and also for Chapter 8, which addresses the need for developing various financial projections. The example uses the sales estimate figures, but it will be framed in generic terms so that you will not get caught up in the actual type of product. Also, a retail business has been selected for the example because it captures a number of the facets that need to be included in the financial part of your business plan. The major differences between a retail business and a service business are in the areas of inventory and payroll. Businesses that sell tangible products usually have considerable capital tied up in inventory. When they sell a product, it is recorded as cost of goods sold. In contrast, payroll expenses are the largest single expense for service businesses. The services the employees provide can be viewed as a service business's products.

If the market is expected to grow by 3 percent this year, then sales for your market segment should be $2,402,784. Now you have to estimate what percentage of sales to your target market you expect to get, whether captured from existing businesses or obtained from new consumers or households entering your area. The number, size, and effectiveness of the businesses that are already competing for the customers in your target market as well as your strategy for creating customers will affect your market share.

If you believe that you can capture 10 percent of the target market, given your planned location, facility, types of services, level of inventory, price strategy, amount and type of advertising, and the other parts of your marketing mix, then you would project sales for your new business to be about $240,000, or $20,000 per month, in its first year. This means that you expect to attract some of the people who are moving into your area and some of the customers of the existing businesses who are still in search of a business, as well as the people who have forgone buying because no business has offered them what they are looking for.

Your first year's sales, however, will probably not be $240,000. Your first year's sales estimate needs to reflect the lag between the time you start your business and the time you generate your first dollar in sales. You will need to set up your business (decorate the facility, bring in inventory, hire and train your staff, and so on) before you open your doors to customers. Your sales estimate also needs to reflect what is called the ramping-up effect, meaning that the initial level of sales will probably not be as high as the level of sales when the business has been up and running for a few months. The SBA worksheet will use $230,000 in this example. The sales estimate of $230,000 reflects sales of $10,000 for the first month rather than the expected average of $20,000 per month because the first 2 weeks will be needed to move into the facility. The example does not reflect the ramping-up effect. In many cases, it may take quite a few months before your business gets up to its projected ongoing level.

There are a couple of other ways to get an idea of your first year's sales. If you are going to start a retail business selling products, you should ask the people who are going to be your suppliers what they think you can generate in the first year. Your suppliers may be calling on and selling to the other businesses in your territory. If they are, they will be in a good position to estimate the "average" level of sales for those other businesses.

One note of caution needs to be provided here. While the suppliers will want to help you, they will also want you to buy what they are selling. Some suppliers may overestimate what you can do just to get you to buy more inventory in the beginning. After all, they may be on commission, and they wouldn't want you to run the risk of running out of inventory if you are successful in attracting customers.

Another approach that you can use to get a feel for possible levels of sales is to see if your type of business is listed in publications like *Annual Statement Studies* (RMA), *Industry Norms and Key Business Ratios* (Dun & Bradstreet), *Financial Studies of Small Business* (Financial Research Associates), and the *Almanac of Business and Industrial Financial Ratios* (published by Aspen Publishers). These books provide financial information about numerous businesses. Some of them categorize firms by total asset size or level of sales. Even though the businesses that report their financial statistics to these publications may not be a perfectly representative sample of all businesses of that type in your specific geographic area or your specific target market, these publications do provide an idea of the percentage of businesses that have assets or sales of less than $100,000, $500,000, $1,000,000, and so on.

The financial tables may indicate that 90 percent of all businesses of your type have sales of less than $250,000. If so, it would be unlikely for your business to exceed that level of sales unless your market was much larger, your competition much weaker, and your business significantly bigger and better than almost all other businesses of that type. The same logic also applies to the amount of assets required to support certain levels of sales. Financial analysis reveals a direct correlation between sales and assets. In other words, it takes a certain level of assets (facilities, inventory, fixtures, and so on) to support a certain level of sales.

The sales-to-assets ratio is an important one to keep in mind. For certain businesses, for every $10,000 in sales, an additional $5000 in assets is needed, of which $2000 will be for inventory, $500 for additional fixtures, $2000 for additional space, and $500 for receivables and cash. The projected sales level will also affect the number of people who will need to be employed and the overall cost for payroll. The relationship between sales and payroll is particularly noteworthy in service businesses. There tends to be a direct and proportional relationship between sales and payroll unless the service can be outsourced or automated. As you can see, if you can estimate your first year's sales, you should be in a position to start estimating your initial capital requirement.

Three other sources of data may be worthwhile. The trade association for your business may have excellent data from its members. Your accountant and your banker may also be in a position to provide you with financial ratios or information about your type of business. Finally, the Small Business Development Center affiliated with the nearest university may be able to provide you with financial information.

IDENTIFYING YOUR CASH OUTLAYS

Now that you have an estimate of your first year's sales, you are in a position to complete the rest of the SBA worksheet. The SBA worksheet asks you to identify and list all the aspects of your business that will require cash outlays. It is helpful because it focuses on cash outlays rather than expenses. Cash outlays are not the same as expenses. For example, if you purchase a major piece of equipment, the cost will be depreciated as an expense over a number of years. The depreciation schedule will affect your profitability and your tax obligation, which will ultimately affect your cash flow. The SBA worksheet, however, views the whole purchase (if it isn't financed) as a cash outlay at the time it is made.

The SBA worksheet divides cash outlays into two categories: regular monthly cash outlays and one-time cash outlays associated with opening your business. The worksheet does not include the amount you will be charged for credit card sales. It focuses on cash outlays that you must make in order to start the business. Credit card charges will be deducted from your sales to give you net cash receipts, so they are not included in the worksheet. They will be reflected in the financial projections in Chapter 8.

Credit card expense for the most popular cards may range from 1 to 5 percent of the amount of sales that customers purchase with their credit cards. The rate may vary with the average amount of each purchase and the overall level of sales by that business that customers place on that particular credit card.

STEP TWO: ESTIMATING MONTHLY CASH OUTLAYS

First, you need to identify and list all the recurring monthly cash outlays. Next, you need to estimate the amount of cash needed for each outlay and record this amount in column 1. Column 2 reflects the cash required to make it through the first few months when your business is getting off the ground. Even though your sales forecast for the first year is $230,000, most of the outlays will be based on what it will take to generate sales of $20,000 per month (or $240,000 in annual sales) because the lack of sales in the first 2 weeks of the first month will hopefully be a one-time lull.

The SBA worksheet encourages you to have at least 3 months' working capital available. You might say, "Surely I will sell something during the first 90 days, so I shouldn't need to start with enough money for 90 days without sales." A better way to look at the 90-day equivalent is to view it as having enough money to cover your first 6 months of operations if sales are only one-half what you expect for that period.

The 90-day equivalent increases your chances of beating the odds because it gives you a buffer against lower-than-expected sales and higher-than-expected outlays. Remember, insufficient funds is the number two reason for business failure. Don't make the mistake too many first-timers make. It is safe to say that if you don't have enough money from the start, you won't be able to obtain it when you run out. Good financial management begins with (1) carefully estimating the amount of money needed, (2) knowing how much will be needed during your first year until revenue from sales can cover your cash outlays, and (3) having good financial controls to ensure that you are using your money in the best way.

Owner's or Manager's Salary

If you plan to manage your own business, you should fill in the amount you plan to withdraw to pay yourself. First-timers are tempted not to include this in the worksheet if they plan to manage the business because they may be willing to forgo taking any money out of the business at first if there is little cash. This is a mistake. If they were hospitalized, they would have to pay someone else to run the business for them. Also, it is good practice to plan to pay yourself from the beginning. If you plan to run your business as a corporation, you will need to pay yourself a salary and report it as an expense.

The SBA worksheet guidelines recommend that you double the figure in column 1 and place this figure in column 2. The rationale for a multiple of 2 is that if your business is running short on cash, you may be able to forgo some or all of your salary until things get better. If you plan to hire someone to manage the business, you should put three times the manager's salary in column 2. The manager may be less willing to postpone his or her paycheck.

If you plan to hire a manager, remember that you get what you pay for. Be sure you hire someone who has already demonstrated the ability to run a successful business and who can be trusted. The best way to avoid the number one reason for business failure—poor management—is to be willing to pay for quality management. Don't cut corners here. The quality of the manager's decisions does more than anything else to determine your business's chances for success.

Salaries and Wages

This amount can be estimated by multiplying (1) the number of people other than the manager who will be employed by (2) the number of hours they will work each month by (3) their hourly wage rates. If you are planning to start a service business, your people will be your "products." Your estimate of salaries and wages is particularly important because this is likely to be your largest cash outlay per month in a service business and your second largest cash outlay (replacing the inventory sold may be the largest) per month in a retail business.

You may be tempted to pay your employees the minimum wage. Again, you get what you pay for. If you plan to be better than your competitors, you should recognize that the quality of your employees will affect your chances for success. If you are trying to create and maintain customers, you must recognize that employee relations and customer relations are closely interrelated. As someone once noted, "If all you offer is peanuts, you should not be surprised when you end up with a bunch of monkeys!" If you cut corners with your people, they will cut corners with you and your customers.

Payroll-Related Outlays

This section of the SBA worksheet includes all payroll-related taxes and charges incurred by the employer. The major outlays are social security, Medicare, unemployment taxes, and workers' compensation coverage. Social security (also known as FICA) and Medicare are paid by both the employer and the employee. The rate for social security is a specific percentage of payroll up to a certain amount of annual income per employee. The rate and ceiling have increased over the years. Who knows what will be the case 5 years from now, so let's play safe here. If your business is formed as a sole proprietorship and you will be working in the business, you will be required to pay a self-employment tax as part of social security. The rate tends to be a little less than twice the individual rate up to the same income ceiling because you are both the employer and the employee. The ceiling for the self-employment tax is the same as the individual social security ceiling. Medicare does not have a ceiling.

Employers are expected to pay a federal unemployment tax. The rate is a percentage of each employee's wages up to a certain level of income. Many states also have an unemployment tax. If a state has an unemployment tax, then state tax rate is deducted from the statutory federal tax rate to determine your actual federal unemployment tax rate. Some states do not limit their tax to the same ceiling used by the federal government. Most employers are also expected to pay for workers' compensation coverage for their employees. The rate will depend on the nature of the business and the number of employees. It may range from less than 1 percent to over 6 percent of payroll.

Rent

Various factors need to be considered when estimating rent. The first question to be answered is how much space you need. Trade association data can be helpful here. Most associations compute average annual sales per square foot. If the trade association for your type of business indicates that average annual sales are $200 per square foot, then you would need a 1200-square-foot facility for your business in order to generate $240,000 in annual sales. Remember, however, that having that amount of space does not guarantee it will generate that level of sales.

You may need more space if you plan to carry more inventory or have more open space than the average business. If you expect your business to grow substantially in the second year, you may need to lease a 1500-square-foot facility so that you won't be forced to seek a new facility if things go well.

The next step is to find a facility that is appropriately located for the type of product or service (specialty, shopping, convenience, or impulse) you will be offering and your target market. The facility will also need to provide the right image and atmosphere and have the right mix of businesses surrounding it to enable your business to attract potential customers. Remember, your decision about a location and a facility must be closely tied to your desire to create a competitive advantage.

Annual retail rent rates may range from $10 to $20 per square foot for most retail space. The rates vary depending on the city, the size of the facility, and ancillary services. Retail space in premium locations like Worth Avenue in Palm Beach or Michigan Avenue in Chicago will be considerably higher.

If an appropriate facility rents for $15 per square foot, you will need to divide the annual rent of $22,500 (1500 square feet × $15/square foot) by 12 to figure your monthly cash outlay for rent. Multiply the $1875 monthly rate by 3 and put the $5625 in column 2. Some lease rates are based on a percentage of sales once your sales exceed a specified level. If you expect your level of sales to exceed the specified level, use the monthly percentage rather than the square foot figure as the basis. Make sure the amount you enter for rent includes all rent-related costs, such as common-area fees.

You may be tempted to save money (and cash) by leasing a vacant facility that is available at a lease rate that is markedly lower than the rate for other locations. Be careful. Most such facilities are vacant because the last business located there went bankrupt. This is not a good omen. Also, any money you save by getting an out-of-the-way location will have to be made up by more advertising, lower prices, and so on. A good rule to remember is, "Out of sight—out of mind!" You don't attract customers by playing hide and seek with them.

Advertising

There are various ways to estimate the amount you need to spend on advertising. One method relies on trade data. Trade data may indicate that businesses offering your type of goods and services spend a certain percentage of their sales on advertising. The percentage varies from one type of business to another. It may also be higher or lower depending on the size of the business. In any event, trade data will give you an idea about what similar businesses, possibly your competitors, may be spending on advertising.

Another approach to determining how much to spend on advertising is to estimate the amount and type of advertising it will take to achieve the desired $240,000 level of sales. As a new business, you will have to create your customers. Advertising will play a significant role in this process.

If you know your target market, you should be able to determine the number of television, radio, newspaper, direct mail, and other types of ads you will need to use to get the attention and interest of your prospective customers. Your advertising will also need to attract potential customers, get them to try your business as soon as possible, and stay on their minds after they have tried your business.

Your estimate also needs to take into consideration the nature, level, timing, and effectiveness of your competition's advertising. If a significant portion of your first year's sales is expected to come from winning customers from your competition, then your advertising budget will have to be larger than your competitors' advertising budgets.

Advertising is not a science, and there are no guarantees. One thing is certain, however: If you cut corners on your advertising, you will probably be cutting your own throat. If your sales goal is $240,000 and trade data indicate that businesses of your type generally spend 4 percent of sales on advertising, spending $9600 a year or $800 a month will not assure you of $240,000 in sales. Your message, media, timing, marketing mix, and competition, among other things, will affect your level of sales as much as your advertising budget. If you plan to have a Web site, make sure you include the monthly operating fee.

Delivery Expenses

Trade association data can be helpful here. Delivery expenses tend to be proportional to sales. Trade data may indicate that 1.5 percent of sales is spent on delivery expenses. Another way to estimate delivery expenses is to figure what you will need to have delivered during the first 3 months. This figure would be placed in column 2. Trade data may be useful for estimating annual delivery expenses, but this approach may be better for the SBA worksheet. If you plan to ship or deliver your products to your customers, then delivery costs will need to be included in the worksheet.

Supplies

This estimate can be handled the same way as the estimate of delivery expenses. You can use trade data or list all the supplies you will need on a monthly basis for the first 3 months.

Telephone

The best way to get an estimate of telephone expenses would be to identify all the long-distance calls you are planning to make. Most of your calls will be to suppliers. The costs for these calls can then be added to your regular monthly phone bill. For many businesses, phone expenses may not be a major outlay. However, some businesses rely extensively on the phone. In any event, the larger the amount of any expense, the greater the need for an accurate estimate of the monthly amount. The charge for your Yellow Pages ad should be listed as advertising instead of as part of telephone expense.

Other Utilities

Your utility expenses will vary with the type and size of your facility. If you are going to be renting a facility that is at least a few years old, the leasing agent or prior tenant may be able to tell you what the utility expenses were in the past. If you are planning to lease new space or build a new facility, the utility companies serving that area should be willing to provide an estimate of the utility expenses for your size and type of facility at little or no charge.

Insurance

Trade data may be helpful here, but this estimate can be better provided by a commercial insurance broker or agent. Ask three different commercial insurers to review your proposed business and to estimate the premium for an all-risk business owner's insurance package. They should provide an estimate at no cost to you. The rate is usually based on the nature of your business, the types of risks associated with it, the type of structure it is located in, and the total value of the assets to be covered. If your business is quite different from most businesses, seek a broker who has an underwriter on the staff. The underwriter may be able to prepare a package that reflects the uniqueness of your business. This will be better, and in some cases less expensive, than a standard package. Insurance is like advertising: Most people would rather not spend money for it, but it is far better to be safe by having too much than to be sorry for spending too little. Too many profitable businesses have gone bankrupt because their owners tried to save a few dollars by not having sufficient insurance coverage. If the annual premium is due up front or quarterly, it should be recorded in column 2. If it is due monthly, it should be handled like the other recurring monthly outlays in column 1.

It should be noted here that you should learn about the availability, rates, and coverage of insurance for your type of business when you are evaluating the merit of the business opportunity. Premiums for some businesses can be susceptible to dramatic increases. Some businesses are finding it difficult to get coverage at all because of growing risks and skyrocketing claims.

Loan Payments

Your monthly cash outlay for interest can be determined only after you have made the first estimate of your initial capital requirement. If the amount of cash you need to start your business is larger than the amount you have, either of your own money or of your own money plus that of a partner or that raised via the issuance of stock, you will probably need to borrow money. Whether you borrow from a bank (which is unlikely unless it is in the form of a second mortgage) or get a loan from a friend or a member of your family, you will have interest payments. If the first estimate of your initial capital requirement indicates that you will need to borrow $20,000, you will have to revise your estimate to include interest (and possibly principal) payments in columns 1 and 2.

If you are able to secure a 5-year loan for $20,000 with only interest due on a monthly basis, you will be expected to make a "balloon" payment of $20,000 for the principal of the loan at the end of 5 years. If you secure a loan with amortized principal payments (which is structured like a mortgage), you will have equal monthly payments covering both principal and interest over the 5 years.

With amortization, there will be no balloon payment due at the end of the loan. For example, if you borrowed $20,000 at 11 percent with monthly payments of interest and a balloon payment of the $20,000 due at the end of the loan, your monthly interest payment in column 1 would be $184. If the loan were amortized, the monthly payment in column 1 would be $435. Obviously, the interest-only monthly payment with a balloon payment due at the end of the loan will reduce your initial capital requirement. If the principal is not amortized, however, you should establish a "sinking fund" from each year's profits to cover the balloon payment when it comes due. The amortized loan reduces the need for self-discipline because it is structured like a sinking fund.

At this time, you are just putting an estimate in the loan payment column. You will not be in a position to put in the exact amount until you have completed the whole worksheet. At that time, you may find that you need to borrow more money than you originally estimated. The revised loan payment would then be included in the worksheet.

Equipment Leases/Service Contracts

More businesses today are choosing to lease equipment rather than buy it. Leasing has two advantages. First, it eliminates the need to come up with the cash up front to buy the equipment. Obviously, leasing your equipment will reduce your initial capital requirement. Nothing is free, so be sure that your attempt to reduce your initial capital requirement does not jeopardize your chances of being profitable. Take a close look at the lease terms and the penalties associated with the lease. Second, products are being improved each year. Having a lease gives you the flexibility to upgrade or change the equipment on a periodic basis as your business grows and changes. This figure should also include the expense for monthly service contracts if you buy equipment.

Legal and Other Professional Fees

Again, trade data may be helpful in estimating outlays for legal and professional services. However, it may be better to get estimates from a few attorneys and accountants. Accounting fees are usually a major professional expense. The monthly outlay for accounting services will be affected by the nature and size of your business. Your fees will also be influenced by whether you or your accountant prepares month-end and quarterly statements and does the tax preparation work. The fees will also vary depending on whether you hire a bookkeeping service, an accountant, or a CPA. Each level and type of service has a different price tag.

You should ask people you know who already are in business for the names of people they would recommend. You can then ask a couple of the recommended accounting services to review your type of operation and give you an estimate of their fee structure for various levels of service.

Legal expenses are the other major type of professional fee. Business operations usually involve contracts. You may also find it necessary to seek legal advice on a regular basis. The same approach you used in selecting an accountant should be used in selecting an attorney. In any event, select an attorney who specializes in commercial law. The estimate for professional fees is important. This outlay could range from about a hundred dollars to over a thousand dollars per month.

Maintenance Expenses

Maintenance outlays will be related to the type and size of your facility. If you are leasing space, your lease agreement may specify a certain amount of required maintenance for your space and for common areas like parking places or restrooms. If it does not, you will need to estimate your monthly cash outlays by contacting potential maintenance services.

Miscellaneous Outlays

This section includes two types of outlays. First, if you will be joining a trade association or will be involved in any organization that has an annual membership fee, you may need to include the fee(s) in column 2. Second, there are always a few things that come up each month that require funds. You may make a contribution to a local charity or buy flowers for an employee who is ill. These cash outlays are labeled "miscellaneous" because you don't know when they will occur from month to month. However, there will always be something that involves a cash outlay. Accordingly, you need to plan ahead and budget for miscellaneous outlays.

STEP THREE: IDENTIFYING STARTING COSTS THAT YOU HAVE TO PAY ONLY ONCE

All your estimates so far have involved recurring cash outlays. The time has come to estimate the one-time outlays that are associated with starting a business. The estimate for each of these outlays will be recorded directly in column 2.

Fixtures and Equipment

You need to determine what fixtures and equipment you will need for your business. You should talk to suppliers and contractors to get estimates for counters, storage shelves, cabinets or display stands, a cash register, special lighting, an outside sign, and so on. Items you buy will be recorded here as one-time outlays. Items you lease will be stated as monthly outlays. Also, make sure that this figure includes any delivery charges.

Installation of Fixtures and Equipment

This outlay is treated separately from the acquisition of fixtures and equipment because first-timers often forget to figure the cost of having these items installed. This illustrates one of the benefits of compiling a list of cash outlays: You reduce the likelihood that you will leave something out and have too little cash to meet your obligations.

Decorating and Remodeling

Almost every facility requires remodeling. Ask two or three contractors for written bids before selecting one.

Starting Inventory

This can be the most significant cash outlay for a new business. If you plan to start a retail business, your inventory could represent at least half of your initial capital requirement. If you plan to start a service business, you may not have much inventory because your people really serve as your inventory.

The best way to estimate your inventory needs will be to figure how much you will need to have on hand in order to support the level of sales you projected earlier for the first year of your business. There is a simple set of calculations that you can use to get an estimate of your initial inventory if you have access to trade data. First, you need to find out what is the average percent markup on cost. Then you need to find out or calculate the stock-turn ratio. The stock-turn ratio indicates how many times your average inventory turns (is sold) during the year. For example, merchandise in an antiques shop may turn two times a year. This means that the average item takes about 6 months to be sold. Merchandise in a clothing store may turn six times. This means that the average shirt is in inventory for 2 months before being sold. The stock-turn ratio is computed by dividing the annual cost of goods sold (based in this case on your projected first year's sales) by the expected average inventory:

$$\text{Stock-turn ratio} = \frac{\text{annual cost of goods sold}}{\text{average inventory}}$$

This ratio can be turned around so that you can estimate the average amount of inventory you will need to carry by dividing the estimated annual cost of goods sold by the stock-turn ratio. Trade data usually provide a breakdown of income statement and balance sheet information. Trade data may indicate that the cost of goods sold in your type of business is 50 percent of sales. If this is what you expect for your business, then you expect that items will be sold for twice the price you paid for them. If trade data indicate that the stock-turn ratio for your type of business is 4 times per year, then you can use the following two-step process to estimate the amount of inventory you will need to start your business:

Step 1

Multiply the projected level of sales	$240,000
by the percentage that cost of goods	
sold is of sales (50%)	× 0.50
to get your estimated cost of goods sold	$120,000

Step 2

Divide your cost of goods sold	$120,000
by the stock-turn ratio	÷ 4
to estimate the average inventory required	$ 30,000

You will need $30,000 in inventory on hand to support annual sales of $240,000. A note of caution needs to be introduced here. This is just a preliminary estimate for two reasons. First, trade data reflect existing businesses. They have learned what sells, and they have calibrated their inventories to reflect this. It will take you some time and experimentation to figure out what sells. Second, starting your business with $30,000 in inventory will not guarantee you $240,000 in sales, just as having a certain number of square feet or spending a certain amount on advertising will not guarantee you $240,000 in sales. The brands you offer, the way you display your merchandise, the effectiveness of your advertising, the appeal of your location, and a host of other factors will influence your level of sales. Your pricing strategy will also affect your stock turns and inventory level. Charging higher prices usually reduces your stock turns. Also, you may have fewer stock turns because your target market may not know about your new business right away.

You also need to consider whether your business is seasonal in nature. If you are starting in a peak season, you will need more inventory. You will also need to carry a larger amount of inventory if it will take a considerable amount of time to replenish the inventory or if the cost of a stock-out (lost business as a result of not having an item in stock when a customer wants it) is high. Suppliers may help you to estimate your inventory needs. They are familiar with the needs of similar-sized businesses. But remember, if the suppliers' people are on commission, they may suggest that you carry more inventory than you really need.

Deposits

Most landlords and leasing companies require deposits up front. Utility (phone, electricity, sewer, water, and so on) providers also require a deposit from new businesses. Contact each utility to learn its deposit requirements.

Legal and Other Professional Fees

Even though you listed professional fees in the estimated monthly outlays part of the worksheet, you still need to record the costs incurred in establishing the legal form for your business and setting up the accounting records. These are one-time expenses that should be treated separately from your ongoing cash outlays. These outlays will vary in proportion to the size, nature, and complexity of your new business.

If you plan to start your business as a corporation, the cost to prepare the articles of incorporation, set up the bylaws, and get the corporate record books and seal in order may run from a few hundred to a few thousand dollars. The same is true for having an accountant set up your books and your software.

Licenses, Permits, and Fees

License and permit requirements vary with the type of business. You should check with state, county, and city offices to learn what is required for your business. Certain businesses need an annual "privilege" license. You may also need to secure a retail or wholesale sales license. There may also be charges for construction permits or inspections.

Grand Opening Advertising and Promotions

Your grand opening advertising includes all the advertising that precedes and coincides with the opening of your business. It also includes the cost of setting up your Web site. This amount is separate from your regular monthly advertising budget. You will need to determine the level of visibility you want for your business. This is an important initial expense, because you want people to start buying your goods or services as soon as your business opens. Remember, the longer it takes to create customers, the more money you will need for your initial capital. Suppliers and media representatives can be helpful here. One rule of thumb for estimating grand opening advertising is that you should spend at least three times the amount you allocated for 1 month's regular advertising.

Accounts Receivable

This may be a good time to encourage you to use caution if you are considering extending credit to your customers. In most cases, there is only one good type of accounts receivable: one with a zero balance. This is one of the most frustrating aspects of running a business. If at all possible, have your customers charge their purchases on their bank credit cards. Credit cards may cost a small percentage of your sales revenue, but monitoring them will take far less time than keeping track of the credit that you extend to customers. You will also reduce the likelihood of having bad debt losses.

If you plan to let your customers charge their purchases "on account" to you, you will need to have more money to start your business. You need to estimate the average balance for your accounts receivable. If you expect to have $2500 in accounts receivable at any time during the year, you will need to include this figure in the initial capital requirement estimate. If you want to be more precise, you could figure what the largest amount of accounts receivable will be during the first 3 months.

Cash

Most businesses need to have cash on hand or readily available to meet unexpected cash obligations and to handle daily operations. Contact the owners or managers of similar businesses in other cities. They should be willing to give you an idea of the amount of cash they have on hand to meet these needs.

Other

It is hoped that your estimates include all of your cash outlays. However, it may be helpful to play it safe by having additional cash on the sidelines. A rule of thumb here is, "The more difficult you expect it to be to raise cash to keep your business going after it is started, the more you need to have money in reserve in the beginning."

STEP FOUR: COMPLETING THE SBA WORKSHEET

You can now estimate your initial capital requirement. Add the one-time cash outlays to the total of the monthly cash outlays in column 2. (See Table 7-2.) The total represents a very rough estimate of the amount of money you need up front to start your business and keep it open until your customers provide enough money to enable you to cover your cash outlays, start generating a positive cash flow, and hopefully become profitable.

The SBA worksheet indicates that you may need $82,060 to start your business. This implies that you will need to either invest that much in the business or get additional investors, a partner, or a loan to cover the part of the initial capital requirement that will not be covered by your personal investment. The SBA worksheet in this example included a $20,000 amortized loan.

The SBA worksheet stresses the need to have sufficient funding for your business from the very beginning. If you have that amount of money or can get it by borrowing or by bringing in one or more partners or investors, then you should proceed to Chapter 8. If you have (or can raise) only $40,000 to $50,000, then the funding gap may be too wide for you to even consider using the more rigorous MBA approach to figuring your initial capital requirement that is profiled in Chapter 8. If the gap is too wide, you may need to (1) increase your funding, (2) find ways to reduce the initial capital requirement, possibly by negotiating with your suppliers to allow you to pay

Table 7-2. U.S. Small Business Administration's Initial Capital Requirement Worksheet*

Estimated Monthly Outlays	Your Estimate of Monthly Outlays Based on Sales of $230,000 for the First Year	Your Estimate of How Much Cash You Need to Start Your Business (See Column 3)	What to Put in Column 2*
Item	Column 1	Column 2	Column 3
Owner's/manager's salary	$ 2,500	$ 7,500	2 or 3 times column 1
Other salaries/wages	2,500	7,500	3 times column 1
Payroll-related taxes	516	1,550	3 times column 1
Advertising	800	2,400	3 times column 1
Rent	1,875	5,625	3 times column 1
Delivery expense	300	900	3 times column 1
Supplies	40	120	3 times column 1
Telephone	100	300	3 times column 1
Utilities	175	525	3 times column 1
Insurance	Quarterly payment	375	Payment required by insurance company
Loan payments	435	1,305	3 times column 1
Equipment lease/ service contracts	200	600	3 times column 1
Legal and other professional fees	100	300	3 times column 1
Maintenance	20	60	3 times column 1
Miscellaneous	100	300	3 times column 1
Starting Costs You Have to Pay Only Once			Leave column 1 blank
Fixtures and equipment		8,000	Talk to suppliers
Decorating and remodeling		6,000	Talk with a contractor
Installation of fixtures and equipment		500	Talk to suppliers
Starting inventory		30,000	Talk to suppliers
Delivery of inventory		600	Talk to suppliers
Deposits with utilities		300	Talk to utility companies
Legal and other professional fees		1,200	Talk to accountant and attorney
Licenses and permits		200	Talk to state, county, and city offices
Advertising and promotion for opening		2,400	Estimate what you need
Accounts receivable		Not expected	Estimate what you need to replenish inventory or cover payroll (service)
Cash		3,000	For special purchases and unexpected outlays
Other		500	Make a separate list
Total Cash You Need to Start Your Business		$ 82,060	Add up all the estimates in column 2

*These figures are typical for one kind of business. You will have to decide how many months to allow for your business.

Modified for this book and used with permission of the SBA.

145

for the inventory over a 90-day period rather than when you start your business, or (3) explore opportunities with initial capital requirements that are more in line with the funds you have available to start a business.

PROCEED WITH CAUTION

You need to remember, however, that your calculations will be only as good as the data you used in making them. These estimates should be fine-tuned if you are thinking about going ahead with the venture. The MBA approach, used in Chapter 8, is far more accurate than the SBA worksheet. It also indicates that the business actually may have a lower initial capital requirement. By projecting the monthly cash flow associated with sales of $230,000, you can use it to estimate the corresponding initial capital requirement.

You also need to remember that most of the calculations have been for the first year of operation. You will need to draw the distinction between when you start your business and when you actually open your business. You may need to disburse cash months before you receive your first dollar in cash from sales. Your sales estimate may actually be based on 8 months of sales if you have to make cash disbursements 4 months before you actually open your doors. Your sales estimate should also reflect seasonality if this is a factor in your business.

8
Projecting Your Financial Status for the First Years

Now that you have developed a preliminary estimate of your initial capital requirements, you are in a position to determine whether you have enough money to start your business. If you don't have enough money, you will have to decide whether you want to (1) seek additional funding by taking on a partner, getting a loan, or selling stock if you can, (2) scale down your business to fit the money you have—which runs the risk of scaling it down to the point where it cannot succeed, (3) postpone starting your business until you have enough money, (4) consider one of the other possible businesses you identified earlier that may have a lower initial capital requirement, or (5) drop the idea of starting your own business altogether.

If you have enough money to start your business or you believe you can raise it, you are ready to go on to the next step of your financial plan: preparing financial projections for the first 3 to 5 years of operation. Several important questions involving profitability, cash flow, return on investment, and the ability to pay off a loan (if there is one) need to be answered at this time.

The first question is, "What kind of profit can be expected for the first year?" You went through a fairly deliberate process to estimate your first year's sales when you figured your initial capital requirement. It incorporated your target market, your competition, and the marketing mix you plan to use to gain a competitive advantage in your effort to create and maintain customers for a profit. Now you need to be sure that your first year's sales estimate will generate a sufficient level of profit to yield a good return on the money you will invest in the business and to provide enough money to expand your operations. If you need to borrow money to start your business, the level of profit you expect to make will be very important to potential lenders. Sales may pay interest, but profits will be needed to pay off the loan.

PROFIT PLANNING: CONDUCTING COST-VOLUME-PROFIT ANALYSIS

The first step in your financial analysis is to estimate the expected profit for your first year based on your projected level of sales. The second step involves figuring the resulting profit or loss for your first year at various sales levels. This is called cost-volume-profit analysis.

In the example used in Chapter 7, you estimated that your first year's sales would be $230,000. You need to identify all your expenses and determine how much each expense will be for the first year. Cost of goods sold may be your largest single expense. In this example, if you buy the items for $5 and sell them for $10, your cost of goods sold will be one-half of sales. This is the same as a 100 percent markup on cost or a markup of 50 percent of sales.

If you expect sales to be $230,000 during the first year, then your cost of goods sold will be $115,000. This tells you that you will have $115,000 left from sales to cover your other expenses and, you hope, provide enough profit to justify your time, risk, and financial investment. Next, you estimate all the other expenses for your business. Most, if not all, of these expenses will be fixed—that is, they will not vary directly with sales from month to month. These expenses include rent, advertising, payroll, insurance, and interest, among others. Adding these expenses for the year to your cost of goods sold for the year will indicate your total expenses.

Remember, when you are estimating your expenses, you do not want to merely plug in the numbers you used when you figured the initial capital requirement. The SBA worksheet was based on cash outlays. It does not accurately reflect the items that will be treated as expenses in this chapter. This is particularly true if you expect to have a loan or purchase equipment. If you have a loan, you report only interest (not principal payments) as an expense. If you buy a major piece of equipment, you will expense or depreciate it over a predetermined number of years instead of treating it as a cash outlay. The IRS does allow you to fully expense certain types of equipment in the first year, however.

At this time, you should check your projections with financial data for similar businesses that may be listed in *Annual Statement Studies*. As noted earlier, trade data provide ratios for cost of goods sold, gross margin, selling and administrative expenses, profit as a percent of sales, and numerous other important statistics that will help you estimate certain figures. These data are also helpful in verifying whether your estimates are in line with the experience of other similar businesses.

Estimating the first year's profit or loss is an essential part of your financial plan. If you find that the first year's sales will not yield a profit, this is not very encouraging. Keep in mind, however, that few businesses, even those that become financially successful, generate a profit in their first year.

If you project a loss, you need to determine whether it is too large for you to handle. If your projections for the second year include a significant increase in sales and a large enough profit to make up for the loss you incurred in the first year while you were learning the ropes and establishing your business, you may still consider going ahead and starting your business. If your projections for the second, third, and fourth years are no better, you should take a good hard look at whether this is the right business to start.

Cost-volume-profit analysis is a particularly helpful approach for evaluating a potential business venture. If you can estimate your cost of goods sold, which will vary with the level of sales, along with the other expenses that are relatively stable or fixed, you can estimate the profit or loss for your business at various levels of sales. You can also calculate the level of sales it will take to break even—to have your revenue cover your expenses.

The following examples illustrate how cost-volume-profit analysis can give you an idea of how to make various estimates. They are highly simplified and do not use the fixed costs, one-time outlays, and other factors included in the SBA worksheet used in Chapter 7. The retail example used in the SBA worksheet will be profiled later in this chapter.

If your cost of goods sold is expected to be 50 percent of sales, then your gross margin will be 50 percent of sales. To compute your breakeven point:

1. Divide the fixed expenses by the gross margin percentage of sales.
2. If your fixed expenses are expected to be $110,000, then you have the following equation:

$$\frac{\text{Fixed expenses}}{\text{Gross margin as a percent of sales}} = \text{breakeven in \$ sales}$$

$$\frac{\$110,000}{0.50} = \$220,000 \text{ in sales}$$

This formula indicates that your breakeven point in sales is $220,000. At your breakeven point, sales will cover your cost of goods sold and annual fixed costs. The breakeven level of sales is reflected in the following simplified income statement:

Sales	$220,000	100%
Cost of goods sold	−110,000	50%
Gross margin	$110,000	50%
Selling, administrative, and interest expenses	−110,000	50%
Profit or (loss) before taxes	$ 0	0%

Your business will not begin making a profit until sales exceed $220,000. Your breakeven point is important, because for every dollar of sales beyond your breakeven of $220,000, you get 50 cents in profit. If your sales forecast falls below your breakeven point, you will probably need to have additional money on the sidelines that you can put into your business to keep it afloat until sales exceed expenses. The actual amount of cash needed will have to be determined by a cash flow analysis. Cost-volume-profit analysis just looks at the relationship between sales and expenses.

Cost-volume-profit analysis has another benefit: It permits you to calculate the level of sales needed to generate a certain level of profit. If you want to know the level of sales needed to produce a $10,000 profit, then you add the desired level of profit to the fixed expenses and do the same computation:

$$\frac{\text{Fixed expenses plus profit goal}}{\text{Gross margin as a percent of sales}} = \text{Sales to generate a certain level of profit}$$

$$\frac{\$110,000 + \$10,000}{0.50} = \$240,000$$

This estimate can be reflected in the following income statement:

Sales	$240,000	100.0%
Cost of goods sold	−120,000	50.0%
Gross margin	$120,000	50.0%
Selling, administrative, and interest expenses	−110,000	45.8%
Profit or (loss) before taxes	$ 10,000	4.1%

Electronic spreadsheets make it possible to determine the level of profit or loss that may occur with various levels of sales. They will also enable you to see the impact that changing the markup may have on your breakeven point and the corresponding profit and loss estimates for various levels of sales. It should be noted that the spreadsheets will not automatically take price sensitivity or elasticity of demand into account. Their calculations are based on the formulas that you provide when you develop them. Electronic spreadsheets can also analyze the impact that changing the fixed costs may have on profit and loss. The following examples may illustrate the point.

Example 1: Varying Your Markup

Let's say that you enter a market in which price competition is intense or you choose to offer lower prices than your competition. You decide to have your markup on cost be 66.7 percent. This is the same as a 40 percent markup on sales. Your cost of goods sold will then be 60 percent of sales. If you paid $5 for an item, your selling price will be $8.33 instead of the $10 used in the previous example. Your gross margin will be 40 percent of sales. Your breakeven level of sales will be

$$\frac{\$110,000}{0.40} = \$275,000$$

If your markup on cost is 66.7 percent rather than 100 percent, you will need to have $275,000 in sales in order to break even. Moreover, if you want to know the level of sales it will take to generate a $10,000 profit, the following calculation will tell you that it will take $300,000 in sales to get that level of profit:

$$\frac{\$110,000 + \$10,000}{0.40} = \$300,000$$

This calculation indicates that with a gross margin of 40 percent of sales, for every dollar beyond the breakeven point, you generate 40 cents in profit, instead of the 50 cents that would come with a 50 percent gross margin.

The question, of course, remains, "Which pricing strategy will be more effective?" Will the percentage decrease in price (having a smaller markup) produce an even greater percentage increase in the number of units sold? This is what is known as the *elasticity* equation. If you believe that by lowering the price by 16.7 percent (lowering your price from $10.00 to $8.33), you can increase the number of units sold by more than 16.7 percent, then you should lower your price. If you are right, you will generate a higher level of sales. This assumes, however, that your competition doesn't also lower its prices and that people will buy more at a lower price. It should also be noted that elasticity addresses only the corresponding sales increase or decrease.

The change in profitability would still need to be calculated to see if the price change increases your profits. If you sell for less than your cost, there is no way you can make up for it in volume.

Example 2: Varying Your Fixed Expenses

Suppose your markup is 100 percent on cost, but your fixed expenses are $120,000 rather than $110,000 because you chose to rent a better or larger facility. Your new breakeven point will be

$$\frac{\$120,000}{0.50} = \$240,000$$

The question then is, "Will I be able to generate at least $20,000 more in sales to justify the additional $10,000 associated with the better location?" If the answer is no, you will probably be better off with the first location. The second location may have some appeal, but the calculations show that it may not be better in terms of its ability to produce profits. The same principle applies to judging the merit of spending more on advertising, expanding the hours for the business, or adding a Web site. For every dollar you spend in each of these categories, you will need to increase sales by $2 just to cover the additional expense.

The increase in fixed expenses associated with this example will also have an impact on the level of sales required to generate a $10,000 profit:

$$\frac{\$120,000 + \$10,000}{0.50} = \$260,000$$

Example 3: Combining the Lower Markup with a More Expensive Location

If your cost of goods sold is 60 percent rather than 50 percent of sales and your fixed expenses are expected to be $120,000 rather than $110,000, your breakeven point will be

$$\frac{\$120,000}{0.40} = \$300,000$$

You can see that both your markup and your fixed expenses have a direct and considerable effect on the level of sales you will have to achieve in order to break even or to make a profit.

The original example is helpful in determining your breakeven point in sales for the typical year of operation. The first year, however, is not the typical year. It also includes various expenses associated with setting up your business, such as grand opening advertising and decorating. These expenses will not be incurred in the second or third year. Consequently, you need to add these to your selling and administrative expenses when figuring your first year's breakeven and profit projections.

Cost-volume-profit analysis is particularly helpful for answering the following four questions about your business:

Level 1: What level of sales is necessary to cover my out-of-pocket expenses? It was demonstrated earlier that if fixed expenses are expected to be $110,000 and the gross margin is expected to be 50 percent of sales,

$$\frac{\$110,000}{0.50} = \$220,000$$

Level 2: What level of sales is necessary to cover my out-of-pocket expenses and pay me for my time? If you are a sole proprietor, your salary or "draw" will be what is left over after all the business expenses are paid. You want to receive $25,000 for your time and effort. (The earlier examples were structured like a corporation, with everyone on the payroll. Since this example is for a sole proprietorship, the owner's salary is not expensed, and so the fixed expenses have been decreased by $25,000.)

$$\frac{\$85,000 + \$25,000}{0.50} = \$220,000$$

Level 3: What level of sales is necessary each year to cover my out-of-pocket expenses, pay me for my time, and retire the debt incurred to finance the business? You estimate that you will need to borrow $20,000 to supplement what you plan to invest from your personal savings to start the business. If the loan is amortized (treated like a mortgage, with monthly payments covering the interest and principal) over 5 years and carries an 11 percent interest rate, then the annual debt retirement payments will total $5220. (This example assumes that the business is the sole proprietorship described in Level 2.)

$$\frac{\$85,000 + \$25,000 + \$5220}{0.50} = \$230,440$$

Level 4: What level of sales is necessary to cover my out-of-pocket expenses, pay me for my time, retire the debt, and earn a fair return on the money I will have invested in the business? You plan to have a 5-year $20,000 amortized note, and you desire a 15 percent return ($6000) on your $40,000 investment. (This example assumes that the business is the sole proprietorship described in Level 2.)

$$\frac{\$85{,}000 + \$25{,}000 + \$5220 + \$6000}{0.50} = \$242{,}440$$

You may be willing to live with Level 1 for the first year if you finance the business yourself and do not need to borrow any money. However, if other people invest in the business or if you borrow money, the business will have to do better than Level 1 if it is to meet the investor's or lender's expectations. The investor or lender will want to know before putting money into the business when and if the business will be able to stand on its own feet and pay everyone involved for their time, risk, and money.

Cost-volume-profit analysis may provide a quick estimate of your breakeven point and profit and loss levels, but two things need to be stressed. First, your calculations will be only as accurate as your estimates of expenses. Second, when the level of sales increases to a certain point, your selling and administrative expenses (advertising, space, employees, and so on) may have to increase to support or foster the increase in sales. Increases in these expenses will need to be reflected in your calculations.

The examples provided have been fairly simplistic. Fortunately, electronic spreadsheets can easily handle complicated financial calculations. If your sales estimate for the first year will provide a sufficient level of profit (or an acceptable minimal loss) for you to still be interested in starting the proposed business, you are ready to work on the remaining parts of your financial plan.

The remainder of this chapter is devoted to providing financial projections for the first 5 years. It should be noted here that the projections have been simplified and contain estimates for most dimensions. The calculations are also based on the following assumptions:

- The business will be started on January 1.
- No cash outlays will occur before January 1 (to simplify the example).
- The firm (business) will be open for business on January 15.
- Sales for January are one-half the sales for the average month, lowering the sales forecast for the first year from $240,000 (10 percent market share) to $230,000.
- The entrepreneur invests $40,000 in the business and is the sole stockholder.
- The business will be a Subchapter S corporation, with taxes paid by the stockholder.
- The business will also be financed via a $20,000 5-year note from a friend. The note will be amortized at 11 percent interest.
- The overall market is expected to grow by 3 percent per year.

- The business's market share is expected to increase by 1 percent per year.
- Some expenses are expected to increase by 5 percent per year. Other expenses are expected to increase by 3 percent per year. A few expenses are not expected to increase.
- The 1500-square-foot facility is more than enough for the first year. By the end of the fifth year, additional space will be needed if the business is to continue to grow.
- The facility is in good shape and will not need extensive decorating.
- An additional part-time employee will be added in the fourth year.
- The facility will need to be redecorated at the beginning of the fourth year.
- Starting in the third year, 35 percent of annual earnings will be distributed as a dividend at the end of each year. The dividend reduces the business's cash position, but it provides the entrepreneur with cash to pay the personal income taxes that are associated with being a stockholder in a Subchapter S corporation.

It should also be noted that the financial projections will be only as accurate as the assumptions that are made and the accuracy of the data that go into them. The projections in the following tables indicate a fairly high rate of profit as a percent of sales by the third year. The level and percent of profit will be reduced dramatically if (1) the business cannot generate the estimated level of sales, (2) the gross margin is less than 50 percent of sales, (3) operating expenses are underestimated, (4) sales for the overall market do not grow as much as anticipated, and/or (5) the business is not able to get a 10 percent market share in its first year and increase its share by 1 percent per year thereafter. The projections are so sensitive that if expenses are underestimated by a few percentage points and sales are overestimated by a few percentage points, the business could lose a lot of money.

CASH FLOW PROJECTIONS

Chapter 7 emphasized the need to have enough money to start your business. Your cash flow schedule attempts to identify when cash will be received from sales and when it will need to be disbursed. The cash flow projections will help you get a more accurate estimate of your initial capital requirement and determine whether you will have enough money to make it through the first year. Cash flow projections are crucial because cash is like oxygen to your business: With it you can keep going; without it you die.

Table 8-1a. First Year's Projected Cash Flow Statement

	January	February	March	April
Beginning balance	$ 60,000	$10,644	$15,918	$16,042
Receipts				
Sales	10,000	20,000	20,000	20,000
Disbursements:				
Payroll	5,000	5,000	5,000	5,000
Rent	1,875	1,875	1,875	1,875
Advertising	3,200	800	800	800
Delivery	900	150	300	300
Supplies	40	40	40	40
Telephone	100	100	100	100
Utilities	475	175	175	175
Insurance	375	0	0	375
Payroll taxes and outlays	516	516	516	516
Licenses	200	0	0	0
Credit card charges	120	240	240	240
Maintenance	20	20	20	20
Legal and accounting	1,300	100	100	100
Miscellaneous	100	75	75	75
Equipment leases/service contracts	200	200	200	200
Fixtures and equipment	8,000	0	0	0
Installation	500	0	0	0
Decorating	6,000	0	0	0
Inventory	30,000	5,000	10,000	10,000
Loan payments	435	435	435	435
Total disbursements	$ 59,356	$14,726	$19,876	$20,251
Cash flow (short)	$ (49,356)	$ 5,274	$ 124	$ (251)
Ending balance	$ 10,644	$15,918	$16,042	$15,791

Your sales forecast for the year may not reflect monthly or seasonal fluctuations in sales, when principal payments on your loan are due, when you will have to pay for replacing the inventory you sell, quarterly insurance payments, and other such factors. The cash flow schedule projects the amounts and timing of cash receipts and disbursements from the time you start ordering your initial inventory, signs, equipment, and so on, to the end of your first year of operation.

The cash flow schedule is particularly important if you have to prepay for some of your assets or expenses. It is also important if you take the risk associated with allowing your customers to put their purchases "on account." If you expect to have accounts receivable, you will have to replace your inventory, pay your rent, and so on, out of the business's cash while you wait for your customers to pay your business what they owe it.

Table 8-1b. First Year's Projected Cash Flow Statement (continued)

	May	June	July	August
Beginning balance	$15,791	$15,965	$16,139	$15,938
Receipts				
Sales	20,000	20,000	20,000	20,000
Disbursements:				
Payroll	5,000	5,000	5,000	5,000
Rent	1,875	1,875	1,875	1,875
Advertising	800	800	800	800
Delivery	300	300	300	300
Supplies	40	40	40	40
Telephone	100	100	100	100
Utilities	125	125	125	125
Insurance	0	0	375	0
Payroll taxes and outlays	516	516	516	516
Licenses	0	0	0	0
Credit card charges	240	240	240	240
Maintenance	20	20	20	20
Legal and accounting	100	100	100	100
Miscellaneous	75	75	75	75
Equipment leases/service contracts	200	200	200	200
Fixtures and equipment	0	0	0	0
Installation	0	0	0	0
Decorating	0	0	0	0
Inventory	10,000	10,000	10,000	10,000
Loan payments	435	435	435	435
Total disbursements	$19,826	$19,826	$20,201	$19,826
Cash flow (short)	$ 174	$ 174	$ (201)	$ 174
Ending balance	$15,965	$16,139	$15,938	$16,112

The cash flow projection is particularly important because it identifies periods when you will not have enough money on hand to meet your obligations. It should indicate whether you need to have cash in reserve when you start your business and/or give you enough lead time to set up a line of credit with a bank (if you qualify) to cover any projected shortages of cash. It will also identify periods when you may have more cash than you need. If you know this in advance, you may be able to put the excess cash in an interest-bearing account or take advantage of cash discounts with suppliers. Table 8-1 indicates the monthly cash flow for the first year.

The lack of balance between disbursements and receipts may cause considerable anxiety and adversity. Quite a few businesses with profit potential go bankrupt because they are unable to meet their financial obligations. Their cash obligations were due early in their first year, and their sales did

Table 8-1c. First Year's Projected Cash Flow Statement (continued)

	September	October	November	December
Beginning balance	$16,112	$16,286	$16,085	$16,259
Receipts				
Sales	20,000	20,000	20,000	20,000
Disbursements:				
Payroll	5,000	5,000	5,000	5,000
Rent	1,875	1,875	1,875	1,875
Advertising	800	800	800	800
Delivery	300	300	300	300
Supplies	40	40	40	40
Telephone	100	100	100	100
Utilities	125	125	125	125
Insurance	0	375	0	0
Payroll taxes and outlays	516	516	516	516
Licenses	0	0	0	0
Credit card charges	240	240	240	240
Maintenance	20	20	20	20
Legal and accounting	100	100	100	100
Miscellaneous	75	75	75	75
Equipment leases/service contracts	200	200	200	200
Fixtures and equipment	0	0	0	0
Installation	0	0	0	0
Decorating	0	0	0	0
Inventory	10,000	10,000	10,000	10,000
Loan payments	435	435	435	435
Total disbursements	$19,826	$20,201	$19,826	$19,826
Cash flow (short)	$ 174	$ (201)	$ 174	$ 174
Ending balance	$16,286	$16,085	$16,259	$16,433

not come in soon enough to cover those obligations. Too many business tombstones display the saying, "The owner went to the well, but it was dry!" In business, it is difficult to get instant cash. You need to plan ahead so that you have enough cash available when you need it.

PREPARING YOUR PRO FORMA FINANCIAL STATEMENTS

You have come a long way in preparing your financial plan. You have estimated (1) your first year's sales, (2) your breakeven point, (3) your initial capital requirement, (4) whether you have enough money to start your business, and (5) your cash flow statement.

You still need to prepare (1) your opening-day balance sheet, (2) a projected income statement for the first year, (3) the closing balance sheet for the first year, (4) the income statements for the second through fifth years, and (5) the balance sheets for the second through fifth years. You should also compute the key financial ratios for the first few years.

At this point you are probably saying, "Do I really need to do all of these calculations and projections? I doubt that many people going into business do all of these things." You are right; most first-timers don't perform these computations. Numerous new businesses fail each year, and some were destined to fail before they were even started. Their founders either did not know how to perform these calculations or were so eager to start their businesses that they were unwilling to take the time to look before they leaped. Financial projections allow you to take the mental journey before you take the actual entrepreneurial journey.

If you want to start a business that beats the odds, you must do a thorough job of financial planning. Running the numbers is an essential part of your business plan. These projections not only give you an idea of what you can expect, but also serve as benchmarks to verify whether things are going as planned after the business is started. Would you like to be a passenger on a plane if the pilot did not check the weather report, check the fuel level, and file a flight plan before taking off? If not, then do not take the same type of risk by not identifying the key financial factors, projections, and indicators that must be taken into account in order to start and manage a successful business.

The following pro forma (projected) financial statements will be helpful as you plan your business. Also, if you plan to borrow money from a bank or someone else or to sell stock to finance your business, you will be expected to have them.

Preparing Your Initial Balance Sheet

The opening balance sheet provides a picture of how the business will be financed and how the money will be allocated. The balance sheet is made up of assets, liabilities, and owner's equity (see Table 8-2). Assets represent the items you need to have in order to operate your business. You will need cash, inventory, equipment, and so on, in order to sell products or services.

When you start your business, every dollar of assets will have to be financed either through debt or with money that you and other people have invested in your business. This is why it is called a balance sheet. Every dollar in assets will have to be "balanced" by a dollar of liabilities or equity. Equity includes the amount you (and others) invested in the business and the earnings you retain in the business after it is started. The balance sheet indicates the amount of the business's assets that are "owed and owned." It is based on the following formula:

Table 8-2. Projected Opening Balance Sheet

	January 1, Year 1
Cash assets	$60,000
Total assets	$60,000
Liabilities (5-year amortized note @ 11 percent, due in year WXYZ)	$20,000
Owner's equity	$40,000
Total liabilities and owner's equity	$60,000

Assets = liabilities + equity

For example, if you plan to start a business with $30,000 of inventory, the $30,000 will have to come from (or be balanced by) a loan or money from you or other investors. Net worth is determined by subtracting the liabilities from the assets. If your business is profitable, you should be in a position to expand the business (increase assets) or pay off the loan(s) used to finance some of the original assets.

The initial balance sheet is important for numerous reasons. It reflects how much money will be needed to start the business and how the business will be funded. It also gives bankers (or a friend or family member) and investors an idea about what will be owned and what will be owed. The balance sheet also provides a picture of whether the assets will consist of equipment, inventory, or land and buildings. Some assets are easier to convert to cash than others if the business falters. The balance sheet thus indicates the downside risk for potential lenders and investors.

Preparing the First Calendar-Year-End Income Statement

The income statement reflects the results of the year's business activity. It indicates the level of sales, the cost of goods sold, the operating expenses, and the resulting profit or loss. If you prepared the cash flow statement, then most of the work of projecting the first year's income statement has already been done. The income statement for the first year is important because it projects the level of profit available for funding growth, reducing debt obligations, or providing a return, which may include paying the investors dividends. Because of the uncertainty of the first year's sales, it may be advisable to prepare your first year's income statement for three different levels of sales: the most likely level, a pessimistic level, and an optimistic level (see Table 8-3).

If the projected income statement indicates that the business is expected to make a profit in the first year, the owner must be prepared to pay income taxes. For this and other reasons, it may be advisable to prepare income state-

Table 8-3. Projected First Year's Income Statement

	Pessimistic*	Most Likely	Optimistic†
Sales	$ 184,000	$230,000	$276,000
Cost of goods sold	92,000	115,000	138,000
Gross margin	$92,000	$115,000	$138,000
Less expenses			
Payroll	60,000	60,000	60,000
Rent	22,500	22,500	22,500
Advertising	12,000	12,000	12,000
Delivery	3,240	4,050	4,860
Supplies	530	480	420
Telephone	1,100	1,200	1,300
Utilities	2,400	2,100	1,800
Insurance	1,500	1,500	1,500
Payroll taxes	6,200	6,200	6,200
Licenses	100	100	100
Credit card charges	2,208	2,760	3,312
Maintenance	240	240	240
Legal and accounting	3,800	3,500	3,500
Miscellaneous	1,110	925	740
Depreciation	2,000	2,000	2,000
Equipment leases and fees	2,400	2,400	2,400
Installation of equipment	500	500	500
Decorating	6,000	6,000	6,000
Total selling and administrative expenses	$ 127,828	$128,455	$129,372
Net profit from operations	(35,828)	(13,455)	8,628
Less interest expense	2,043	2,043	2,043
Net profit‡	$ (37,871)	$ (15,498)	$ 6,585

*80% of most likely sales
†120% of most likely sales
‡This is a Subchapter S corporation, so stockholders pay the taxes.

ments on a monthly basis for the first year. The Internal Revenue Service and your state's department of revenue will expect estimated income tax payments on a quarterly, or in some cases monthly, basis when you start making a profit. The income statement will enable you to identify when the business will generate a profit, how much that profit will be, what your tax obligations will be, and when you will need to have funds available in order to meet your tax obligations.

Another tax factor should also be noted. The Internal Revenue Service wants small businesses to use the calendar year for tax returns. If you start your business in May, your first year's projected income statement should reflect your expected levels of sales, expenses, and profit or loss for that calendar year, even though it may not be for 12 months.

PREPARING YOUR FIRST CALENDAR-YEAR-END BALANCE SHEET

It will be beneficial for you to project the balance sheet for the completion of your first calendar year of operation. This balance sheet will reflect the change in financial condition from the initial balance sheet as a result of your cash flow and your profit or loss. Unless you added more debt, paid off debt, invested more in the business, or were involved in a major expansion during the first year, most of the changes between these two balance sheets will be reflected in the income statement.

If your business is expected to make a profit and have a positive cash flow, your assets and equity should increase. Conversely, if the business is expected to lose money and you do not expect to have enough cash available to meet your financial obligations, you may need to seek additional debt or equity financing in order to provide a sufficient level of cash to continue operations.

In any event, the first calendar-year-end balance sheet will provide a picture of the amount of assets involved in the business and the extent to which they are owned versus owed. In most cases, if the business made a profit, your balance sheet will indicate that you own a larger portion of the business than when you first opened its doors (see Table 8-4). This is how businesses create wealth.

Preparing the Income Statements for the Second through Fifth Years

It is advisable to prepare income statements for at least the first 3 years of operation. The second and third years are particularly important. As noted earlier, most businesses do not make a profit in their first year. Projecting

Table 8-4. Projected First Year's Balance Sheet

	December 31, Year 1
Assets	
Cash	$16,433
Inventory	30,000
Equipment	8,000
Less accumulated depreciation of equipment	(2,000)
Deposits with utilities	300
Total assets	$52,733
Liabilities	
5-year amortized note payable in year WXYZ	$16,825
Owner's equity	$35,908
Total liabilities and owner's equity	$52,733

your second- and third-year income statements will give you a better idea about whether your company will be profitable, when you may achieve profitability, and the level of profit or loss you may expect each year. The income statements may also indicate when you will be able to give yourself a raise! (See Table 8-5.)

Your sales estimate is the most important part of your projected income statements and corresponding cash flow. You will need to forecast whether your sales will increase from year to year. Many businesses experience a continued increase in sales from the first to the second year of operation. While you will be continuing your effort to create more new customers in the second year, you may already benefit from repeat customers from the first year. Even though the income statements in Table 8-5 are annual projections, you should project your business's second-year income statement on a quarterly basis. Each quarter should reflect both any growth in sales

Table 8-5. Projected Income Statements for the Second and Third Years

	Year 2	Year 3
Sales	$271,920	$305,540
Cost of goods sold	135,960	152,770
Gross margin	$135,960	$152,770
Less expenses		
Payroll	63,000	66,150
Rent	23,175	23,870
Advertising	9,888	10,383
Delivery	4,079	4,583
Supplies	544	611
Telephone	1,260	1,323
Utilities	2,205	2,315
Insurance	1,575	1,653
Payroll taxes	5,940	6,192
Licenses	100	100
Credit card charges	3,263	3,666
Equipment leases/service contracts	2,520	2,646
Maintenance	240	240
Legal and accounting	1,200	1,200
Miscellaneous	900	900
Depreciation	1,716	1,226
Decorating	1,000	1,000
Total selling and administrative expenses	$122,605	$128,059
Net profit from operations	13,355	24,711
Less interest expense	1,675	1,266
Net profit*	$ 11,680	$ 23,445

*This is a Subchapter S corporation, so stockholders pay the taxes.

and any seasonality that affects your business. Quarterly income statements will also be helpful if you want to project your cash flow for the second year of operation. The quarterly statements may then be consolidated into the year-end income statement for your second year. The second year's income statement will also be important if your business will be operating on a calendar year. If you plan to start your business in May, your first year's income statement will reflect only 8 months of business. Your second year's income statement is important because it will reflect the complete business cycle, from January through December. The income statements for the following years can be projected on an annual basis.

It is also worth your time and effort to project the income statements for the third, fourth, and fifth years (see Tables 8-5 and 8-6). These do not need to be done on a quarterly basis unless your business will have wide seasonal fluctuations in sales. The third through fifth years' income statements will

Table 8-6. Projected Income Statements for the Fourth and Fifth Years

	Year 4	Year 5
Sales	$340,930	$378,170
Cost of goods sold	170,465	189,085
Gross margin	$170,465	$189,085
Less expenses		
Payroll	79,500	83,475
Rent	24,586	25,323
Advertising	11,447	10,500
Delivery	2,557	2,836
Supplies	682	756
Telephone	1,389	1,458
Utilities	1,735	1,822
Insurance	1,735	1,822
Payroll taxes	8,155	8,513
Licenses	100	100
Credit card charges	4,091	4,538
Equipment leases/service contracts	2,778	2,917
Maintenance	252	252
Legal and accounting	1,200	1,200
Miscellaneous	1,000	1,000
Depreciation	874	700
Decorating	6,000	1,000
Total selling and administrative expenses	$148,081	$148,212
Net profit from operations	22,384	40,873
Less interest expense	808	298
Net profit*	$ 21,576	$ 40,575

*This is a Subchapter S corporation, so stockholders pay the taxes.

provide a picture of the projected level of business activity and profits. If you borrowed money to start the business, the loan officer (or a friend or family member) will want to see if the business will be making enough money to pay off the note in 5 years. The people who invested in the business will also want to know what they can expect in return (via increased value and/or dividends) for their investment.

The third through fifth years' income statements will also be important because they should indicate whether you expect the business to level off or continue growing. If your business plan involves opening an additional store, offering additional goods or services, or expanding your sales territory, your projected income statements should reflect these changes. They should indicate the resulting increases in sales, expenses, and profits.

The projected income statements will be based on numerous assumptions. You will have to estimate the rate of inflation in expenses, the nature and extent of competition, whether you can increase your prices, and whether your target market is expected to grow, stay about the same, or shrink. Electronic spreadsheets may make doing the financial projections easier, but you will have to give a lot of thought to what the future may hold, who your competitors will be, and what your business should be doing in the years to come.

Preparing the Balance Sheets for the Second through Fifth Years

The projected income statements will enable you to prepare the projected balance sheets beyond the first year of operation (see Tables 8-7 and 8-8). The projected income statements will indicate the level of profits projected

Table 8-7. Projected Second- and Third-Year Balance Sheets

	December 31 Year 2	December 31 Year 3
Assets		
Cash	$21,805	$30,164
Inventory	33,990	38,192
Equipment	8,000	8,000
Less accumulated depreciation of equipment	(3,714)	(4,938)
Deposits with utilities	300	300
Total assets	$60,381	$71,718
Liabilities		
5-year note payable in year WXYZ	13,282	9,330
Total liabilities	$13,282	$ 9,330
Owner's equity	$47,099	$62,388*
Total liabilities and owner's equity	$60,381	$71,718

*35% of the third year's earnings will be distributed as a dividend of $8,205.

Table 8-8. Projected Fourth- and Fifth-Year Balance Sheets

	December 31 Year 4	December 31 Year 5
Assets		
Cash	$35,113	$ 52,559
Inventory	42,616	47,271
Equipment	8,000	8,000
Less accumulated depreciation of equipment	(5,812)	(6,512)
Deposits with utilities	300	300
Total assets	$80,217	$101,618
Liabilities		
5-year note payable in year WXYZ	4,920	0
Total liabilities	$ 4,920	$ —
Owner's equity	$75,297*	$101,618†
Total liabilities and owner's equity	$80,217	$101,618

*35% of the fourth year's earnings will be distributed as a dividend of $8668.
†35% of the fifth year's earnings will be distributed as a dividend of $14,172.

for each year. Each year's profit or loss and cash flow will affect the corresponding year's balance sheet.

The balance sheets will also reflect the extent to which various assets have been depreciated. If you bought a piece of equipment for $8000 that had a useful life of 7 years, then each year's balance sheet will reflect the declining, or depreciated, value of that asset. The balance sheet thereby gives the net book value of the business's assets.

The balance sheets give a picture of what the business is expected to look like at the close of each calendar year. Each balance sheet will show the size and composition of the assets, the liabilities, and the net worth of the business to its owners. The balance sheets will also reflect whether the business will need to borrow money or whether some of its profits can be distributed to the owners.

The balance sheet for the fifth year will be particularly relevant if you signed a 5-year note to help start the business. The fifth year's balance sheet will indicate what your business will look like in financial terms when the note is paid off. If you have not borrowed any additional money and you have the cash to retire the 5-year note as it comes due, you will own the whole business at the end of 5 years. The preceding example reflected an amortized note that was being paid off on a monthly basis. If the loan had not been amortized, then it would have had to be paid off with a balloon payment of $20,000 at the end of the 5 years. In either case, when people start a business and get a loan, 5 years may seem like a long time, but your financial projections let you see if there will be light at the end of the 5-year tunnel.

The idea of owning the business at the end of 5 years is an exciting prospect and will make the time, effort, and anxiety associated with starting a new business more worthwhile. Table 8-8 indicates that by the end of the fifth year, the business will have $101,618 in assets and no debt. This means that the $40,000 you invested in the business will have grown to $101,618. The appreciation in the value of your business is noteworthy because the projections include a dividend of 35 percent of each year's profit starting in the third year. The annual dividend is important because it should provide you with the cash you need to pay the personal income taxes that are associated with being a stockholder in your S corporation.

While the numbers appear to be very encouraging, they are merely the product of various assumptions. As noted earlier, if any of the assumptions about the rate of growth, market share, stock turn, or expenses vary by even the smallest percentage, the corresponding cash flow, income statement, and balance sheet projections will change. Remember, things rarely go as planned. You need to run the numbers, but you cannot afford to believe that they are a perfect projection of what will actually happen.

RUNNING THE NUMBERS IS AN ESSENTIAL PART OF THE BUSINESS PLAN

This part of the business plan can be viewed as a financial road map for charting the future direction of your business. A considerable amount of your time will have to be spent analyzing your business and making the financial calculations. These activities are an essential part of your business plan. Few people who start a business have an in-depth understanding of financial accounting. Nevertheless, running the numbers is a part of starting and managing a business that cannot be ignored or left to an accountant.

Almost every business decision has a financial dimension. You will not be able to make good decisions without a good understanding of financial statements. If the number one reason for the failure of small businesses is mismanagement and the number two reason is financial problems, then you need to develop your financial competence in order to increase your chances of beating the odds. If you don't understand cash flow, income statements, balance sheets, and how they are interrelated, then learn about them before your lack of knowledge causes you to make the wrong decisions.

Part 3
Sources of Funding, Alternatives to Starting from Scratch, and Entrepreneurial Do's and Don'ts

9

Sources of Funding

"SHOW ME THE MONEY!"

This classic line from the film *Jerry Maguire* is particularly appropriate when it comes to starting a new venture. The success of a start-up is contingent on numerous factors. There must be a market opportunity, the entrepreneur must have the skills and a strategy for serving the people or businesses that are not having their needs met, and the venture must have enough money to get up and running so that it can create and maintain customers for a profit.

When most people compute their initial capital requirement, they find that they do not have enough money to start their business. If you find that you do not have enough money, don't give up. There are numerous avenues available for obtaining external financing for your business.

This chapter can be viewed as the "facts of life" for funding a new venture. It emphasizes the need to develop a funding plan and the importance of bootstrapping. It also profiles various sources of funding and some of the criteria used by these sources. While some of the sources may not have a track record in funding start-ups, you should still know about them so that you can consider them later to fund your venture's growth.

The following facts of life shed light on the challenges that entrepreneurs face when it comes to funding a new venture:

FACT 1: FEW ENTREPRENEURS HAVE ALL THE MONEY THEY NEED

Many entrepreneurs find that there is a gap between the personal funds they have available and their projected initial capital requirement. This gap may range from a thousand dollars to substantially more money. In some cases, the funding gap can be bridged using some of the avenues presented in this chapter. If the gap cannot be bridged or if the costs or risks associated with bridging the gap are too high, then the venture should not be started.

FACT 2: ENTREPRENEURS HAVE TO BE WILLING TO ACCEPT RISKS

Funding a start-up involves risk. When you start a new venture, you are gambling that the money you put into it will make money. You are going to have to commit your own money in order to make that happen. If you want others to ante up, you have to be the first one to ante up. If you need funding from other sources, you will have to show those sources that you are willing to take the risk and that it is worth it to them to take the risk of helping you start your venture. If you are unwilling to commit and risk your own funds to provide the first dollars for your business, it is very unlikely that other people or institutions will put their funds into the venture.

If you are married, make sure your spouse is truly committed to the venture. You may have to cash in your certificates of deposit, liquidate part or all of your stock portfolio, get a second mortgage, tap your 401(k) plan, and/or draw from your kids' college fund. Your spouse may also be expected to cosign for a loan and various other business obligations.

FACT 3: DON'T EXPECT TO GET A LOAN FROM A BANK

Getting a loan to start a new venture is not like getting a mortgage. While bankers seem to be very nice people who sound as if they are supportive of the idea of your starting your own business, do not expect them to provide a loan for your new venture. Banks rarely lend money to start-ups. When the business is up and running and shows promise, they may help finance its growth. Banks are possibly the most risk-averse source of new venture funding. They may get involved when the business shows that it can repay the loan, but until then, don't expect them to actually provide a loan.

Banks really do not want to make business loans for a small amount of money. Generally speaking, banks charge 4 percent more on a loan than the money they lend costs them. If the loan is for $20,000 at 12 percent, the bank will make only $400 per year. It doesn't really make even that much because it has to pay the banker's salary and all the corresponding overhead. Also, it would like to have some profit left over to make the time, effort, and risk worthwhile. Since it often takes the same amount of time to review an application for a $200,000 loan (on which the bank will collect $24,000 in annual interest) as it does to review a $20,000 loan request, it makes sense for the bank to focus its attention on larger loans.

Banks would rather refinance your house to free up some of the equity you have in it so that you can start your business than provide you with a business loan. It is a lot easier for the bank to determine the market value of your house than to determine the likelihood that your business will be a success while it is merely an untested concept. It is also much easier for the bank to put your house on the market if you fail to make your monthly mortgage payments than it would be to get its money back if your venture goes down. In most cases, if the bank has to foreclose on a business loan, it has to sell whatever is left of your business's assets. Banks risk not getting a dollar back for each dollar in the business loan.

It may be worthwhile to review the criteria that banks use in reviewing loan requests, especially the 50/50 rule or 80/20 rule, which are profiled in the last section of this chapter. Many of the potential sources of funding will apply some of the same criteria (character, capability, capacity, conditions, context, and collateral) when they consider funding your business.

FACT 4: TAKE A GOOD LOOK AT YOURSELF . . . ARE YOU CREDIT/INVESTMENT-WORTHY?

Potential lenders and investors will investigate your trustworthiness and creditworthiness. If your credit history, employment history, or legal history is tarnished, your ability to attract funding will be jeopardized. You should expect to have potential investors or lenders run a credit check on you. If you have declared bankruptcy, have been the target of major litigation, or have a criminal record, you will not garner the level of trust you will need in order to attract funding.

FACT 5: SOMETIMES YOU HAVE TO GIVE UP SOMETHING TO GET SOMETHING

If you really want to be your own boss, you'll need to provide all the funds yourself. If you have to rely on outside funding, you will have to make certain sacrifices in order to bridge the funding gap. Any time you use "other people's money," there will be some strings attached. If you use some form of debt, you will have to operate within certain restrictions. Securing some type of credit or a loan has merit because it does not dilute your ownership, but there are expectations that must be met. If the venture does not meet those expectations, your business could face litigation, seizure of assets, or foreclosure, which could result in personal bankruptcy. If you need investors, you will have to dilute your ownership (and management) in the venture. It should be pointed out that dilution of ownership is not necessarily bad. If you want your business to get up and running and to grow quickly, you may need to issue stock to others. You have to ask yourself, "Would I rather have a 100 percent stake in a $100,000 business, a 60 percent stake in a $250,000 business, or a 40 percent stake in a $500,000 business?"

FACT 6: RAISING MONEY TAKES CONSIDERABLE TIME

Raising money takes a considerable amount of time, information, and effort. It cannot be relegated to "when time is available" or postponed until the last minute. It may take months of prospecting to bridge the funding gap. Veteran entrepreneurs stress the need to start the search for funding well before you need it, to have backup plans because life is full of surprises, and to never assume that the deal is done until the money is actually in your bank account.

FACT 7: YOU WILL NEED TO BE A SALESPERSON TO GET FUNDING

Entrepreneurship involves selling people on the merits of joining your venture, of buying its products and services, and of forming alliances with you as well as putting their money into your venture. If you have a real aversion to selling, then forget about starting a business.

FACT 8: RAISING FUNDS ALSO TAKES RESILIENCE

Entrepreneurs must have the ability to handle rejection—especially when it comes to getting a loan or attracting investors. Howard Schultz, who led Starbuck's growth, noted that the hardest part of fundraising was keeping an upbeat attitude when he encountered rejection after rejection. Schultz recalls that, in the course of the year he spent trying to raise money for Starbuck's, he spoke to 242 people and was turned down by 217 of them. He noted, "Try to imagine how disheartening it can be to hear why your idea is not worth investing in."[1]

FACT 9: NOT ALL MONEY IS ALIKE

Money is not a commodity. There is *smart* money and there is *dumb* money. Entrepreneurs who have a big ego or who want to run their own business frequently seek funding from friends and family. In a sense, they just want the money. This is called dumb money. Smart money is value-added money because it comes from people who will add value to your venture through their experience and contacts. Smart money comes from people who can help you make better decisions because they understand the nature and dynamics of business and they are in tune with the marketplace. Smart money is also in a position to recommend people for your management team, suppliers, distributors, prospects for joint ventures, and/or sources of additional funding. Angels, venture capitalists, and commercial lenders are considered to be sources of smart money.

FACT 10: YOU NEED AN "F-PLAN."

It should be clear by now that raising money cannot be left to chance, nor should its importance be underestimated. Insufficient capital is one of the primary reasons why new ventures fail. David Evanson and Art Beroff note that most new enterprises don't fail because they can't generate enough business—they fail because they just plain run out of money.[2]

DEVELOPING THE F-PLAN FOR YOUR VENTURE:

The need to have a business plan for starting and growing your business was stressed earlier in the book. The business plan needs to include a financing plan, or what will be referred to for the remainder of this book as the *f-plan*. The f-plan must identify how much money will be needed to start the venture and how much will be needed at certain stages of its evolution. It must also identify what the money is needed for, where it will come from, and what conditions will be attached to it.

Keith Schilit stresses the need to estimate your capital requirements, to balance your debt and equity, and not to overrely on one source of funding. He also emphasizes the need to maintain a liquid position, to avoid excessive fixed assets, to avoid excessive inventories, to maintain adequate working capital, and not to seek more funding than you need.[3]

Like most plans, the f-plan will not be foolproof. There is no way that it can project all of the firm's financial needs or the exact timing of those needs. The value of the plan is that it forces you to take the mental journey before you take the physical journey. It helps you identify in advance issues that will need to be addressed. It also gives you lead time so that you can find the funding source that best fits the venture's needs.

The amount, timing, and type of funding play a critical role in the f-plan. The f-plan also has to identify the specific uses for the funds sought and the type of returns the funds will generate for the source of funding. If debt financing is sought and is possible, then the f-plan will have to show how the money will be used as well as when and how the interest and principal will be repaid. If the venture is seeking equity funding, then the f-plan will have to show potential investors the type of return they can expect. Investors, whether they are angels or venture capitalists, will also be looking for a "liquidity event" that will enable them to get their money out with a substantial return. The three most common liquidity events are the acquisition of the venture by another firm, a management buyout, or an initial public offering that will eventually allow you to sell your stock on the open market.

You will never have enough money to do all the things you want to do. There will always be opportunities you would like to pursue, people you would like to hire, information systems you want to use, and so forth. You must approach your venture from a capital budgeting perspective. You need to identify the activities, products, services, territories, customers, and so on, as value-added investments. The f-plan needs to identify the areas that have the highest yield per dollar invested over the life of the action so that you can allocate the venture's limited funds accordingly.

BOOTSTRAPPING: PROACTIVE WAYS TO RAISE AND CONSERVE CASH

Bootstrapping is not considered a source of funding, but it affects the amount of funding needed and where it is sought. Because most new ventures are undercapitalized, they must get the greatest mileage out of each dollar available. The term *bootstrapping* reflects *resourceful* efforts made by the entrepreneur and management team to raise and conserve cash. This section highlights a few ways to conserve cash. The remainder of the chapter will highlight various ways to raise cash.

Almost every entrepreneur will have to resort to bootstrapping at some point in the new venture's evolution. Bootstrapping is particularly important in the start-up and early growth stages. It plays a key role in the success of the venture for at least five reasons. First, it may be the only way to get the funds needed to start the venture. Second, it forces you to be more frugal in using funds. When you have to fight for each dollar of funding, you develop a keener appreciation for each dollar and are more cautious about spending it. The accounting concept that you make a dollar profit for every dollar you can cut from your costs also applies to managing the emerging venture's cash position. In theory, every dollar that you can cut from your cash outlays is a dollar that you will not need to raise in order to pay for operations and/or expansion.

Veteran entrepreneurs know that reducing expenses or cash outlays by a dollar has a far greater impact on a business's profitability than increasing sales by a dollar. Chapter 8 noted that if a business's gross margin is 50 percent of sales, it takes $2 of sales to make a dollar. However, you can make a dollar by reducing your fixed costs by a dollar.

Third, bootstrapping makes you a better businessperson. In addition to making you more frugal, operating with a hand-to-mouth cash flow forces you to have good financial controls in place and to monitor operations more closely. When you are operating at the edge, you tend to see things more clearly. You also tend to deal with things right away rather than postpone them.

Fourth, bootstrapping may allow the venture to grow to a point where it is more attractive to lenders and investors. Bootstrapping may enable the firm to get up and running. Bankers are more willing to lend money to businesses that have a track record. Bootstrapping may pay big dividends if you seek outside investors. Generally speaking, you should make every effort to postpone seeking outside investors as long as possible. The greater the value of the business, the easier it is to attract investors. Higher valuation is particularly beneficial because it means that you can attract more money and you will not have to give up as much ownership of the business to get that money.

Fifth, you need to focus your attention on getting the business up and running. This means hiring and directing personnel, creating and maintaining customers, having the proper systems in place, and dealing with the nearly endless stream of problems and challenges that pop up. If you must also devote considerable time to courting bankers and investors, the other dimensions of the business may suffer. If you can bootstrap the venture and postpone the need to attract funding, you can invest your time and energy in the business.

BOOTSTRAPPING TECHNIQUES

Bootstrapping is a two-dimensional strategy, and it can take many forms. The second dimension, *creative funding,* involves trying to raise money to get the venture up and running and to keep it going. The first dimension, *resourceful austerity,* involves trying to minimize amount of the money the venture needs in order to operate so that it can go further with the funds that are available. Entrepreneurs need to have a firm grasp of their venture's "burn rate." The burn rate represents the amount of cash it takes to keep your business open on a daily basis. Diligent purchasing and budgeting play a key role in bootstrapping efforts.

The first rule of conserving cash through resourceful austerity is that you need to have your act together. If the overall business plan has addressed the crucial who, what, and where questions, you should be in a position to have the f-plan project funding needs. Having your act together reduces trial-and-error methods that burn cash. The second rule of conserving cash is, "Don't spend it unless you have to." Every cash expenditure/outlay should be subjected to the "Is it really necessary?" test. Entrepreneurs must make every effort to ensure that every dollar of cash goes into areas and activities that add value to the venture. The third rule of conserving cash is that if you do need that item or activity, you should make sure that you are getting it at the lowest reasonable cost and on the most favorable terms.

The fourth rule is to lease rather than to buy. The fifth rule is that if you can get it used, don't waste valuable cash on buying new stuff. The sixth rule is that if you have to buy it, finance it for the longest period of time possible so that it places the least drain on your monthly cash outlays.

Jeff Bezos demonstrated his frugality when he started Amazon.com. Instead of buying the typical mahogany desk for his office, he got an old door and put it on two-by-fours. He wanted to demonstrate that Amazon.com was committed to spending money only on things that added value to its customers and investors. Even when he was worth more than $10 billion, he drove a Honda sedan.

A note of caution may be appropriate here. Be resourceful and frugal, but don't be obsessive. Entrepreneurship is not about being the world's best bootstrapper. Entrepreneurship is about creating a successful venture. The clock is always ticking. Don't let your bootstrapping efforts divert your attention from building your business.

Creative funding takes many forms. The most common form of bootstrapping is for the entrepreneur to use every bit of his or her own balance sheet to get the firm up and running. This may involve selling one's house and moving into an apartment, taking out a second mortgage on one's house, or selling almost all of one's possessions. Every dollar that can be freed up from the entrepreneur's balance sheet represents one less dollar needed from outsiders.

Bootstrapping may well be the theme song for most entrepreneurs. Numerous well-known ventures were started with minimal funding and resourceful bootstrapping by their entrepreneurs. Steve Jobs and Steve Wozniak started Apple Computer with $1350. Ross Perot started EDS with $1000. Ben Cohen and Jerry Greenfield started Ben & Jerry's with $12,000. Michael Dell started Dell Computer with $1000. Phillip Knight started Nike Inc. with $1000.

Fred Smith went to Las Vegas with $100 in his pocket and won $27,000. His winnings helped him meet Federal Express's payroll and buy fuel for its planes. Ben & Jerry's offered a carpenter and a plumber membership in its "Ice-Cream-for-Life Club" if they would make the repairs needed to fix the gas station that served as the company's first location so that it could open for business.[4]

Edward DuCoin started Impact Telemarketing at the age of 18 with $100, a used desk, and a cheap answering machine. His first office was his bedroom in his parents' home. By 1997, his company was generating $12 million in revenue.[5]

FUNDING SOURCES COME IN ALL SHAPES AND SIZES

There are a variety of funding sources for start-ups and emerging ventures. There are three primary ways to finance a start-up: (1) founder funding, (2) bringing in additional owners (partners, members, or stockholders), and (3) getting a loan. Once the venture is up and running, its retained earnings may provide an avenue for funding the venture's growth, in addition to issuing debt and bringing in outside investors.

You should be aware of the merits and drawbacks of potential funding sources so that you are in a position to seek the right funding source at the right stage of the venture's evolution. Each of these sources has benefits and drawbacks. The following list of funding sources provides a brief overview of various ways to fund a venture or to reduce its need for cash.

Founder Funding
Founder funding is considered essential and is often the sole source of funding. You should make every effort to have enough money to get the venture up and running. Every dollar you can put into the venture is one less dollar that has to be borrowed or raised from other sources. You should avoid committing your last dollar to the venture, however. You should keep some money or liquid assets on the sidelines in case of emergencies or unanticipated funding gaps, which are almost inevitable. When time is of the essence, having some money on the sidelines can mean the difference between staying alive and dying on the vine.

Bringing In a Partner
About 10 percent of all start-ups are formed as partnerships. In some cases, a partner may be brought in because that person has skills that are critical to the venture's success. In other cases, one or more partners are brought in because of a funding gap. Partners can also help run the business. If they are

limited partners, then their involvement is limited to their investment in the venture.

Friends and Family

Friends and family are one of the most common sources of funding. George Dawson, president of Growing Your Business, noted that your friends and family are the first people you should look to for financing your new business. Not only are they the most likely to believe in you and your business idea, but they are less likely to saddle you with the kinds of personal guarantees that banks demand.[6] Friends and family therefore play a key role by providing funding when the venture is in the start-up stage and it is nothing more than an untested concept.

Funding from friends and family is frequently referred to as "love money." They usually lend money or invest in a venture because of their relationship with the entrepreneur. While they may consider the loan or purchase of stock to be a business deal, they usually do not exercise the same degree of due diligence or have the same level of expectations as other funding sources. Numerous ventures received crucial funding from friends and family. Jeff Bezos's parents played an instrumental role in getting Amazon.com off the ground. Fred DeLuca's desire to have a shop that would provide submarine sandwiches (Subway) was made possible when a family friend provided a loan for $1000.

Looking for financing from friends or relatives has at least three major drawbacks. First, they may not be willing or able to lend you the money. Second, they may need their money before you or they expected. Third, you may be jeopardizing your friendship and family goodwill. When friends and family lend you money or buy stock in your company, relationships tend to change. Instead of asking, "How are you?" they will ask, "How's the business doing?" When you borrow money from friends and relatives, it rarely strengthens those relationships.

If you borrow money from friends or family, make sure it is clear whether the loan is to you or to the venture. Make sure that the terms and conditions of the loan are documented, and be sure to charge a fair rate of interest. The IRS has strict rules about loans from family members and even from the entrepreneur to the venture. You also need to be sure that you comply with Securities and Exchange Commission (SEC) guidelines if you plan to sell stock. The issuance of stock also needs to be carefully documented.

Failure to carefully structure and document the loan or issuance of stock could come back to haunt you when you approach other funding sources later on. Most of the other funding sources are far more diligent than friends and family. The way you handle funding from friends and family will reflect your professionalism.

Third-Party Guarantees

Friends and family can help you get funding without actually having to put up their own money. They can do this by cosigning a loan or guaranteeing the payment for goods and services. This is important because your venture has a limited credit history and few assets to serve as collateral. It should be recognized that the person who is cosigning or personally guaranteeing payment must be creditworthy.

Credit Cards

Credit cards may play a crucial role in getting the firm up and running. While they may charge a painful rate of interest, they are often the only means of bringing money into the venture. A study by Arthur Andersen indicated that credit cards are also used well after the start-up stage. The study indicated that credit cards are a source of financing for 34 percent of America's small to medium-sized businesses.[7]

It is easy to get overextended with credit cards. Banks, investors, suppliers, and prospective members of your management team may run a credit check on you. Don't jeopardize the future of your venture by creating a bad credit history at this time. Carrying a lot of credit card debt may affect your ability to get a loan from a bank or to attract investors even if your accounts are in good standing

Leasing

Leasing equipment and other assets is usually preferable to buying them. When you purchase an asset, you are using valuable capital. It also reduces your flexibility. Leasing gives you the opportunity to try something to see if it works before you make a major commitment.

Sale/Leaseback

If you start your business by committing some of your own personal assets to it, it may be worthwhile to enter into a sale/leaseback arrangement. Selling the asset frees up valuable capital. You may also be able to arrange for a flexible lease payment schedule.

Discounted Fees or Fee-for-Equity Propositions

Many things are negotiable in business. If your venture has considerable growth potential, it may be possible to negotiate lower fees and more favorable payment terms from top-notch accounting firms, consultants, law firms, banks, public relations firms, and other service providers. These firms want to get a foot in the door, so they may be willing to make certain concessions if they believe they will benefit from the venture's growth. Service providers may even be willing to take equity in exchange for services. Accounting firms, however, are not permitted to take an equity interest.

Supplier Financing

Credit terms should be a major factor that you consider when you select suppliers. Entrepreneurs should talk to all their potential suppliers about financing and extended credit terms. A supplier's willingness to extend credit for inventory and other tangible assets and provide flexible terms may be more important than its prices for a cash-strapped venture. The ability to get extended terms on inventory is particularly valuable. If the inventory can be sold and cash collected from the sale before the supplier has to be paid, the venture will need far less capital to run its operations. Jeff Bezos found this very helpful when he started Amazon.com. By having his customers purchase books with a credit card, he was able to get cash for the books before he had to pay the publishers for them. This reduced his need for working capital.

Customer Prepayment

If customers are willing to pay cash or leave their payables to the venture outstanding for a shorter time, the venture may not need to borrow as much money or owe as much to its suppliers. It is even better if your customers will prepay for their goods and services. If they are given an incentive (a small discount, free shipping, preferential treatment) to pay in advance, they may be interested in doing so.

Customer Investment

Customers may actually be a *source* of funding. A few emerging ventures have generated funds by asking their customers if they would like to invest in the venture. This approach has been tried with brewpubs, wineries, and restaurants. In addition to having stock in the venture, the customers get special benefits. Along with owning stock, the customers may also gain *most preferred customer* status. This may be particularly beneficial to the customer if the venture has limited capacity and the customer wants to be assured of supply.

Factoring

If you plan to extend credit to your customers, you may consider factoring. Factors will buy all or part of a venture's accounts receivable. They will pay cash for a percentage of the value of the accounts receivable they buy. This is rarely the preferred source of cash, but it is one way to free up capital. The amount of money provided depends on the extent to which the accounts receivable are collectible by the factor. Factoring should be viewed as a stopgap measure rather than a regular source of funding.

Bartering

Some emerging ventures barter their products or services as a form of payment for what they need to buy. A start-up service firm may offer to provide its service to one of its suppliers in exchange for the goods or services it needs to buy from that supplier. Occasionally, the barter arrangement may involve third parties who have common interests. Ventures that are considering bartering should consult with their accountant to make sure that these cash-free transactions do not violate IRS. or sales tax regulations.

Management Team Taking Pay Cuts in Exchange for Bonuses or Stock

Emerging ventures frequently rely on stock options and/or performance bonuses to attract and reward members of their management teams and other key employees. To conserve cash, they offer stock options in return for lower salaries. Performance bonuses also represent a way to put off paying money to key people until it has been earned. People tend to be more committed to a business and more resilient in dealing with its ups and downs when they have a piece of the action.

Banks

As noted earlier, borrowing money from a bank for a start-up is entirely different from getting a mortgage on your house. Banks rarely provide funding for start-ups. The risks are just too high to justify their involvement. They are more likely to offer to refinance your house in order to free up some of the equity in it for your business. Banks should be seen as a source for growth funding. The final part of this chapter profiles the criteria that banks use in reviewing loans after your venture demonstrates that it is a viable business.

The Small Business Administration (SBA)

The U.S. government has been a major player in funding emerging ventures for decades. The SBA has various lending programs in which it actually serves as an underwriter rather than the provider of loans. Most SBA loans are actually provided by commercial banks. In most cases, the venture must approach a bank seeking a conventional business loan. If the venture comes close to meeting the bank's lending criteria, the bank may suggest that the venture seek an SBA loan. If the venture meets the SBA's lending criteria, the SBA will indicate to the bank that it will underwrite the majority of the loan. Since this reduces the bank's downside risk, the bank may provide the loan. A number of banks have earned the distinction of being certified or preferred SBA lenders. SBA certified lenders still need SBA approval before a loan can be granted. SBA preferred lenders are authorized to review and approve SBA loans without consulting the SBA. The preferred status obviously speeds the approval process. The SBA Web site lists certified and preferred banks.

The SBA's 7M microloan program may have merit for businesses that are unable to get funding from conventional sources. The loans are provided through a network of intermediaries that consider loan requests from $100 to $35,000. The intermediaries may also be in a position to provide management and technical assistance to loan recipients.

Government Grants

The federal government and numerous states provide funding grants for various types of businesses. Small Business Innovation Research (SBIR) grants are a common source of funding for firms in technology-related fields. These grants come with strings attached and may include an equity interest in the venture. *The Small Business Guide to Federal Research and Development Funding Opportunities,* published by the SBA's Office of Innovation Research, provides an agency-by-agency breakdown of federal R&D programs. You should also check with your state's department of commerce to see if it provides funding.

Business Incubators

Government agencies, corporations, and universities have established business incubators. These incubators are designed to assist start-ups and emerging ventures. Government-sponsored incubators usually provide a lower rent rate, some form of management assistance, and a common infrastructure (secretarial services, meeting rooms, etc.) to help ventures in their first year or two. For-profit incubators frequently provide these benefits, more sophisticated professional services, and the potential for an equity investment. These incubators function like a vertically integrated venture capital firm. They provide considerable support for promising entrepreneurs and ventures. Their assistance accelerates the venture's growth by helping it ramp up operations and get funding. Business incubators were very popular in the past, but they have had mixed success in recent years.

Strategic Alliances and Corporate Partnerships

Emerging ventures that have promising technology may consider establishing an alliance or forming a corporate partnership with one or more firms. Alliances and partnerships are very appealing today because they can provide an avenue for funding and other forms of support for ventures that are not in a position to secure a loan or attract investors on favorable terms.

Licensing or Royalties

A number of emerging ventures have found that offering licensing or royalty arrangements can be a good way to get an infusion of capital. Emerging ventures that do not want to go (or are not in a position to go) the debt, equity, or ally/corporate partner route may consider attracting capital by offering a licensing or royalty arrangement to one or more parties. The arrangement is fairly straightforward. The emerging venture receives cash from the other party in return for a commitment to provide the other party with a percentage of the venture's revenue when it comes in.

One company used royalties to help finance the development of its product. One of the company's entrepreneurs noted, "Because we didn't have the money, we didn't have the ability to develop software [the company needed]. We knocked on the doors of technology companies and invited them to participate based on the potential rewards—on royalties rather than equity in the company." Sprint accepted the emerging venture's invitation because it wanted to get into the sports market.[8]

Small Business Investment Companies (SBICs)

SBICs are privately owned investment firms that are licensed and regulated by the SBA. These firms use their own funds plus funds obtained by borrowing at favorable rates with SBA guarantees or by selling their preferred stock to the SBA. Many banks have their own SBICs, which function as the banks' own venture capital funds. Most SBICs provide funding via convertible subordinated debt or loans with options for an equity interest. Some SBICs will do equity deals. Over the years, SBICs have been early investors in Callaway Golf, Outback Steakhouse, Staples, Federal Express, Apple Computer, America Online, and Intel.[9] For additional information on SBICs, contact the National Association of Small Business Investment Companies in Washington, D.C.

Issuing Stock to Individuals

Stock may be issued to various types of investors in many ways. It can be issued to friends and family, to members of the management team, and to the venture's employees, customers, suppliers, and corporate partners/allies. It can also be issued to angels, venture capital firms, investment banks, and SBICs. Stock can also be sold to the public if certain conditions are met.

The issuance of stock has both its advantages and its drawbacks. The major advantage is that it is not a fixed liability. Unless it is a condition at the time of issuance, the venture does not have any obligation to pay dividends or to redeem the stock. Issuing stock has two major drawbacks. First, it dilutes the entrepreneur's ownership position and possibly weakens the entrepreneur's control of the business. Second, issuing stock can be like walking through a minefield. If it is not done right, it can cause serious legal problems. Make sure you get good accounting and legal advice before you even consider issuing stock.

Angels

Angels can be described as wealthy individuals who invest in and/or lend money to emerging ventures that have considerable potential. They can play a key role in the creation and growth of a new business. They are different from friends and family in at least four ways. First, they tend to be more diligent in reviewing the prospects for a business. They will insist on financial projections, and they may require you to provide personal guarantees. Second, they will also place more emphasis on getting a healthy return on their funds. Angels are very selective. They know that most new ventures have a very precarious existence and that few new ventures go on to make substantial profits. Angels look for ventures that have the potential to at least triple their money within 5 years. Some angels will not invest unless they think that they can double their investment on an annual basis over a 3- to 5-year period. If your business is more of a lifestyle business than a high-potential venture, do not even think about seeking an angel.

Third, angels represent smart money. Most angels have considerable business experience. Some angels are former entrepreneurs. They may be in a position to open doors with distributors, suppliers, corporate allies, and other funding sources. Fourth, they usually can commit more money to the emerging venture. Their involvement may range from a few thousand dollars to hundreds of thousands of dollars. The time commitment that they make to the firm will vary from one angel to the next. Some angels will actually help manage the firm. Others will merely want to be kept posted on the firm's performance and to have a seat on the board of directors. While nearly every community has angels, they usually keep a low profile. If you are interested in going the angel route, you should make an effort to network with entrepreneurs, bankers, accountants, and attorneys who may know angels.

The SBA's Office of Advocacy sponsored the development of the Angel Capital Electronic Network. ACE-Net is a nationwide Internet listing service that provides information to small, dynamic businesses seeking $250,000 to $5 million in equity financing. ACE-Net is not a matching service. It merely provides information.

Angel Networks

A number of angels have come out of the shadows and taken a more visible and proactive approach to looking for good investments. If you are near a metropolitan area that has considerable entrepreneurial activity, there may be an angel network in that community that solicits and reviews investment packages. Some networks have their own fund or portfolio for investing in emerging ventures. Other networks merely provide a forum for individual angels to do their own deals. These networks function almost like small and less formal venture capital firms. However, their "wealth-enhancing expectations" tend to be lower than those of venture capital firms.

Venture Capital Firms (VCs)

Venture capital firms may be the most controversial and least understood form of funding. The phrase, "I'll get venture capital funding" is freely bantered about by naïve entrepreneurs. Few firms meet the lofty expectations set by venture capital firms. VCs will only consider funding firms that have "hockey stick" projections and that offer the potential for lucrative liquidity events. In return for early-stage funding, which involves a high degree of risk, VCs expect to have a 20 to 40 percent interest in the emerging firm. VCs rarely try to take a controlling interest in an emerging venture. The terms and conditions they attach to a deal and their ability to replace the entrepreneur if the venture does not meet their expectations has given them the less-than-endearing label of "vulture capitalists."

Venture capital firms should not be considered for initial financing. They rarely invest in a new business until it has demonstrated high growth potential. These firms have extremely high expectations because they live by the "20-60-20" rule when reviewing a deal. They know that only one (10 percent) or two (20 percent) of every ten investments they make may be highly profitable. The 10 to 20 percent that provide lucrative returns (if they are fortunate enough to have them) must cover the 60 percent of their investments that yield only a marginal return and the 20 percent that are total losses.

Venture capital firms look for firms that have the potential to dominate a market and to be sold or go public within a few years. The average investment or "deal" today is between $1 million and $3 million, with the venture capital firm getting a 30 percent ownership position in the business. One other point needs to be noted about venture capital firms: They tend to specialize in a particular industry or market. If you get to the point where you may be seriously considered by a VC, do your homework and look for a VC that invests in your type of business and has a good reputation.

Private Offerings

Selling stock to the general public is not a simple proposition. The U.S. Securities and Exchange Commission is charged with protecting the public from investment scams. The SEC has relaxed some of its rules in the last few years so that smaller businesses can issue stock. Entrepreneurs who are considering the possibility of issuing stock should consult with an attorney who specializes in the issuance of stock.

Investment Banks

Investment banks are a hybrid source of funding. They help firms put together major funding deals. They may provide debts as well as equity packages. They may be the primary investors and/or lenders, or they may put together a syndicate to provide the package. Investment banks play a critical role in putting together initial public offerings.

Initial Public Offering (IPO)

Only a few emerging ventures go public each year. Doing an IPO is a big deal. Some entrepreneurs consider the IPO to be the culminating point of their entrepreneurial journey. They see having their firm publicly traded as the ultimate accomplishment.

Unless your venture has the potential to capture a large part of a high-growth market and to garner a pre-IPO valuation of at least $100 million, do not even think about it. While a few entrepreneurs have tried to do an IPO over the Internet, most emerging ventures that attempt to do an IPO will use a team of specialized accountants, attorneys, and investment bankers and a specialized printer. Most IPOs involve raising tens of millions of dollars. The associated fees and charges can easily exceed 10 percent of the offering.

Financial Intermediaries

A number of individuals and firms help entrepreneurs put together funding packages and search for funding sources. They usually charge 5 percent for their efforts. If you do not have a clue as to how to get funding, if you need the money soon, or if your business is quite unique, then an intermediary may be worth considering. Caveat emptor applies here, as it does in most cases. Make sure that the intermediary comes highly recommended.

Internet Search Engines

A number of search engines have surfaced in the last few years that are designed to help entrepreneurs find funding sources. Some of these Web sites just provide information. Others use search engines to match ventures with potential funding sources. Some of the Web sites are tied to specific industries. Others are directed to specific regions of the country. Don't confuse technology with integrity. As with intermediaries, look for credibility when using any source of information and practice due diligence when considering any source of funding.

CRITERIA THAT BANKS USE WHEN CONSIDERING A LOAN REQUEST

As noted earlier, banks rarely provide loans to start-ups. However, it may be helpful here to describe the criteria that banks use when they review a loan request so that you can be prepared when your venture reaches the point in its evolution when it may be possible for you to get a commercial loan.

You may have heard people say, "Banks will only lend you money if you don't need it." This is not necessarily true. Banks are in the business of lending money. However, banks make their money by making loans to people who pay them off with interest. If someone applies for a loan to start a business and is turned down, this means that the bank determined that the risk of default outweighed the bank's expected interest income. Banks recognize that risk is part of any business proposition, but they are very cautious when it comes to lending their depositors' money. They know that most start-ups fail, especially start-ups by first-timers.

A good way to prepare for applying for a loan is to know the criteria that loan officers use when they review loan requests. Loan officers tend to evaluate a loan request using what are commonly called the "six Cs" of commercial lending.

The First C: Your Character

The first and foremost thing that loan officers look for when reviewing a loan request is evidence of your trustworthiness. This is crucial. Banks place a premium on integrity because they rely on your statements about your business and the corresponding financial projections. If your financial, professional, or personal background has any significant blemishes, your chances of borrowing money from a bank are diminished. Loan applications usually include a section that permits the bank to initiate a thorough credit check on you. If there is anything in your background that indicates a lack of integrity, loan officers will usually reject your loan application without even reviewing your proposed business idea. The bank may also check out the principal officers and directors of your business. Be prepared to identify all the people who will be an important part of your new business. In baseball, when you get three strikes, you are out. In commercial lending, the lack of integrity almost automatically means that you are out!

The Second C: Your Capability to Manage the Business

Banks know that mismanagement is the number one reason for the failure of new businesses. Your loan proposal must demonstrate that you and everyone else who will be making the various decisions have what it takes to make your business a success. Banks prefer to lend money to a business that will be managed by someone who has extensive business experience. Loan officers are very reluctant to lend money to first-timers, so it is important for you to communicate that the people involved have the skills needed and will not be using a trial-and-error approach to managing. If you are a first-timer, but you can show that you have extensive experience and been very successful in that field as a manager or an employee, that will help your chances of getting funding. If you do not have much experience, then you must demonstrate that you have surrounded yourself with capable advisers and experienced personnel. Your loan proposal should indicate how each person is suited for his or her position. It should also include a biographical sketch and a résumé for each key person.

Two examples demonstrate the value of having experience. A person was very successful as a residential realtor when he worked for one of the most respected and successful real estate firms. When he approached the bank to start his own firm, the bank realized he really was not starting from scratch. The banker knew that he would be bringing the goodwill associated with being known in the community and that he would benefit from referrals from former clients.

The same situation applied to a person who worked in a high-end men's clothing store. He had developed considerable rapport with the store's customers for a number of years. He knew his customers and what they wanted. He also noticed that they were not entirely pleased with the store's current selection of products and brands. When he approached the bank for a loan to start his own store, the bank provided a loan because the loan officer knew that that person had what it takes. In both cases, the fact that the bankers had been clients of the entrepreneurs helped the entrepreneurs secure funding.

A rule of thumb to remember is that if you have limited experience in the field, then your chances of getting a loan are also limited. This is why banks may look more favorably on a first-timer who is starting as a franchisee rather than as an independent business. Most well-respected franchises (1) are selective in whom they allow to acquire franchise rights, (2) offer training to key people before the business opens, and (3) provide management assistance on a regular basis. If you lack relevant experience, you should consider going the franchise route, gaining the experience by working for a similar business, or hiring someone who already has a proven track record to manage your business. You could also consider bringing in a partner instead of hiring a manager, if the partner has the appropriate experience. In any event, bankers know that there is a direct relationship between previous experience and new business success.

The Third C: Your Business's Capacity to Pay Off the Note

Banks operate under the very simple rule, "We make money only if we lend to businesses that make money." If the loan officer feels comfortable with your personal background and your ability to exercise good judgment when making business decisions, then the loan officer will focus on the ability of your business to make a profit.

The financial part of your business plan will be an integral part of your loan proposal. Your financial projections will provide the type of data that the loan officer will need in order to review your business idea. Loan officers will be particularly interested in (1) how soon you can generate a positive cash flow, (2) when you will show a profit, (3) how large that profit will be, (4) whether it will be lasting, and (5) whether various assets will be financed via debt or equity.

Banks, unlike investors, may be more concerned about your venture's cash flow than about its profitability and its ability to generate wealth. Bankers want to be sure that your business will have the ability to pay the monthly interest (and principal payments if the loan is amortized) and to pay off the note when it comes due. You should be prepared to present the cash flow projections for at least the first 2 years and the projected balance sheets for the next 3 to 5 years. Bankers' risk-averse nature makes them reluctant to do long-term funding unless it is for durable and marketable assets. Generally speaking, the more quickly your business can generate positive cash flow, the greater the likelihood of qualifying for a loan.

Your ability to prepare, present, and support your financial projections is an indication of your capability to manage a business. If you have an accountant help you prepare the financial part of the business plan, be sure that you understand the nature and logic of the financial projections. This is one of the reasons why you should have a working knowledge of accounting and finance. If every time the loan officer asks you a question about the basis for certain figures, you respond by saying, "I don't know, you'll have to ask my accountant," this will reduce your chances of getting a loan.

The Fourth C: The Conditions or Terms of the Loan

Even if the loan officer is satisfied with the first three Cs, the nature of your loan request will also influence the bank's willingness to lend you money. Your loan request will need to provide answers to the following four questions: (1) How much money are you requesting? (2) What will it be used for? (3) How long will it be needed? and (4) How will the loan be paid off?

The first question has considerable bearing on whether you will get the loan. If your balance sheet shows that you expect the bank to finance more than half of the venture's assets, you are likely to encounter difficulty. Loan officers do not want to provide more than one-half the value of the business. If a loan exceeds 50 percent of the venture's assets, the business would be more the bank's than yours

Banks expect most of the assets to be financed by you or other investors for three reasons. First, they want the owners to be committed to the business. They feel that you will be more responsible if you have money riding on the business's success. Second, if you don't have enough money and you are unable to get other investors to commit their money to the business, why should a bank put its depositors' money into your business? Bankers feel that if you are unwilling to commit your own money or are unable to convince other individuals to invest in your business, then either your business lacks merit or you lack the selling skills that will be more important for your business to succeed.

The third reason bankers do not want to finance more than half the assets is that they want to cover themselves in case your business fails. When businesses fail, the creditors frequently get to sell (liquidate) the business's assets in order to recover what the business owes them. In the past, loan officers used the 50/50 rule when considering a loan request. Their reasoning was that if the business failed, they would probably still be able to liquidate the assets for 50 cents on the dollar. The 50/50 rule was their "financial parachute." If they could get 50 cents per dollar of assets, they would be able to recover the amount of the loan's outstanding balance. The growing reluctance of banks to lend money to start-ups has caused some banks to use an 80/20 rule, limiting the loan to only 20 percent of the assets.

As you can see, you and other investors are at the end of the line when the assets are liquidated. Bankers do not like to take excessive risks. They reduce their risks by limiting the amount of the loan to a certain portion of the business's assets, using those assets as security, and being as close as possible to the front of the line to get their money out of the business if it is unable to meet its financial obligations.

The loan request should answer the second question, "What is the loan to be used for?" It should indicate (1) the type and amount of assets your business has, (2) the amount of assets already financed by debt from others, and (3) the amount of assets funded by investors. Loan officers also want to know if the money you want to borrow will be used to purchase fixtures and equipment, to buy a building, to pay for inventory, to finance your receivables, or to cover your monthly expenses if you do not consistently have a positive cash flow.

Loan officers prefer to lend money for items that can be identified, that can last for a number of years, and that can be repossessed and sold if all else fails. If your loan request is for money that will be dissipated (disappear) quickly—for example, to pay for advertising, rent, and salaries—you may find the bank reluctant to lend. Also, if the other tangible assets are leased or financed specifically by the manufacturer or distributor, these businesses may be in front of the bank when the line forms to pick up the pieces if you don't beat the odds.

The third question, "How long will the money be needed?" is related to the preceding question. The length of the loan is affected by the nature of the assets you are trying to finance. If you are using the money to buy inventory, you should not expect a loan to run for more than a few months. If you plan to use the money to buy equipment, the bank may be willing to lend the money for a couple of years. If you are planning to buy a building, you may be able to secure a loan for at least 10 years. Loan officers look at the useful life of the assets they are financing. They rarely lend money for longer than the assets are expected to last.

Borrowing money for a business is quite different from getting a mortgage to finance the purchase of a house. You will be expected to have a lot of equity up front. A 5 percent down payment will not get a loan officer's attention. Moreover, banks rarely lend money for more than 5 years unless it is to be used to finance a building. You may have been able to get a 20- to 30-year mortgage for your home, but you will have to demonstrate to the bank that your business has the ability to pay off the loan within 5 years.

Your answer to the fourth question, "How will the loan be paid off?" should indicate whether you will use profits, refinancing, or the issuance of stock at a later date to pay off the note.

Two other conditions also need to be kept in mind when you are borrowing from a bank, First, you will have to carry enough insurance on your business's assets to cover them in the event of a fire or some other type of business loss. Second, the bank will place various restrictive covenants on the operation of your business. You will be expected to provide certain financial records on a regular basis that reflect the financial health of your business. You will need to maintain certain levels of inventory, receivables, and cash. The restrictions may include getting prior approval from the bank if you are thinking of making any major changes in your balance sheet, such as selling or purchasing assets or altering the business's equity or debt configuration.

The bank may not technically be a partner in the business, but it may seem like a senior partner in certain instances. Borrowing money involves more than filling in a loan application and shaking hands. It needs to be addressed as a rigorous process. If you approach the bank in a casual manner, the loan officer is likely to (1) infer that you are not serious about your business, (2) infer that you are unwilling or unable to do your homework, or (3) assume that you will not be able to make a favorable impression on potential customers. With any of these assumptions, your chances of getting a loan are minimal.

The Fifth C: The Context of Your Proposed Business

Lending is not a science because no business exists in a vacuum. Loan officers have to exercise judgment when they lend money to a business. There are a myriad of factors that have to be considered when sizing up the merit of a business proposal and the risk associated with it. Loan officers also have their own perceptions and preferences.

You need to recognize that loan officers have attitudes about most types of business. Some loan officers get excited about manufacturing or technology businesses. Others seem to favor retail or service businesses. This may also be true for banks. Smaller banks tend to be more "retail" oriented. They actively seek opportunities to lend to promising local businesses. Many large banks have a reputation for avoiding start-ups and early-stage ventures. Some banks also avoid making loans for less than $100,000.

Banks that have been successful in lending to certain types of businesses are more open-minded when they review a loan proposal for a similar business. Conversely, some loan officers and banks have had bad experiences with certain types of businesses. If you are in a similar business, you may encounter considerable skepticism on the part of the loan officer.

Look for a loan officer who has extensive experience in your business's field or has had a good track record in lending to that type of business. This may be to your advantage. If your idea is very foreign to the loan officer, or if it falls into the category of "I'll be darned if I ever lend money to that kind of business again!" then you may be better off looking for another loan officer or approaching a different bank. Many loan officers are known to avoid lending to restaurants, video rental stores, and women's clothing boutiques.

You should expect loan officers to look at the *context* in which you will start your business. They may pay particular attention to potential economic, legal, regulatory, employee, supplier, or environmental problems. You may have financial projections that demonstrate your business's capacity to pay off the loan. Loan officers, however, place a premium on the local, regional, and national economic picture. Their feeling about whether there will be inflation, a recession, tight money, high unemployment, and so on, will influence your likelihood of getting a loan. Loan officers can get cold feet if the overall economic outlook is not good. Even if your target area has growth potential, loan officers may still have cold feet. If your type of business is recession-proof and inflation-proof, you may be in good shape.

Loan officers are also interested in whether your business is competition-proof and obsolescence-proof. They will be particularly interested in whether the market is already saturated—that is, whether too many businesses are already competing for too few customers. This usually results in intense price competition that destroys profitability. They will also be interested in whether you will be competing with chains and franchises or will be up against small independent businesses.

Loan officers tend to look more favorably on your business plan if (1) you have a fairly new product or service that people already want to buy, (2) there is little competition, (3) the competition is made up of small independent businesses, and (4) few businesses of your type have failed. Loan officers don't seem to be bothered by other similar businesses being started. They are far more apprehensive when similar businesses are starting to fail. Loan officers prefer a situation in which a growing opportunity exists, even if there is competition, to a situation in which the market is showing signs that it is waning and businesses are failing. Loan officers frequently contact their headquarters to learn about the success rates for your type of business. The bank's headquarters staff usually has access to trade data as well as to the track record for similar businesses in the bank's loan portfolios, so it has a clearer picture of the merit of that type of business.

Loan officers also look at barriers to entry—the ease with which other people can start your type of business. If your type of business requires extensive experience, rigorous licensing requirements, and considerable capital, and you are one of only a few people who meet all the qualifications, the bank will be more willing to lend you money. Conversely, if almost anyone could start your type of business with no experience and minimal investment, this would be disconcerting to a loan officer.

Legal issues also concern loan officers. Certain types of businesses have come under closer scrutiny and faced increased regulation in recent years. Billboard businesses have encountered considerable regulation in many towns. Some municipalities have passed ordinances requiring billboard businesses to reduce the number and size of their signs. Some towns have gone so far as to require that all billboards be removed within the decade. Day-care, exercise, pest control, and other businesses are expected to encounter additional licensing requirements and regulations in the years to come. If your business is expected to have numerous employees, the loan officer may be concerned about the likelihood of unionization. The potential for a strike can give a loan officer cold feet. The potential for employee accidents and the business's liability may also affect the loan officer.

The loan officer may be concerned about your vulnerability to suppliers. Many small businesses fail because their suppliers went out of business or failed to continue providing for the needs of those businesses. Restrictive covenants between one of your competitors and a supplier to not provide service to your business may be illegal, but informal practices of this type continue in many fields.

The ability to get insurance coverage is another area that concerns businesses and loan officers. Insurance premiums for some types of businesses have more than tripled in the last couple of years. Some businesses have had to reduce their coverage or go without coverage because the costs have increased so much. A few businesses have even closed their doors because they could not get insurance coverage. Some of these businesses did not even have a checkered past. The insurance companies simply decided to discontinue coverage to that kind of business. Neither you nor your loan officer wants your business to die on the vine because you cannot get what you need in order to do business. The greater the risk of your failing to get services or products from any type of supplier, the greater the likelihood that the loan officer will not approve your loan request.

Environmental factors may also make the loan officer apprehensive about financing your business. If your business can be adversely affected by the weather (hurricanes, tornadoes, floods, droughts, or unseasonable conditions), the loan officer may not want to risk the bank's depositors' money. Loan officers like to finance businesses that are influenced by their managers rather than by Mother Nature. Loan officers also tend to shy away from any business that could be involved in any type of ecological disaster. If your business will be dealing with anything that is flammable or toxic, or that has the potential to be a pollutant, the loan officer may steer clear of your proposal.

The fifth C indicates that your loan proposal can be rejected because of the nature and context of your business, regardless of the strength of the other Cs. In such a case, you will have to provide even more documentation in your business plan and loan request to substantiate your optimism and demonstrate the viability of your business idea. For this reason, it may be advisable for you to set up an appointment with your bank's commercial loan officer when you are in the early stages of preparing your loan application. You may be able to get an initial impression of the loan officer's interest in such a business. You may find that the bank has adopted a policy of not lending to that type of business. It is hoped, however, that you will find the loan officer to be enthusiastic about your business. If that is the case, the loan officer may be able to get or recommend some sources of information to help you prepare your loan request. You may find that the loan officer can provide helpful advice. This may pay off later. The more the bank helps you from the beginning, the more likely it is that it will approve your loan request.

The Sixth C: Your Collateral

Most people who apply for a loan place too much emphasis on their collateral. Your collateral is important, but loan officers do not put it at the top of their criteria when they review a loan request. Loan officers want to finance businesses that will make money. If they have reservations about the business's potential profitability, they may require a large amount of collateral to cover their risk. Nevertheless, banks tend to operate on the policy, "If it takes a lot of collateral to cover the bank's position, don't approve the loan."

Your collateral represents a "financial parachute" for the bank. Both you and the bank hope that it will never have to be used. As with parachutes, the bank will look for collateral that is large enough to break the fall. Banks also prefer collateral that can be easily converted to cash. If your business's collateral will be custom manufacturing equipment that may be difficult to resell and that has minimal value once it has been used, your banker may place little value on it as collateral. The same may also be true if your personal collateral is a 200-acre family-owned farm in Kansas.

If your business is unable to meet its loan obligations, the bank is placed in a couple of awkward situations. First, the loan officer has to admit to not exercising good judgment when he or she loaned you the money. Second, the officer has to go through the process of converting assets into cash in order to recover the bank's money. This takes time and diverts the bank from what it is in business to do. It also alienates your employees, customers, investors, suppliers, and creditors.

Your loan request will need to reflect what assets can be used as collateral for the bank loan. If your business is to be a sole proprietorship or a partnership, the bank will probably ask you to include personal balance sheets for yourself and any partners. Remember, you are the business. If it fails to meet its obligations to the bank, the bank will look to your personal assets for settlement of the loan. If your business will be set up as a corporation, don't be surprised if the bank and other creditors ask you and the other major stockholders to provide personal balance sheets. The bank may also expect you and the other major stockholders to personally co-sign the loan. This will create the same personal financial obligation as if the business were formed as a proprietorship or partnership.

Collateral may be one of the six Cs, but it rarely makes up for weaknesses in any of the other five Cs. You will need to provide enough collateral to reduce the downside risk for the bank, but don't treat collateral as the primary selling point in your loan request.

OTHER FACTORS TO CONSIDER WHEN YOU SEEK A LOAN

As you begin the process of applying for a loan, you should keep in mind the following points: First, it may be worth your time to approach a few banks, not just the one you are using now. Some banks are more receptive to emerging ventures than others. Also, loan terms often vary from bank to bank. You may be able to find a bank that offers a lower interest rate, a more flexible payback schedule, or fewer restrictive covenants. Second, be prepared to scale down your request to fit what you can borrow.

CONCLUSION: ANITA RODDICK WAS RIGHT— FINDING FUNDING CAN BE A REAL CHALLENGE

Anita Roddick, co-founder of The Body Shop, noted, "There are only two ways of raising money: the hard way and the very hard way."[10] There are as many sources of funding as there are facets on a diamond. The same applies to the criteria used by each source when it considers funding and the terms or conditions associated with the funding package. The need for a comprehensive funding plan and the need to have sufficient lead time when seeking funding cannot be overemphasized.

There is no one best source of funding for all ventures—one size does not fit all ventures! Each stage of the emerging venture's growth has particular needs. The challenge for entrepreneurs is to find the source of funding that fits its particular needs at that particular point in time. What is right at one stage in the venture's evolution may be totally inappropriate for another stage. The key is sensing in advance what is needed and having the time, contacts, information, and skills to put together the best funding package.

A few points may be helpful in closing this chapter on funding. First, life is full of surprises, and few things will go as planned. It is always wise to have backup sources of capital. Try to keep some money in reserve to cover unforeseen opportunities or problems. Don't commit all your money to the venture in the beginning, and don't commit every last dollar of the venture's funds to its operations. Remember Murphy's Law, "If anything can go wrong, it will, and at the most inopportune moment." You will need to have some water in the well when you need to put out fires. It would be a tragedy for the venture to go down for the lack of a few dollars. If you get into a situation in which you desperately need funding, it will be very expensive even if you get it. Backup sources may include (1) having a line of credit with a bank, (2) having untapped credit cards, or (3) having an angel investor who wants to be part of your venture.

Second, remember that you will probably be the last person to be paid. Your employees, your suppliers, and your bank will demand that they be paid—even if it means that you have to go without a paycheck or without getting any return on the money you have put into the venture. Entrepreneurs need to remember Harry Truman's words, "The buck stops here!"

Third, don't drain the venture. If you are one of the fortunate entrepreneurs who has revenue beginning to roll in, make sure that you don't drain the venture of the funds that will be so critical to its growth and continued success. Lillian Vernon stresses the need to keep three rules in mind when starting a business and keeping it going. They are, "Reinvest, reinvest, and reinvest."[11]

Fourth, some entrepreneurs have a real aversion to borrowing money. Debt funding has at least three advantages. For one thing, if you are using other people's money to start and grow your business, when your business eventually pays off its debts, you will get all of its profits and own all of its assets. When you create and maintain customers at a profit, you will be transforming debt into net worth. Also, when you borrow money, you do not dilute the ownership of the business. Lenders are creditors, not owners. Finally, interest payments are also tax-deductible as a business expense. When a business pays dividends to its shareholders as a return on their investment, those dividends are not treated as tax deductions. The deductibility of interest expenses reduces your tax obligation, which reduces your cash outflow.

Fifth, most people who are involved in funding emerging ventures are not entrepreneurs. They look at things differently, have different objectives, and have different expectations. Don't expect them to be as optimistic as you are about your chances for success or as emotionally involved in your venture. The more that you can see the world through their eyes and provide them with the type of information that they consider relevant, the greater your chances of getting funding.

NOTES

[1] Howard Schultz and Dori Jones Yang, *Pour Your Heart into It* (New York: Hyperion, 1997), p. 73.

[2] David Evanson and Art Beroff, "Many Golden Returns," *Entrepreneur,* March 2000, pp. 66–71.

[3] W. Keith Schilit, *The Entrepreneur's Guide to Preparing a Winning Business Plan and Raising Venture Capital* (Englewood Cliffs, N.J.: Prentice-Hall 1990), p. 235.

[4] Vance Trimble, *Overnight Success: Federal Express and Frederick Smith, Its Renegade Creator* (New York: Crown, 1993), pp. 161–162.

[5] Martha Visser, "Phone-omenon," *Success,* September 1998, p. 62.

[6] James Morrow, "Secrets of a Start-Up," *Success,* September 1998, p. 68.

[7] Ibid.

[8] Debra Phillips, G. David Doran, Elaine Teague, and Laura Tiffany, "Young Millionaires," *Entrepreneur,* November 1998, p. 119.

[9] Jeffrey H. Birnbaum, "Uncle Sam, Venture Capitalist," *Fortune,* May 24, 1999, p. 66.

[10] Anita Roddick and Irene Prokup, *Body and Soul: Profits and Principles—The Amazing Success Story of Anita Roddick and the Body Shop* (New York: Crown, 1991), p. 73.

[11] Lillian Vernon, *An Eye for Winners: How I Built One of America's Greatest Direct-Mail Businesses* (New York: HarperCollins, 1996), p. 66.

10

Buying an Existing Business

SOMETIMES IT'S BETTER NOT TO START FROM SCRATCH

So far, this book has focused on starting a business from scratch. Like most things in life, this approach to getting into business has advantages and drawbacks. The primary advantages of starting from scratch include being able to develop a business that will capitalize on a unique opportunity or business idea and having the pleasure of knowing that you did it on your own. The major disadvantage of starting from scratch is that you need to come up with the answers to the hundreds of questions involved in starting a new business. This may represent a challenge, but it also poses a considerable risk, especially for the first-timer.

Even a thoroughly prepared business plan will not provide all the answers, nor will it identify all the questions that will need to be addressed. When you start a business from scratch, you will be engaged in a lot of trial and error. You cannot be assured that suppliers will fulfill their commitments, that the location you choose will appeal to prospective customers, and that the people you hire will work out.

Your business plan is based on assumptions about whether there are customers in search of a business, what the appropriate products or services to offer will be, what advertising will work, and so on. Quite a few of your assumptions will not be right on target. This is why so many start-ups fail.

The business plan will help you to be more systematic in analyzing the market. It will also force you to collect data to test the validity of your assumptions. Nevertheless, when a first-timer attempts to start a business from scratch, that person is usually taking the most risky path for going into business.

There are two other ways to go into business: You can buy an existing business, or you can acquire the rights to a franchise and become a franchisee. Both alternatives give you the opportunity to bypass many of the questions you must answer before you start a business from scratch. In each case, assumptions about the business idea have already been field-tested.

While these avenues may reduce the likelihood of failure, each of them has a corresponding cost. Moreover, neither approach can guarantee success. This chapter addresses the pros and cons of buying an existing business. The next chapter covers the benefits and drawbacks associated with becoming a franchisee.

WHY BUY AN EXISTING BUSINESS?

In many instances, it may be advisable to buy an existing business rather than start one from scratch. The greatest benefit of buying an existing business is that the business is a tangible entity. When you start a business from scratch, you have to estimate the levels of sales, costs, and profits. When you are considering buying a business, the seller can provide actual financial data that reflect the business's performance. Instead of having faith that people will buy the products and services the business offers, you will have a record of how many people bought what and when that you can review.

When you start a business from scratch, you are dealing with an almost endless list of unknowns. When you buy an existing business, one of the things you are buying is the answers to questions that could not be answered prior to starting a business from scratch.

One of the interesting things about buying a business is that the process is not all that different from the process of starting a new venture. First, you need to identify an area in which a substantial and lasting opportunity exists. Second, you must have or must develop the necessary skills and resources to capitalize on the opportunity. Third, there must be sufficient profit potential or potential return on the amount of money to be invested in the business to justify the risk. The first few chapters of this book stressed the need for these three factors to be present and the importance of developing a thorough business plan. It was also noted that getting into a business is not something that can be done overnight. Starting a business from scratch is a very time-consuming process. The same is true for buying an existing business.

While it may take less time to buy a business than to start one, it may still take 4 to 12 months from the time you start looking for opportunities until you actually own a business. It could take more than a year to find a business that fits with your personal preferences and meets your financial objectives.

The major advantage of buying an existing business is that everything is already in place. Instead of hoping that people will be interested in your new business, you have customers who are accustomed to buying from that business. Instead of having to contact suppliers and negotiate with them to provide merchandise and trade credit, you get established relationships. Instead of having to hire and train people, you get a seasoned group of employees.

There are numerous other potential benefits to buying an existing business. Presumably, you are securing a positive cash flow rather than having the anxieties associated with waiting for cash receipts to cover cash disbursements. If the business has that ideal one-of-a-kind location, it may offer an opportunity that you could not have if you were to start a business and had to wait for an acceptable location to become available. If you believe that an opportunity exists for starting a new business of the same type, for the same target market, and in the same geographic area as the business you are considering buying, then one of the benefits of buying a business rather than starting one is that there will be one less competitor.

Buying an existing business has at least six other potential advantages. First, an existing business has a financial track record, which may make it easier to get a loan and/or attract investors. This may be particularly important if it is a novel type of business. People are often unwilling to finance an unusual idea or an untested concept. However, they may be interested in investing in a unique business that has proven its viability. Second, seller financing may be possible. Seller financing is an alternative that is not available when a business is started from scratch. The reluctance of banks to extend loans to start-ups increases the appeal of buying an existing business. Third, the seller's terms (interest rate, payment schedule, covenants, and so on) may be better than those that you could get from any conventional lender. The terms of the deal may actually be more important to the buyer than the price. The ability to structure the financing so that the business's cash flow is synchronized with payments to the seller can make a real difference.

Fourth, in some cases, you may be able to acquire the assets you need for less money than you would have to pay if you had to buy all of them new when you start your business. Fifth, if the business has been successful, then either the owner or the manager has been making the right decisions. If you do not have the level of experience necessary to manage the business, you may be able to arrange a contract in which the seller stays on as a consultant for a few months after you purchase the business to teach you the ropes.

If the business has been managed by someone other than the owner, that person may be interested in staying on. If you do not have enough money to buy the business, you might consider asking whether the manager would be interested in investing in the business or becoming a partner. This could be a mutually advantageous proposition. You receive additional capital and management capability, and the manager is able to stay on the job. You may not own 100 percent of the business, but you will have a higher probability of making a profit. Some people may ask how you can afford to have both the manager and yourself on the payroll. The answer is that if you buy and manage the business yourself, you will be spending most of your time learning the business. If you keep the manager, then the two of you can concentrate on strengthening and expanding the business.

Sixth, an existing business may have unique features or exclusive assets. If the business includes a facility (either owned by the business or with a lease that you can assume) that no one else can match, then buying the business provides a competitive advantage that would not be possible for you to have if you were to start this type of business from scratch. The same can also be true for the name of the business or its logo, or it may have exclusive territorial rights to a popular brand or have a patent or license privileges.

In some cases, it would be impossible, extremely time-consuming, or cost-prohibitive for you to try to develop these advantages from scratch. If so, it may be better to buy an existing business. Conversely, if you believe that you can create a competitive advantage, achieve superior financial performance, and do it with less capital, then you should start a business rather than purchasing an existing one. In many cases, first-timers will have a better chance of beating the odds if they buy the right business.

SOME BUSINESSES ARE FOR SALE, OTHERS CAN BE BOUGHT

There are more than 18 million businesses in the United States. Over 90 percent of these businesses are small businesses. At one time or another, nearly every owner thinks about selling his or her business. The average business changes hands every 4 years. The businesses for sale section of the classified ads and the listings by business brokers are only the tip of the iceberg. As one entrepreneur put it, "My business isn't for sale, but if someone comes along with the right offer, I'll sell it!" Ironically, some of the businesses that are listed for sale may not really be for sale. Some owners list their businesses periodically as a matter of curiosity, to see if someone bites!

At least 20 percent of existing businesses are formally or informally up for sale. For every business formally listed, there may well be two or three businesses of the same type in your geographic area that could be purchased. This rule of thumb tells you that it may be worth your while to check the network of people who know which businesses are not formally on the market but can be bought. Attorneys, loan officers, accountants, and trust officers are frequently aware of their clients' interest in selling their businesses. Business owners may also have an idea about other business owners who may be interested in selling their businesses. Commercial realtors may also know of people who may want to sell their business. You may even consider running a "want to buy a business" classified ad that describes your interests in general terms.

If you are willing to move, it may be worthwhile for you to contact business brokers in other cities and check the business for sale Web sites listed in the appendix.

BUYER BEWARE: ALL THAT GLITTERS MAY NOT BE GOLD!

There are about as many reasons why owners want to sell their businesses as there are businesses for sale. Unfortunately, many of the reasons owners give for wanting to sell their businesses are not the real reasons. The reasons for selling include retirement, health problems, the desire to live in a different location, and sons or daughters who do not want to take over the business. In some cases, these may be the real reasons. In other cases, however, they are merely socially acceptable smoke screens to cover the real reason: The business is in trouble or its future is not very promising.

Every business may be unique, but the following seven categories cover most of the businesses for sale:

1. Successful businesses with the potential to continue to be at least as prosperous
2. Businesses that have been successful but have diminishing potential
3. Businesses that have been moderately successful but have the potential to be very successful
4. Businesses that have been moderately successful and are likely to continue their "lukewarm" existence
5. Businesses that have been moderately successful but are destined to decline and ultimately fail

6. Businesses that have experienced difficulties but have the potential to stand on their own feet
7. Businesses that have experienced difficulties and are destined to fail even if new management and additional funds are injected into them

Businesses in the first, third, and sixth categories are worth considering if the price and the terms are right. The fourth category may be acceptable if you are not ambitious and are looking for a "lifestyle" business. Owners of businesses in the second category usually want as much money for their businesses as the owners of businesses in the first category. Many sellers in the fifth and seventh categories are anxious to find a buyer while there is something left to sell. If you are considering buying a business that has had problems, recognize that it may be more difficult to turn a troubled business around than to start one from scratch.

The sale of a business is similar to the sale of stock in that the buyer is more optimistic about the future than the seller. The moral to this story is that you may ask sellers the reasons why they want to sell, but you need to carry out a thorough investigation of the business, its market, and other related factors to be sure that you are not about to buy a lemon. Also, if a deal seems to be too good to be true, it is probably a deal that you should pass up. Occasionally a business can be bought for a fraction of its worth because of a death or illness, but these situations are rare. When a business is for sale because of the owner's illness or death, you should realize that troubled businesses frequently contribute to health problems. Make sure that the business you buy won't put you in the same predicament within a couple of years.

There are at least four other rules of thumb to keep in mind when you consider buying a business. First, you should develop a target business profile. Before you go looking for a business to buy, you should have a specific set of criteria for what you expect. You need to identify how much you are willing to invest in a business, what level of risk you are willing to accept, what minimum return on investment you are willing to receive, and how much time you are willing to commit to learning and managing the business.

Second, resist the temptation to buy the first business that looks good. Too often, people are so anxious to get into business that they buy the first business that comes along. This is particularly true if the business has considerable emotional appeal. If this happens, force yourself to step back and look at the business objectively. Don't let the seller play the car salesperson's game of pressuring you to make an offer on the spot because someone else is also interested. Experience shows that people who maintain some objectivity and have patience eventually find the right business. First-timers frequently find it difficult to remain cool, calm, and collected. They should heed the Japanese saying, "The first person who speaks loses!"

You should pursue buying a business with something like the deliberation that you would exercise when considering marrying someone. Emotions will obviously be a factor, but staying power should be a high priority. If you are excited about a particular business, make an effort to check out at least one other business. Checking out another business will give you a chance to settle down and be more objective. You may also find that it is an even better opportunity than the first one.

The third rule of thumb applies to looking at businesses that have been around long enough to have a track record. Most businesses will not make a profit in their first year. If the business is not operating at least at its breakeven level by the end of its second year, it may never make a profit. Moreover, a business that does not have a positive cash flow may need additional financing after you purchase it. A business with a positive cash flow will help you meet the financial obligations you incurred in buying it.

You should concentrate your attention on businesses that have been operating for at least 2 years. The fact that a business has its head above water after 2 years is no guarantee that it will continue to be profitable, but you will be increasing your odds of buying a business with a future. Someone once said, "It may take 2 years to know if you have a lemon, but it takes an oyster 7 years to produce a pearl."

The fourth rule of thumb is to adopt the sky divers' motto, "Don't jump from the plane without a good parachute!" Make sure that each business you consider buying can be sold if you find that you were not meant to run a business or if you find that it doesn't have as rosy a future as you thought. Check to see how long the business has been for sale and what price or financing adjustments had to be made to induce you to buy it. Make sure you are buying a business with a future rather than getting stuck with a liability.

GUIDELINES FOR ANALYZING A BUSINESS

If you find a business that appears to have been able to create and maintain customers and that matches your capabilities, you will need to do a thorough analysis to determine its real merit. The time has come to go beyond your initial impressions and do what is called *due diligence*. Now you have to roll up your sleeves and look at the business from every possible angle.

The purchase of a business involves numerous players. The seller may be represented by a business broker. The seller will also consult with an accountant, an attorney, and investors in setting the asking price and negotiating the final terms of the sale. You should go into the process with (1) an accountant who is good at financial analysis and is experienced in business valuation, (2) an attorney who is experienced in business buyouts, and (3) a good idea of what you and the other investors are willing to commit to buying the business.

If a business broker is involved in listing the business you are pursuing, that person should be able to provide you with the asking price, whether the owner is willing to provide financing assistance, what the terms of the sale and financing will be, a list of the assets and liabilities involved in the business, and an income statement and balance sheet for at least the last 12 months. Some business brokers are not willing to provide financial information unless you make an initial offer to show your sincerity. This offer may simply involve signing a statement of confidentiality and disclosing certain personal and financial information.

Some brokers may ask for an earnest deposit before they will provide any financial information. They want to deal with "qualified buyers," so the check is the price you pay to learn the specifics for that business. The practice of asking the inquirer to sign a statement of confidentiality and, in some instances, requiring a deposit does two things. First, it protects the seller from casual inquiries, through which people, including competitors, can gain access to the seller's confidential financial information. Second, the statement and deposit indicate that the prospective buyer has the financial wherewithal to buy the business if the deliberations result in a formal offer. At first glance, this appears to be a tedious and cumbersome process, but it makes sense when you realize that it may take 3 or more months to close a deal, even if it goes fairly smoothly. The broker minimizes casual window-shopping by expecting a tangible commitment from a prospective buyer early in the process. The deposit, if required, may be refunded under certain conditions if you do not buy the business.

THE BOOK VALUE APPROACH TO VALUING A BUSINESS

At this point, your major concern is determining what the business is worth. Unfortunately, there is no universally accepted formula for determining the worth of a business. The traditional approach for setting selling price has been to take the book value, or possibly the market value, of the business's tangible assets and add a certain amount for "goodwill." Goodwill represents the intangible side of the business. A successful business is more than the sum of its assets. As stated earlier, an ongoing business has an established name, a set of customers, relationships with suppliers, experienced employees, and so forth. Goodwill can be viewed as the price you pay for reducing the amount of trial and error and avoiding the risk associated with starting a business from scratch.

The value of goodwill and its bearing on the asking price are the most emotional and controversial elements of the purchase of a business. Sellers place a premium on the value of their business's goodwill. It reflects their contribution to the business. Buyers are aware of the importance of goodwill; however, they usually prefer to have their money go for assets such as inventory and equipment, which can be converted into sales and depreciated to enhance cash flow. Tangible assets may also make it easier to get a loan from a bank.

The traditional approach to valuing a business concentrates on the business's balance sheet. The book value of the assets and the amount of goodwill are important because when most sole proprietorships and partnerships are sold, the buyer purchases the assets and the seller uses the proceeds of the sale to pay off the business's liabilities.

While there may be varying opinions on how to value goodwill, valuing the tangible assets is fairly straightforward. The current balance sheet reflects the book value of the assets. Book value is the assets' original purchase price less accumulated depreciation.

If the current market or replacement value of the assets is greater than their book value, the market value of the assets may be used instead of book value to set the asking price. However, just as there are cases in which the market value exceeds the book value of the assets, there can also be instances in which the assets are worth less than their book value.

You will need to have your accountant determine the true value of the assets. Your accountant will pay particular attention to the percentage of accounts receivable that can be collected, whether the inventory is seasonal or out-of-date, and whether the accumulated depreciation truly reflects the change in the value of the equipment. Your accountant will probably request a financial audit and a physical audit. If the business has a substantial amount of assets or if the assets are unusual, it may be advisable to have a professional appraiser estimate the market value of the assets. In either case, it is advisable for you to choose the auditor or appraiser.

The value of goodwill can range from a modest 10 or 20 percent of the value of the tangible assets to a multiple of their dollar value. If the business has not made money or if equivalent assets and employees can be acquired easily, the goodwill may have minimal value. In other businesses, particularly service businesses, the value of goodwill may exceed the value of the tangible assets.

Two of the most valuable components of a service business are its customers and its employees. They play a crucial role in the business's future growth and viability. Service businesses such as insurance agencies, realty offices, employee placement businesses, beauty salons, and so on, do not have much in the way of tangible assets. The owners of service businesses are selling their "book of accounts." Service businesses are actually selling their customers and their employees' relationships with those customers. Their customers are their goodwill. If you were to start one of these businesses from scratch, you might be able to match an existing business's tangible assets, but it could take thousands of dollars of advertising and years of effort, among other things, to develop a comparable customer base and customer relationships. Even with an investment of this much time and money, there would be no guarantee that you could match the existing business. It is for this reason that you should have the seller sign a "noncompete and confidentiality (nondisclosure)" agreement as a condition for the sale of the business to you.

The traditional assets plus goodwill approach to establishing the asking price for a business has its merits. It also has some drawbacks. Even if you can decide on the best way to value the assets, you still have to determine an appropriate value for the business's goodwill.

THE CAPITALIZATION-OF-EARNINGS APPROACH TO VALUING A BUSINESS

The more popular capitalization-of-earnings approach to valuing a business looks at the business's income statement more than at its balance sheet. The major difference between the two methods is that in the traditional approach, the emphasis is on buying the assets of the business. The capitalization-of-earnings approach is concerned with buying the business's future profit potential. This approach is used more than the book value approach because two of the most important questions for the prospective buyer are, "At what level of profit is the business presently operating?" and "How much (profit) is it capable of generating?" Assets are important, but they are merely the means to an end—generating a profit. With the capitalization-of-earnings approach, the business is valued according to what it is capable of doing rather than the assets it has on hand at the time of the sale.

The capitalization-of-earnings approach is consistent with the prospective buyer's interests. While the seller may want to get cash for his or her investment in the business, the prospective buyer wants to know what level of return he or she can expect on the investment in the business. Unfortunately, the capitalization-of-earnings approach presents two major challenges. First, you need to determine the business's true profitability. Second, you need to determine the appropriate capitalization rate to apply to the earnings. The capitalization-of-earnings approach to determining the value of the business is based on the following formula:

$$\text{True net income} \times \text{capitalization rate} = \text{value of business}$$

This approach requires that the business's true net income be determined. Most first-timers assume that the net income from the last 12 months as reported on the business's income statement is an actual figure. In fact, this figure may not reflect the business's true profitability.

If the business is a sole proprietorship or a partnership, profit is defined as what is left after all the expenses are deducted from revenue. The business's profit is actually what the owner gets for running the business. The following example illustrates the point. The sole proprietor of a retail shop asked a consultant to give her an idea of how much she should ask for her business if she put it up for sale. The consultant asked, "How much money did your business make in the last 12 months?" The owner said that the business made $10,000. This sounded like a reasonable profit for a business with only $80,000 in sales. The capitalization-of-earnings approach might use a rate of 4 for this business and yield the following value:

$$\text{Profit of } \$10,000 \times 4 = \$40,000$$

Herein lies one of the reasons why you need to be certain that the profit figure in the formula reflects the true level of profit for the business. When you are valuing a sole proprietorship or partnership, you need to be sure that the figure represents profit after the owner's salary has been deducted.

The $10,000 profit figure should be modified to reflect the 40 hours a week for 50 weeks that the owner worked at the business during the last 12 months. If the owner were to have been paid a modest $10 per hour, then $20,000 ($10 times 2000 hours) should have been deducted from sales revenue as an operating expense. Wages for every employee, including the owner, must be deducted as an expense for a corporation. The same adjustment should be used if you are valuing a sole proprietorship or a partnership. If the owner had not worked there, someone else would have been needed to carry out those tasks. The cost of labor, whoever performs it, needs to be reflected when determining true profitability. The salary figure should reflect that person's skill and time committed to the job.

If the $20,000 for the owner's time and effort is deducted from the previously reported $10,000 profit, it will provide the following value for the business:

Profit of $0 (or actually a $10,000 loss) × 4 = $0 value for the business

At this point, you should say, "Wait a minute. Even though the business did not make a profit or actually lost money, it must be worth something." Obviously the business is worth something. It may not be making a true profit, but its balance sheet indicates that it has $20,000 in assets and no liabilities.

In this instance, the owner should use the assets plus goodwill approach for figuring the asking price. The minimum asking price for a business should be the market value of its assets. In this case, an asking price of $24,000 was recommended for the retail business.

This price included $4000 (20 percent of the assets) for goodwill. The business may not have made a profit, but (1) it had an established set of customers, (2) the market was expected to grow, and (3) it had 3 more years of an assumable lease for a location that could not be matched.

The business was sold in 4 months for $21,000. The owner agreed to make a $3000 concession because the buyer's accountant determined that some of the inventory was seasonal. The owner also accepted the offer because the buyer was prepared to pay cash. This was important because the seller did not want to provide financing. The fact that the seller was anxious to move to Florida also expedited the sale.

This example may not be typical, but it illustrates the complexity involved in determining the actual level of profit and the true value of a business's assets. If the business had been profitable, the capitalization-of-earnings approach might have been more appropriate. With that approach, the capitalization rate, or multiple, is the most important part of the equation. If the business is profitable and has the potential to be even more profitable, its present profit level will be multiplied by a higher capitalization rate. If it is a moderately profitable business and it is expected to continue being stable or lukewarm for the next few years because it is in a stagnant market or because competition will be increasing, then a lower capitalization rate will be used.

The capitalization rate and the value of goodwill used in the book value approach are similar in concept. If the business is more profitable than comparable businesses, it must have some advantage. The more profitable it is, the greater the value given to goodwill or the higher the capitalization rate. It is wise, however, to determine the extent to which the seller's personal goodwill is taken into consideration. You don't want to be left with the empty shell of a business when the seller leaves.

The capitalization-of-earnings approach is similar to the approach used by most investors in the stock market. Investors in stock frequently use the price-earnings ratio to determine an appropriate price. If the business is making $4 per share and is expected to double its profits within 4 years, investors may be willing to pay more for the stock than for a company with less potential. In this case, investors may apply a capitalization rate of 8 to the $4-per-share profit. Thus, they would be willing to pay up to $32 a share for this business. If the business is not expected to do better, it might warrant a capitalization of 3 or 4. Investors would probably not be willing to pay more than $12 for a share of this business.

When you buy a business, you are buying it for what it will do, not what it has done. The capitalization rate places considerable weight on future potential. Capitalization rates may be as low as 2 or as high as 20, depending on how long the business has been operating, the growth of its market, its competition, and its present profit level. In a start-up business, there is no profit, so future profits become the basis for what a person may be willing to invest in the business.

The following example demonstrates how the capitalization rate can be used in valuing an established and profitable business. A wholesaler of plumbing fixtures wanted to sell his business. He was 65 years old, and he planned to retire during the coming year. He had started the business 30 years earlier, and it had grown into the leading wholesale plumbing fixtures business in the area. The asking price for the business was set at $800,000.

The prospective buyer for the business had experience in manufacturing plumbing fixtures and wanted to relocate in that area. The prospective buyer requested the financial statements for the last 5 years. The prospective buyer's accountant reviewed the figures and brought in a professional appraiser to determine the true value of the assets.

The business was a corporation and had no long-term debt. The income statement for the past 12 months indicated that the business had had a pretax profit of $150,000. The previous income statements revealed that the business had averaged $120,000 in profit for each of the 4 preceding years. The appraiser valued the assets, which included inventory, fixtures, equipment, supplies, receivables, metal building, and land, at $560,000. This meant that the owner wanted $240,000 for goodwill.

At this point, the prospective buyer had to decide whether to (1) make an offer, (2) try to start a similar business from scratch, (3) look for a similar business to buy, or (4) look for a different opportunity. The prospective buyer made an offer for $720,000. The offer was based on the following factors. First, the area had considerable growth potential. Housing starts were increasing, and the trend was expected to continue for the next few years. Second, even though the prospective buyer might have been able to match the assets for $560,000 by starting from scratch, he knew that he would be at a competitive disadvantage to the existing businesses. Third, this business had an established relationship with plumbing contractors in the area. Fourth, the business had exclusive regional distribution rights for the leading brand of plumbing fixtures. Fifth, the prospective buyer wanted to hire the general manager to run the business while he learned the ropes. The general manager was considered excellent and was interested in staying on following the transfer of ownership. Sixth, the business had an extensive inventory of plumbing fixtures that were no longer being manufactured. These fixtures were valuable because homes and other buildings that had been built 30 years earlier now needed replacement fixtures. This business was the only wholesaler in the area that had these items in inventory.

The steady stream of profits, the large amount of goodwill, and the potential improvement in profitability provided the basis for this offer. The owner, however, rejected it. He knew that the business was worth $800,000, and he was not willing to negotiate.

The buyer had made the original offer of $720,000 because he was not looking for the owner to provide financing assistance. The prospective buyer was also "fishing" to see whether the owner would be willing to accept 10 percent less than the asking price.

The prospective buyer returned a week later with an offer of $800,000. He had no reservations about offering $800,000 for the business because the capitalization-of-earnings approach indicated that it was worth at least that price.

The capitalization formula indicated

$$\frac{\$800,000 \text{ asking price}}{\$150,000 \text{ current profit}} = 5.33 \text{ capitalization rate}$$

This capitalization rate would be appropriate for a business that is generating a good return and has a promising future. If the business were to continue earning $150,000 each year, it would be generating an 18.75 percent return on the $800,000 investment. This would be a very good investment.

The prospective buyer considered the future to be even brighter than the present. He also felt that the business warranted a capitalization rate of 7 or 8. He believed that the business would have been a good buy even at 7 times $150,000, or $1,050,000. Furthermore, the prospective buyer believed that the $150,000 profit did not reflect the firm's real profit for the past 12 months. The income statements indicated that the owner had taken $120,000 out of the business as the "president's salary" for each of the past 5 years. This amount was recorded as an expense, not as a dividend.

The prospective buyer felt that this produced an understatement of earnings, since the owner lived in another state and was barely involved in business operations. The buyer did not expect to draw that large a salary. Instead, he planned to use part of the $120,000 to make it lucrative for the general manager to stay and teach him the ropes. The prospective buyer believed that the business's true profitability for the last year was closer to $190,000 or $200,000. This meant that even if a conservative capitalization rate of 4 was used, the business was worth at least $800,000.

The capitalization-of-earnings approach can be summarized as, "How much money are you willing to pay to buy a certain level of earnings?" In the preceding case, the prospective buyer was willing to pay $800,000 to buy a $200,000 return. At this price, he would be getting a 25 percent ($200,000 divided by $800,000) return on his investment. This was a very good deal, and it had the potential to be even better. But this offer was also turned down. The seller concluded that the business was worth more than the $800,000 asking price. He took it off the market because it would serve as an excellent pension vehicle for him. The prospective buyer did not get any return on the time and money he invested in due diligence. The moral of the story is that buying a business is not a simple process and that no deal is done until a contract is executed.

THE CASH FLOW APPROACH TO VALUING A BUSINESS

Cash flow plays a crucial role in the operation and valuation of a business. While the business's assets and earnings need to be part of the valuation formula, many buyers consider the business's cash flow to be more important in determining the value and appeal of a business. The increased focus on cash flow is the result of two major factors. First, income statements and balance sheets can be blurred by depreciation schedules and book values. Second, more buyers are using either seller financing or loans from others to do the deal. While earnings may be important, they look at the cash flow to see whether it will make the deal possible and financially worthwhile.

Valuation based on cash flow may be done in two different ways. The first approach is similar to the capitalization-of-earnings approach in that a multiple of annual cash flow is used to determine the value of the business. The multiple will vary with the nature of the business, how successful it has been, how it is positioned for continued success, and other factors, including goodwill. Many businesses are valued at 2 to 4 times their cash flow. The second approach involves projecting the cash flow for the next few years and discounting it to the present. Obviously this approach is a challenge because you need to project cash flow as well as determining the appropriate discount rate and the number of years in the future that will be discounted.

VALUATION MAY BE A HYBRID OF VARIOUS APPROACHES

The valuing of businesses is not a science because each business is unique, accounting information has limitations, and there is no certainty as to what the future holds for any business. The best way to value a business may be a hybrid of reported earnings, cash flow, a capitalization rate, and the value of goodwill. Each month, *Inc.* magazine profiles a business that is for sale. It is interesting to see how each business is described in financial and nonfinancial terms, its selling price, and the writer's comments about its merit to a potential buyer.

The term *EBITDA* (earnings before interest, taxes, depreciation, and amortization) is being used more often to provide a better representation of the business's financial situation. Capitalization rates continue to be a source of frustration and ambiguity. They vary from one industry to the next and from business to business within each industry. The extent and nature of seller financing will also affect valuation, as will a proprietary position or other factors that give the business a sustainable competitive advantage.

CLOSING THE SALE: DON'T FORGET YOUR ACCOUNTANT AND YOUR ATTORNEY

It should be obvious that buying a business takes a lot of time, knowledge, and patience. You must have a good idea of what you are looking for and what you are willing to do in order to buy a business. In many cases, it is easier, quicker, and better to buy an existing business than to start one from scratch. But remember, there are no guarantees. Just because the business has done well is no assurance that you or anyone else will make a profit. The business will be different once you own it.

If you are thinking about buying a business, be sure that the three basic ingredients are present: (1) A market exists in which customers are in search of a business. (2) You have the ability to make the right decisions to create and maintain customers. (3) There is a sufficient financial return to justify the risk.

Buying a business involves more than just agreeing on the selling price. You will need to have the advice of your accountant and your attorney on numerous aspects of the purchase agreement. Your accountant will need to review the business's financial records and tax returns for the last few years. She or he will be trying to determine the accuracy of the records and to develop a clear picture of the business's revenues, expenses, profits, assets, and liabilities. Your accountant will also be in a position to help you make financial projections for the next 2 or 3 years. You should pay particular attention to the cash flow. Hopefully, the business will be able to generate enough cash to meet the financial obligations you will incur in buying it.

Your attorney will play a major role in helping you establish the terms for purchasing the business. Your attorney will be involved in

1. Checking to see if there are any liens or chattel mortgages on the business's assets.
2. Drafting a noncompete and confidentiality clause for the seller to sign.
3. Establishing an indemnity agreement in which the seller agrees to protect the buyer from any claims made by creditors.
4. Making sure that an escrow account is set up by the seller to cover any claims.
5. Having the seller sign an affidavit indicating that all creditors have been notified of the sale of the business.
6. Drafting a clause in which the seller guarantees all accounts receivable.
7. Checking to see that all leases can be assumed.
8. Making sure that all warranties, contracts, and sales agreements by the seller are known.
9. Having the seller indicate that no litigation or government investigation is currently under way.
10. Having the seller verify that the business is in compliance with all EPA and OSHA regulations.

11. Checking on the status of all license agreements, patents, customer lists, recipes, formulas, processes, copyrights, logos, etc.
12. Reviewing all zoning requirements and permits.
13. Drafting a casualty clause whereby the buyer can get out of the agreement if there is a major calamity such as a fire or a flood that affects the future of the business before the title to the business is formally transferred.
14. Establishing the final terms for the sale of the business. This includes listing the assets, including serial numbers (where applicable) and the liabilities to be assumed, determining how inventory and accounts receivable adjustments will be made, and setting the actual date and conditions for completing the sale.

Your attorney will also establish certain conditions to ensure that the seller continues doing business as usual up to the date of the sale. It is important that goodwill with customers, suppliers, creditors, and employees not be allowed to deteriorate. Your attorney also may put a clause in the purchase agreement stating that any disputes between the buyer and the seller arising after the sale will be handled by the American Arbitration Association if the two parties are unable to resolve them.

Marc Diener, who is an attorney, emphasized the value of having experienced people help guide you through the process of buying a business. He noted, "Professionals can be a tremendous asset in reading between the lines. Savvy brokers, agents, bankers, CPAs, and attorneys are already well-versed in the 101 ways you can get bamboozled. When they tell you something doesn't smell right, you should pay attention."[1] He also noted, "Transactional attorneys have a particularly effective technique for smoking out the other side; representation and warranties. Basically you make the other side promise in writing that the specific facts you are counting on in making the deal are true. If their representations later turn out to be false, they could get nailed for fraud, with numerous unpleasant consequences. However, don't look the other way just because the other side swears it's so. . . . Even the tightest representation and warranties can't act as a stand-in for due diligence and plain old common sense."[2]

NOTES

[1] Marc Diener, "Can't Fool You (Anymore)," *Entrepreneur,* May 2002, p. 92.
[2] Ibid.

11

Acquiring a Franchise

BUYING SOMEONE ELSE'S FORMULA FOR SUCCESS

People are often frustrated because they lack the experience and skills to start a business from scratch. When they consider buying an existing business, either they feel like they are buying a used car (possibly a lemon) or they do not want to be limited to the businesses that are available for sale. Fortunately, there may be a happy medium. Franchises offer the excitement of starting one's own business while reducing the trial-and-error process experienced by most first-timers.

There are over four thousand organizations that offer franchise rights in the United States. Franchises are available for nearly every type of business. If you are considering the retail market, where businesses sell goods or services to the ultimate consumer, a franchise may be a good way to get into business. There are over 600,000 franchise units worldwide. Franchises account for nearly half of all retail sales in the United States. Whether you believe that you see a market opportunity for chimney sweeping, residential landscaping, parking lot striping, or operating a fitness center, there is at least one franchise available to help you beat the odds.

When you buy a franchise, you are buying someone's formula for success. This is similar to the reason why many people buy an existing business. Buying a franchise is like buying goodwill. Two of the major strengths of a franchise are that (1) most franchisors have already tried their business idea in the marketplace to see whether they could create and maintain customers for a profit and (2) the franchisors have developed a formula for improving the franchisees' chances of being successful.*

The failure rate for people who purchase a franchise is lower than that for independent business start-ups. While there is no guarantee that every franchise, even a McDonald's, will succeed, their track record makes a case for considering the franchise route. The benefits of a franchise are particularly noteworthy if you have limited experience.

In many cases, the franchising company (franchiser) has been operating that type of business for at least 2 or 3 years. During that time, the franchiser has moved along the learning curve by testing the product or service concept and developing information systems that give it a better understanding of what does and does not work. Franchises therefore offer the first-timer the opportunity to hit the ground running. The franchisee does not have to take the time and risk associated with reinventing the wheel.

THE BENEFITS OF BUYING A FRANCHISE

The franchisor sells the franchisee a license that offers certain privileges. The privileges can vary dramatically, even among franchises in the same industry. In some cases, the franchisee has the opportunity to receive management assistance and to buy supplies and inventory from the franchisor at favorable prices. In a few cases, the franchisee can buy a complete business package. The franchisee purchases the supplies, fixtures and equipment, inventory, and even the land from the franchisor. Some franchisors may even help with financing through their own financing division or by providing assistance in getting a loan from financial institutions.

As noted at the beginning of this book, the number one reason for small business failure is the lack of management experience and education. The founders of these businesses made too many wrong decisions because they used a trial-and-error approach rather than good management. This explains why franchises have been so popular in the past 30 years.

---

*Disclaimer: This chapter should not be considered a blanket endorsement of franchises. You should use the same degree of due diligence in analyzing a franchise that you would exercise in buying a business. You should also use the services of an attorney and an accountant who are experienced in franchise contracts and operations.

The most successful franchises offer training programs for the franchisee and his or her employees. Training programs and other forms of management assistance cover various aspects of opening and operating the franchise. The formula and training may not guarantee success, but they usually offer the first-timer a higher probability of being successful than by starting an independent business from scratch.

Most franchises offer numerous other benefits. The franchiser may help the franchisee select the appropriate site for the business, provide centralized purchasing to take advantage of quantity discounts, and offer a computerized accounting system to simplify paperwork. One franchise has its own construction division. This takes a lot of the uncertainty out of building a facility. It also reduces the time it takes to open it.

Franchisors often provide cooperative advertising arrangements whereby the franchisor subsidizes a portion of the franchisee's advertising. Franchisors frequently provide franchisees with prepared artwork for their advertising. This enhances the quality of the franchisee's advertising and reduces the expense for artwork.

Some franchisors send specialists to help the franchisee with the grand opening; these specialists stay on the scene to help the franchisee through the first week or two. These franchises usually have "circuit riders" who visit franchisees on a periodic basis to provide additional management assistance. One restaurant franchise helps franchisees find managers. Some franchisors also provide newsletters and conferences that offer ideas on how to improve various aspects of the business. A few franchises even offer a "franchise hotline" to provide answers to pressing questions.

THE DRAWBACKS OF BUYING A FRANCHISE

The saying, "There is no free lunch" certainly applies to the franchise concept. In return for franchise fees and the acceptance of various restrictions, franchisees learn the franchisor's formula for success and receive other privileges. Franchisees pay one or more franchise fees in order to secure the right to conduct business under the franchisor's name. This may be viewed as more of a trade-off than a drawback. Nevertheless, you need to recognize that it may take more money to buy a franchise than to start a business from scratch. Franchise fees will increase your initial capital requirement and affect your income statement.

The initial franchise fee is the fee most commonly paid by franchisees. The franchisee pays a specific amount of money for the right to use the franchise name. This fee may range from a few hundred dollars for a new service-type franchise to over $100,000 for a leading hotel franchise. A few franchisors either do not charge a franchise fee or waive it as a special promotion to generate interest.

Quite a few people are attracted to franchises that have low initial franchise fees. These people see the low fee as meaning that it will not cost them a lot of money to start their business as a franchise. Two popular sayings may be worth noting when reviewing the initial franchise fee for various franchises. The first saying is, "You get what you pay for." In many instances, the franchise fee merely lets you use the franchise's name on your business card, letterhead, Yellow Page ad, and sign. The franchisor may not provide any other benefits or assistance. A rule of thumb for initial franchise fees is that the more established and successful the franchise, the higher the initial franchise fee. The franchise fee is like goodwill. If the franchisor is going to provide you with a competitive edge and a higher probability of making a profit, you should be willing to pay for those benefits.

It is not unusual for a new franchise to have a very low initial franchise fee. When a franchise is being established, the franchisor incurs considerable legal, promotional, and accounting expense, not to mention the overhead associated with the franchise team's related expenses. New franchisors are so eager to get some money back into their checking accounts and to have a few franchises as the lead dominos to show that the formula works that they will offer the first franchisees a low initial franchise fee. A restaurateur once told the story of a franchisor who called him one night and offered him the exclusive rights to two states for a new fast-food hamburger franchise for just $10,000. The restaurateur turned down the offer because he thought that there were already too many hamburger franchises. This restaurateur regretted his decision for the rest of his life. That hamburger franchise is now one of the top fast-food franchises in the country. It has over a hundred locations in those two states. The restaurateur would have become a multimillionaire within 5 years merely by selling franchise rights in various locations in the two states.

While this is not the typical situation, it does illustrate the fact that the franchise fee is usually a product of supply and demand. When there are only a few franchisees, the fee may be low, but as more people want that franchise, the fees usually increase in proportion to the demand.

The second popular saying, "Look before you leap," encourages the prospective franchisee to put things in perspective. The franchisor can make money in only three ways: by selling franchise rights, by collecting ongoing fees, or through a combination of the two. If the initial franchise fee is very low, then the franchisor usually has a higher fee structure for the operational side of being a franchisee. For example, Subway charges a low franchise fee in order to keep the cost of starting a Subway Restaurant more affordable. This is one of the reasons why Subway has so many units.

Operational fees may come in various forms. The most common type of operational fee is the royalty fee. The royalty fee is usually a percentage of the franchisee's sales. It is usually between 2 and 6 percent of sales, although the royalty for some franchises can be as high as 15 percent of sales. Some franchise agreements stipulate that the royalty rate will fluctuate with the level of sales.

First-timers sometimes wonder if it is worth being a franchisee if they have to pay the franchisor a percentage of sales. They view the royalty fee as an expense that an independent business would not have to pay. After all, if the average business's profit is less than 4 percent of sales, how can a franchise make a profit if it has to pay a 5 percent royalty fee?

The best way to view this situation is to ask yourself, "Is being a franchisee going to give me a significantly higher level of sales because the franchise will have name recognition?" and, "Will I have better training than the owners of most independent businesses?" The prospective franchisee also needs to ask, "Will my other expenses be lower than an independent business's expenses because the franchisor provides me with economies in record keeping, supplies, fixtures and equipment, and so on?" If the answer is yes, the royalty fee may be justified. The key here is to look at the overall net effect of being a franchisee, not just at the fees.

First-timers also express concern that the royalty fee is based on sales rather than profits. Franchisors base the fee on sales for one very simple reason: They want their money right off the top; it's up to the franchisee to make a profit.

The second most common operating fee is the advertising fee. Most franchisees pay a percentage of their sales to the franchisor for regional and national advertising. This fee also enables the franchisor to sponsor franchisewide sales promotions. Franchisors recognize the need for their franchisees to be visible in the marketplace. Anyone who has children who watch television will acknowledge that fast-food franchises own Saturday mornings. Most of the commercials are designed to get the children who are viewing the cartoon shows to want to go to at least one of the franchises during the weekend, if not that morning!

Some first-timers have mixed emotions about paying the advertising fee. Research has shown that independent businesses tend to be reluctant to spend much money on advertising. It has also shown that when they do spend money on advertising, they tend to do it in a haphazard manner. It has been said that you have to spend money to make money. This definitely applies to advertising—provided that you spend it wisely. The advertising fee makes sense because it keeps franchisees from shortchanging their advertising budgets. It also means that franchisees will have professionally researched and prepared advertising packages. Franchisees may also benefit from the franchisor's economies of scale. The franchisor can secure regional and national television time and magazine space at lower rates than small independent businesses could get. The same applies for radio spots and graphic art.

Two other aspects of franchise advertising are worth noting. Most franchisers expect, and in many cases require, each franchisee to spend a certain percentage of sales on local advertising and sales promotions each year. Some franchisors have an interesting approach to handling the advertising fee: They use part of the fee to subsidize each franchisee's local advertising expenses. For every dollar of local advertising, the franchisor may rebate a certain percentage. This is the franchisor's way of encouraging franchisees to advertise more extensively than their local competitors.

Franchisors want to establish automatic name association. When potential customers think of fast food, McDonald's wants customers in search of a business to think "McDonald's." When a couple is thinking about selling their house, Century 21 wants them to think "Century 21." The same applies to pizza and Domino's, printing and Alphagraphics, ice cream and Baskin-Robbins, and mufflers and Midas. In the competitive marketplace, franchisees often overwhelm independent business with their advertising and brand identity.

There are a few other franchise-related fees. These are referred to as the "hidden" fees. Franchisees may have to purchase all their equipment, supplies, and inventory from the franchisor. In some cases, they may be required to buy the building and the land from the franchisor. The franchisor may charge the franchisee a monthly fee for maintaining the franchisee's records on a computerized accounting system. The franchisee may also be required to travel to franchisor-sponsored training meetings and conventions and pay a registration fee to attend.

Franchisors receive quantity discounts from vendors when they buy fixtures, equipment, inventory, and supplies. They may pass on their economies of scale to their franchisees. Conversely, they can make a profit from these items when they sell them to the franchises. If the franchisor passes the discounts on to the franchisee, then the franchisee may have a considerable cost advantage over competitors. If it does not, the added costs of doing business as a franchisee may make it difficult for the franchisee to make a profit.

Franchise agreements that require franchisees to buy certain goods and services exclusively from the franchiser reflect the monopoly power of some franchisors. These restrictions are the second drawback of being a franchisee. As noted earlier, when a person acquires a franchise, that person is buying a formula for success. While the formula has its benefits, prospective franchisees need to recognize that it may be a formula that they won't be able to change.

Franchise formulas almost always have numerous restrictions attached to them. These restrictions may include (1) the hours the unit must be open, (2) the prices to charge customers, (3) the location of the franchise, (4) the design of the building, (5) what goods and services can be sold, and (6) to whom the franchisee can sell the franchise. Franchisees may also be required to personally run the franchise unit, and there may be limitations on the franchisee's owning more than one unit or any other business. These restrictions are the franchisor's way of increasing the franchisee's likelihood of success. Franchisors also establish these guidelines to assure consistency from one franchisee to another. At one time, Holiday Inn used this consistency as the basis for its advertising campaign. Holiday Inn's television spots stated, "At Holiday Inns, there are no surprises. You can expect the same quality rooms and service at each location."

Some franchisees find the guidelines very constraining. Consistency has its merits, but each local marketplace has its own unique aspects. Every business endeavor, whether it is a franchise or an independent business, needs to tailor its market offering and operations to the particular needs and interests of its target market. Most fast-food franchisors do not allow their franchisees to create their own entrees or to add other popular items to their menus. One of the leading fast-food franchises operated for more than 30 years before it added chicken to its menus. When chicken became popular, many franchisees were frustrated. All they could do was watch their customers go to other restaurants to eat what the franchisee could have prepared for them.

The restrictive nature of many franchise agreements prohibits franchisees from owning additional franchise units or other businesses. Some agreements stipulate that the franchisee must be present for at least 48 weeks of the year. This is constraining to some franchisees. It keeps them from capitalizing on other opportunities and from taking a lot of vacation time. A few franchisees have been known to exclaim, "I went into business so that I could be my own boss, but these restrictions do not permit me to make my own decisions."

Many people who become franchisees do not find these restrictions to be cumbersome, however. They need the formula, the training, the management assistance, the advertising ideas, the computerized accounting system, and the standardized operating procedures provided by the franchisor. Franchises may be the best way for inexperienced people to go into business. In a figurative sense, the franchiser acts as a senior partner.

Not everyone, however, is cut out to be a franchisee. If you are the type of person who constantly identifies market opportunities, has extensive experience, and prefers flexibility and creativity over assistance and structure, then you may be better off starting your own business. If you are a very enterprising person and you have a dream of doing things on a grand scale, you should find an emerging market opportunity that will permit you to become a franchisor rather than a franchisee.

FINDING THE RIGHT FRANCHISE OPPORTUNITY

If you have come to the conclusion that the franchise route is the best avenue to take in order to have your own business, the next step is to begin the process of searching for the most appropriate one. The process of selecting a franchise is similar to that of starting a business from scratch or buying an existing business. It starts with identifying areas of opportunity, goes on to determining whether you have or can develop the capabilities to create and maintain customers, and is concluded with estimating whether there will be enough return to justify the time and money to be invested in the business.

The first step in finding the right franchise is to identify markets with growth opportunity and geographic areas where customers are in search of a business. Someone once said, "When you are looking for a house to buy, find a neighborhood where you would like to live and then look for a house you would like to have as your home." The same rationale applies when looking for a franchise.

The process of identifying the right franchise begins with identifying the right type of business. If you were planning to go sailing, you would find it easier to sail if the wind were to your advantage and the water was not rough. The nautical saying, "May you always have the wind at your back" is good advice for the prospective franchisee. It is easier to sail with the wind than against it. It is also better to check the weather report before setting sail. The forecast may indicate that the calm may be merely the calm before the storm.

Too many people are attracted to industries that are already saturated with competition. It is difficult for a new franchisee to make a profit under these conditions. A popular franchise in a saturated market may have less chance of being successful than an emerging franchise in a new market with greater potential. As in surfing, the key is to catch a wave early (when it isn't crowded) that has the potential for a long and pleasurable ride. One enterprising person noted that he found that starting a new business from scratch was too risky. He attributed his success to finding promising franchises when they were in their formative years and then buying "master franchise" rights so that he could open (or sell others the right to open) franchises in a large geographic area. He also focused his attention on food-related franchises. He figured that these were less risky than other franchises because "people have to eat." That individual's success can also be attributed to knowing when to cash out. When he sensed the inevitability of intense price competition, he sold most of the 30 pizza franchise outlets he had set up.

Windows of opportunity open and close. Prospective franchisees need to make a deliberate effort to keep their eyes and minds open for lasting business opportunities. All too often, people are impressed with the fame of international franchises or seduced by new franchises that offer riches within 6 months.

Even though most franchises have good track records, none can guarantee success. The prospective franchisee should be reminded of the saying, "It takes a good jockey and a good horse to win the race. No jockey has been known to win a race by carrying a horse over the finish line!" In this analogy, the horse is the market opportunity and the jockey is the franchisee.

The prospective franchisee needs to answer two questions. The first question is, "What is the best opportunity?" The second is, "Which is the best franchise to help me capitalize on that opportunity?" You may find it useful at this time to refer back to Chapter 2, which describes the step-by-step process for identifying business opportunities. The only difference in the process discussed in that chapter and the process of acquiring a franchise is that once you have identified the top two or three opportunities, you will investigate the franchises available to determine which ones offer the capability to create and maintain customers for a profit.

If your market research reveals good opportunities in the areas of child care, residential landscaping, employment agencies, and printing services, your next step is to learn about the franchises available for each type of business. The place to begin your investigation of available franchises is the nearest public or university library. *The Franchise Annual* (published by Info

Press) and *Bond's Franchise Guide* (published by Source Book Publications) provide information on various franchises. *Inc.* magazine and *Entrepreneur* magazine provide profiles of newly formed as well as established franchises in their magazines and on their Web sites. They also list the most popular franchises.

In your preliminary research, you should look for the year the franchise was established, the number of operating franchise units, the number of franchiser-owned units, and the geographic areas served by the franchise. You should also look for the initial investment required, the fee structure, the average number of employees per unit, the services offered by the franchiser, whether the franchisee has exclusive territorial rights, and whether the franchisor provides financial and management assistance.

The prospective franchisee should contact numerous franchisors in the fields that appear to have potential and ask them for a franchise packet. Most franchisors welcome the opportunity to send people information about their businesses. However, some franchisors will not send a complete franchise packet until you have demonstrated that you are a qualified prospect.

The prospective franchisee should also contact the International Franchise Association. The IFA provides information about franchising and specific franchises. You should also go to your library and review the *Business Periodicals Index* for the past 2 years to learn what has been written about the franchises that interest you. Internet search engines like Yahoo! and Google may also provide useful information. The Better Business Bureau, Dun & Bradstreet, and the U.S. Small Business Administration may also be able to provide background information on various franchises. Your accountant, attorney, loan officer, and local chamber of commerce may also be in a position to assist you in investigating a franchise.

The next step is to review the information for the franchises that have initial appeal. Some of the franchises may be eliminated from consideration because they require a higher franchise fee than you can afford. Other franchisers may not have territories or individual units in the area where you want to locate.

This step requires a fairly rigorous and objective analysis of each franchise. Your accountant can help you by reviewing the financial information in the franchise packet and from other sources. You may check to see if your bank has done business with any franchisees and to learn whether they are doing well.

Quite a few franchises will be dropped from your list of alternatives because they do not have good track records or because there is little information available to review. This is why it may be advisable to consider only franchises that have been operating for at least 3 or 4 years. The chapter on buying a business stressed the need to review at least 3 years of financial records. One or two years of operating results may not provide sufficient information to determine the franchise's potential.

The "look for a neighborhood you want to live in and then find the right house" approach may also apply in another way when it comes to finding the right type of franchise. There is no point in looking at houses you cannot afford. A little research will indicate whether you can afford certain types of franchises. Some franchisors require the franchisee to make a considerable investment in fixtures and equipment as well as the franchise fee. A number of franchisors will not even discuss the prospects for securing franchise rights unless the inquirer has a net worth above a certain level. For example, the franchisor for an auto-service type of business requires that prospective franchisees have a net worth of at least $300,000. This is its way of ensuring that the prospective franchisee is not undercapitalized.

People usually look for a home that reflects who they are and their lifestyle. The same situation may apply to finding the right franchise. You should look for a franchise that appeals to your interests and will use your talents. This is called "goodness of fit." For example, when a couple in their forties with extensive airline experience was looking into possible franchises, they focused their attention on franchises that (1) would use their professional experience with information systems, (2) would capitalize on their ability to interact well with employees and customers, and (3) did not require technical skills or experience in that field. After considerable research, they decided to become franchisees in a hair-cutting franchise. In a short time, they had five franchise outlets.

CHECKING OUT THE FRANCHISORS

At this point, you have probably narrowed your interest to four or five franchises. More than likely, the franchisors have called you to follow up on the franchise packet they sent to you. If not, it may be time to contact them. You should request specific information about the availability and terms for a franchise unit. You should also request a copy of the franchise agreement and any other contractual obligations between the franchisor and the franchisee.

One of the advantages of buying a franchise rather than buying an existing business is that federal and state laws require franchisors to provide potential franchisees with a disclosure statement. The Federal Trade Commission prohibits franchise units from being sold to franchisees without a disclosure statement known as the Uniform Circular Offering. The FTC also stipulates that the franchisee must have the document at least 5 days prior to any exchange of money and before the franchisee signs the franchise agreement.

The disclosure statement contains a considerable amount of information on the franchisor's background. The statement must identify the franchisor's officers, directors, and principal owners. Any criminal convictions, civil judgments, bankruptcies, or administrative orders by or against these people must be contained in the disclosure statement. The statement must also include a description of these people's business experience.

The disclosure statement should list the names and addresses of franchisees. It should also include the number of units opened that year and the number of units that were reacquired or terminated.

The disclosure statement must indicate the nature of the licensing agreement, the fees to be paid, the types of assistance the franchisor will provide, a description of any territorial protection for the franchisee, and conditions affecting the sale or loss of franchise rights by the franchisee. It needs to include a copy of the franchise's latest income statement and balance sheet. These financial records must have been audited by a CPA. The disclosure statement is not reviewed by the FTC, but the franchisor is liable for any errors in it. Franchisors are also required to substantiate any figures on earnings by their franchisees that they cite. The FTC's Web site offers a lot of information on the nature of franchising and its corresponding regulations.

Numerous states require franchisors to provide franchisees with additional information or place other restrictions on the promotion and sale of franchise units. Prospective franchisees have far more information about franchise agreements and protection from unscrupulous or fly-by-night franchisers than they did years ago, when franchises started to gain in popularity. Nevertheless, you should not limit your investigation of franchises to just the material that federal and state guidelines require them to provide.

You should review the sales and profit figures for a cross section of existing franchisees. Do not rely only on the figures provided by the franchiser. Select a representative group of franchisees and visit them. You should observe their operations and ask each franchisee about the competition, the franchisee's perceptions of the assistance received from the franchiser since signing the franchise agreement, and what you might expect in the way of financial results.

It will also be worth your time to check out the extent to which franchisees have their own organization to represent their interests (like a union) with the franchisor. Franchisors that are abusive prompt the formation of such groups. You should also check out the number and nature of lawsuits by franchisees against the franchisor. The lawsuits and settlements may indicate whether there is considerable ill will between the franchisees and the franchisor.

It may also be worthwhile to contact some of the people who sold their franchise units to learn why they did so. Suppliers of existing franchise units may also provide some interesting views on the value of that particular franchise. This would also be a good time to determine what avenues for recourse may be available to you if the franchiser fails to fulfill the terms of the franchise agreement.

LOOK BEFORE YOU LEAP

While the failure rate for franchisees may be relatively low, it pays to be selective. Franchising is similar to a marriage. You should look for a franchise that will stand the test of time. If the franchisor goes under, you will be left in an awkward and lonely situation. To be successful, you will need a market opportunity that will last and a franchisor that will be there to help you create and maintain customers for a profit. The right franchise is the one that will strengthen your business without forcing you to make too many sacrifices.

The best way to review a franchise opportunity is to view it from all angles. Reviewing a franchise takes considerable effort. It also takes time and money. It may take 4 to 6 months from your initial inquiry to reach agreement on the final terms. It may then take an additional 6 months to open your business. It should be apparent that you will need to have your CPA, your attorney, your investors, and possibly your commercial loan officer with you from the beginning. These people will encourage you to look before you leap. They are in a good position to give you professional advice on the relative merits of the franchises you are reviewing. Having the right attorney is particularly important. Going the franchise route is like traversing a minefield. You should have an attorney who has extensive experience in franchise law. The American Bar Association's membership directory lists attorneys who are members of its franchise division.

Epilogue
Entrepreneurial Do's and Don'ts

If you have gone through all the steps of analyzing the market, identifying opportunities, and developing a business plan, you have made substantial progress toward preparing yourself to start your own business. However, if you are like most people, you have probably found that for every question you answered, more questions surfaced that needed to be answered. At this point, your situation is similar to that of a person who has just graduated from college. You've learned a lot, but you still don't know all you need to know. There is a lot more for you to learn if you want to beat the odds.

The preceding chapters provided numerous helpful insights, examples, tips, and guidelines. It is easy for people to be overwhelmed, however, when they are presented with so much information on so many different areas. The following list of do's and don'ts has been provided to help you put things in perspective and to highlight many of the most salient points that you need to keep in mind as you continue your entrepreneurial journey.*

These tips were provided during interviews with over 150 entrepreneurs from a wide range of businesses. Before getting to the list, it may be helpful to provide a noteworthy observation by one of the entrepreneurs.

Life in a startup is similar to the cycle of manic-depressive behavior where you feel you are on the top of the world one day and waking up terrified in the middle of the night on the next.

*This list was generated by interviews conducted by students enrolled in my entrepreneurship classes at the University of North Carolina at Wilmington and Duke University.

TAKE A GOOD LOOK AT YOURSELF, YOUR LIFE, AND WHAT IS DRIVING YOU

Think about and be clear about your motivation for starting the venture.

Realize that your business is a 24/7 adventure. You can't call time-outs, and there are no real vacations.

Don't fail to recognize the impact of starting a business on your family and social life.

Don't do this without the support of your personal network (family, and so on). You will need their support, and it will cost them something too (in money as well as time).

Make sure your personal life is in order. You cannot afford to let personal problems interfere with the business.

Don't expect to maintain your same lifestyle and standard of living. Your cash flow may not be what you expect, and you may need to make some sacrifices in order to remain in business.

Save enough money to live on for the first 2 years that your business is open so that you can take all the profits you make and put them right back into your business.

Make sure that you and your family can recover from the financial setback if things do not go as well as planned. Things normally don't go as well as planned.

Don't go too far with the personal sacrifices. Try hard to maintain some balance in your life.

Don't dive in half-heartedly. Go all out or go home!

Have your heart and soul in the business. If you don't believe in it, no one else will.

Don't go into a venture just because you are tired of what you are doing.

Don't start a business just because someone else has been successful at the same business. You will never be able to copy that person's decisions (good and bad) or luck.

Make sure you really want to be an entrepreneur ... too many hours ... too much stress.

Don't expect it to be easy ... or that it will be easier now that you are your own boss.

Don't think you will be your own boss.

Be prepared to work harder than you ever thought.

You must be willing to do most of the work when you are starting out.

Realize that you will wear many hats, especially when you are first starting. You will do a variety of tasks that you never envisioned doing and would not do if you were working for someone else.

The life of an entrepreneur is one that requires a lot of self-imposed discipline. You will not have a boss to say "Let's call it a night" or to give you encouragement when things get rough.

Don't underestimate the power and importance of having prior experience or knowledge.

Don't assume that expertise in one area will easily translate into business savvy in another area.

Don't get into things you know absolutely nothing about.

Don't go into business as a get-rich-quick scheme. Get-rich-quick schemes usually backfire.

Don't let other people's skepticism draw you away from accomplishing your own goals and dreams.

Always be willing to take a chance.

Don't let the fear of failure hold you back from something you really want to do.

Don't quit your full-time job until you know you can make a living at the new enterprise.

Don't burn your bridges when you leave a company, and don't talk negatively about your former employer—it's a small world, and this detracts from your professionalism.

TIME: YOU WILL NEVER HAVE ENOUGH

Don't underestimate the amount of time that it is going to take to be an entrepreneur.

You must be able to budget your time carefully.

You will work harder and longer hours than ever before.

Don't think success will come quickly or easily.

Develop a presence in the market. Spend a lot of time building relationships with suppliers and sources of customers.

Focus on those things that are important to the business. Don't spend a lot of time on office paperwork instead of meeting prospects or improving your network of contacts.

Don't forget about running the business while you are out generating new business.

PREPARATION: STACK THE ODDS IN YOUR FAVOR

You should invest considerable time in finding new business.

Don't share your idea with everyone. Be discreet with those you talk to about your idea.

You need to be at least 40 years old to have enough experience to start, but if you're older than 40, you may not have enough energy to persist.

If possible, work in that type of business before starting a venture. The best way to research a business is to work in that business for a while.

Find an idea or industry that excites you. It will help with the long hours associated with a new business venture.

Don't start a business based on something you like to do or want to do just to have a business of your own. Make sure there is a market for the product or service.

Don't be afraid to start the new venture. If your planning and research are thorough and you feel confident about the prospects, then start your own business.

Set up some type of advisory committee or board for advice well before you start your business.

These advisers can go beyond providing advice to providing business services, providing introductions to other companies and opportunities, and even becoming investors themselves.

Contact professional advisers (an accountant and an attorney) before you do anything else.

Hire professionals who know what you do not know.

Get a good accountant. An accountant can tell you areas where you can save money that a bookkeeper cannot. This is especially important with taxes and deductible expenses.

Network, network, network . . . develop as many contacts as you can. You will need all the help you can possibly muster.

Talk to other entrepreneurs in the area.

Visit people in other cities who have started similar ventures like the one you are considering . . . pick their brains.

Learn from others who have gone before you. Learn from successful people by examining both their successes and their failures.

Take advantage of the many groups that provide assistance to new ventures.

Join industry groups that share best practices. Leverage their members' ideas.

Have a mentor. Find someone who can help you with knowledge of your business or of running a business in general. You need a reality check from time to time.

Research your product or service idea and make sure that a market exists.

Before you start, know the answer to the question, "How am I going to make money?"

Don't wait for the perfect opportunity to present itself. If you wait for the home run, you'll never make it to the plate.

MANAGEMENT: WHO EVER SAID IT WOULD BE EASY?

Don't think you will survive just because you are smart.

Don't think you know everything, because you don't.

Recognize and understand how much you know and how much you don't know.

Challenge your assumptions.

Continuously analyze where you are and where you should be going in business.

Be perceptive and flexible. The marketplace can change. Be willing to adapt your strategy. Preconceived ideas can be disproved. New opportunities can develop. Unless you have a frame of mind to be flexible, you will miss these opportunities and changes, and this can negatively affect your success.

Develop an understanding of what the critical success factors for the business will be.

Learn to say NO.

Don't be afraid to make mistakes.

Learn from your mistakes.

Do what you think you should do instead of what everyone else thinks you should do, but don't get so cocky that you think you do not need the help and advice of advisers and experts.

Don't rely too heavily on learned behaviors from your previous life—i.e., corporate America.

Don't be afraid to make a major decision on gut instinct when there is no other choice.

Do be prepared. You can never be too prepared.

Don't wait too long to act on ideas.

Be prepared to have big responsibilities, make quick decisions, and resolve problems.

Do your homework—research the variables and perform due diligence.

Don't ever let your guard down or stop paying close attention to quality and details. Execution is often the key. Attention to details can put you ahead of the competition.

Continuously cover all of the bases. A new venture is fragile. Employee morale, cash flow, customer relations, finances . . . everything needs to be monitored constantly. Any problems that arise need to be addressed immediately.

Don't bite off more than you can chew. Know your limits and pace yourself.

Don't assume that your way is always right or always the best way.

Listen to customers' and employees' complaints and ideas.

Don't trust another person's estimates of revenue or profits unless you can be sure that they do not have a vested interest in your starting the business (franchises come to mind). Do the analysis yourself if you can, or hire an independent consultant.

When starting a business, it is important that you listen to all the inputs from business acquaintances, friends, and family. They will all have good advice. Always remember, however, that this is your business and you must make the final decision.

Be flexible and have fun—enjoy the ride.

A high level of energy and a high level of infectious enthusiasm are essential.

Your persona becomes the persona of your business. Your drive, stamina, attitude, and behavior become the attributes of your business. Any action you take in front of employees or customers is a representation of your business. Always put your best face forward.

Don't throw in the towel at the first sign of adversity—be prepared to face tough times.

Don't get discouraged when you hit obstacles or things do not go as planned. There will be bumps in the road.

Don't get overly optimistic in the good times.

Don't think you can do it by yourself.

No matter what successes you have, stay humble.

No matter what failures you have, learn from them.

Be prepared to motivate yourself because you will be your own boss and there will be no one there to tell you what needs to be done.

Don't compromise your integrity.

Honor your commitments. Don't promise anything you can't deliver.

Never lie to customers or employees. Lies will always come back to haunt you.

Do the right thing even when it hurts.

Never be satisfied with your current state. Always look for ways to improve the business.

Track key operating and performance metrics carefully.

Hone your management skills and have people available to you who are good managers.

Continually look for ways in which you can do a better job. Your job will need to evolve as your business grows.

Be prepared to learn, to change, to delegate, and to solicit constructive criticism.

Use technology to improve your performance and enhance your personal productivity.

THE BUSINESS PLAN: THE MENTAL JOURNEY MUST PRECEDE THE PHYSICAL JOURNEY

Prepare a real-world business plan. Period!

Don't expect your business plan to be 100 percent complete. You cannot plan for all possibilities. However, play the chess match in your head and try to anticipate as much as possible what might happen and what your response might be.

Formalize a business strategy, even if only as a mental exercise. While mid-course corrections are to be expected, starting operations by the seat of your pants will probably not produce a sustainable business.

Translating a good idea into a profitable business is the key.

Identify the potential pitfalls and risks and build a risk management plan around them. Focus more attention on the risky areas than on the no-risk components.

Don't treat the risks associated with being in business like a gamble. Business success is not a game of chance; it is a game in which careful preparation and analysis can lead to significantly better outcomes.

Just because something looks good on paper doesn't mean it will work in a competitive environment

Paranoia is good. Eventually either you will be copied or someone else will do the job better.

Don't expect reality to match your initial concept. Be realistic.

There is no fixed formula for success in a new business. No "blue light special" guaranteeing success is ever going to be offered because each business is different. The critical success (or failure) factors will vary among businesses, even those operating in the same industry. Some businesses are successful in spite of themselves simply because someone steps up to fill an unmet need.

Don't fall into the idealism trap. Murphy's Law happens—even with thorough planning and preparation. Things cost twice as much and take twice as long as you expected.

Don't overanalyze potential opportunities; if you do, the window of opportunity could be closed by the time you are ready to launch the venture, or you will lose your competitive advantage.

Hard work carries you only so far—you need resources in order to be successful. Recognizing what those resources are and finding a way to get them is critical to any new venture.

Don't believe the old adage, "If you build a better mousetrap, the world will beat a path to your door." Ideas are a dime a dozen; it is skilled people and a well-thought-out plan that will turn a good idea into a business success.

Don't rely on home-run plans. If everything has to happen exactly as planned for the venture to be successful, it will probably fail.

STRATEGY: HOW DO YOU PLAN TO GAIN SUSTAINABLE COMPETITIVE ADVANTAGES?

Dare to be different! Those businesses that are different are the ones that stand out. As Sam Walton said, "Break all the rules, swim upstream, and go the other way."

Be opportunistic, receptive to feedback, and flexible when you are launching a new business. It may not be until you are in business that you fully understand the business you are in.

Know the business you're in and stick to it. Resist the temptation to be everything to everyone. Differentiate your business on the basis of quality, service, and other value-added functions.

Don't cut corners. Build a reputation for excellence. Quality and service may cost more up front, but they pay back over time multifold.

Most products work because of one or two simple features. Figure out what those features are and execute them extremely well.

Start small, gain some experience, then expand.

Don't expand too rapidly or grow for growth's sake.

Don't get distracted. You'll see lots of interesting ideas, but to be successful, you must stay focused.

Be committed to continuous improvement and continuous innovation.

Expect to spend most of your time attracting new business.

Be prepared for change. Nothing remains the same. Even if you do everything right, your business can still fail.

HUMAN RESOURCES: YOUR BUSINESS WILL BE ONLY AS GOOD AS YOUR PEOPLE

Find someone you trust to help you with the business. You will want days off, and most people do not want to be a slave to their business.

Hire the best and compensate them well. Don't hire cheap—hire the best you can find and afford.

Know your own strengths. Hire talent to fill in your weaknesses.

Choosing the right employees to hire is the most important thing. The difference between good and great people is the difference between success and failure. Mediocrity is the death of a new venture.

Don't be afraid to quickly fire an employee who is not working out.

Delegate based on your shortcomings.

Don't go into business with friends because you think it will be easier. It may be harder if you have to tell your best friend that he or she is wrong, is not performing up to expectations, or is fired.

Don't take on a partner unless you absolutely must. If you do, make sure that he or she is as committed as you are.

LEGAL: IT'S A MINEFIELD OUT THERE!

Consult legal counsel when starting a business. Make sure that all the details of starting a business are covered with him or her.

Don't make verbal agreements with clients. Make sure that you have written work agreements with clear expectations of the work to be accomplished. This will ensure that there are no misunderstandings later.

Don't rely on anyone else (i.e., a partner) when starting your new venture unless you have a formal legal agreement.

Don't try to represent yourself in legal matters.

Be sure that you incorporate. This way someone can sue only the business, not the partners as individuals.

Follow all regulations and obtain all permits that are needed.

FINANCIAL SIDE: MONEY IS LIKE OXYGEN—YOU NEED IT TO LIVE

Make sure that you have the proper funds to cover unexpected spending. Get the necessary capital in the beginning. The last thing you want to have to worry about while you are working hard at getting your business off the ground is how you are going to pay for everything.

Resist the temptation to spend profits freely. As you begin to move from the red to the black, do not immediately spend the extra cash. Reinvest it in the business as part of your growth plan.

Be realistic about your expectations for income.

Don't expect to make a lot of money right from the start.

Forecast how long your business will have negative cash flow before it will have a positive cash position. Arrange financing so that you can last that long. If you think you are going to have negative cash flow for 6 months, be prepared for 9.

Get a line of credit immediately. You never know when you will need it. You will not get money when you need it because banks hate cash flow problems.

Don't invest all your money at the start of the business. Save some for growth or survival.

Don't risk or jeopardize all of your life savings by investing it in your business.

Don't mortgage your life away. Credit cards and second mortgages are not good funding sources.

Don't expect the bank to lend you money to start your business.

Don't pay for what you don't need. Never spend capital on something unless it adds true value to the business.

THE BUSINESS OPPORTUNITY: ANALYZE THE MARKETPLACE AND DO THE RIGHT MARKETING

Select a product or service for which there is demand in the area where you are establishing your business. Don't choose something just because you personally like it or think it might work; know what is needed and what will succeed.

Find something that people need and want in any economy. If your product and/or service is attractive only when the Dow Jones Industrial Average is breaking new ground, you are in for many long, sleepless nights.

Look for a niche in an existing market that is not being served.

Don't overlook existing markets that need revitalizing or that may have become stagnant in a market with new needs.

Don't enter a market with a product that is readily available and inexpensive (a commodity). Seek a high-margin, high-growth business.

Fill a real need. Making the best widget in the world is of no avail if no one is buying widgets.

Don't get into an oversaturated market. Make sure that you offer your customers a unique product or service. It's easier to be successful if you are the only one in town offering a certain product or service.

Don't attempt to compete in a mature industry unless you have particularly strong experience, creativity, contacts, and/or funding.

Exploit opportunities in emerging or changing industries.

Focus on the one thing that will differentiate you from your competition and do all you can to be the best at that one thing.

Find something to offer that your competitors can't offer.

Build competitive advantages and barriers to entry.

Build a brand name to deter competitors (particularly for products that are easily copied or imitated).

What holds true for one geographic market does not necessarily hold true for another, even one in close proximity.

Don't wait for customers to come to you. Don't simply hang out your shingle. Get commitments from several key prospective customers before you actually launch your business.

Be willing to start with small contracts and lower hourly fees while you build a roster of clients and build your reputation. Remember that potential clients are taking a chance by trying your business. Make the decision easier for them by reducing their risk or cost.

Don't assume that everyone will love your product or service.

Know your competitors. What services do they offer, and what rates do they charge? How do you compare?

Don't underestimate your competition.

Identify potential retaliatory actions from competitors.

Don't yield to unscrupulous competitors—keep your values and be respected in your community.

Don't get so busy running the company that you lose sight of your customers.

Quality service is the most important attribute in launching a business.

Don't jeopardize your reputation or your customer relationships for short-term gains.

Don't accept more customers than you can handle.

SUPPLIERS: YOU CAN'T LIVE WITHOUT THEM

Shop around for suppliers and vendors.

Make sure that you have all of your vendors lined up in advance.

Value and establish relationships with your suppliers.

Don't tie your whole business to any one vendor.

Don't be afraid to ask your suppliers for a lower price.

CLOSING POINTS

Start a business that someone else will be willing to buy if you want to cash out or just get out.

Know when it is time to exit. Sell when things are good . . . and if things are not good and they cannot be fixed, then minimize your losses so that you have something left for your next venture.

Remember the first tip: Don't forget why you wanted to start a business in the first place.

Carpe Diem!
Carpe Futuram!

Appendix
Sources of Helpful Information

BUYING A BUSINESS

BizBuySell.com (www.bizbuysell.com) lists businesses for sale.

Business Resale Network (www.BR-Network.com) provides information and lists businesses for sale.

DOING BUSINESS IN FOREIGN MARKETS

The Trade Information Center of the U.S. Commercial Service (www.usatrade.gov) offers market information on foreign countries.

FRANCHISE INFORMATION

American Association of Franchisees and Dealers (www.aafd.org).

Entrepreneur magazine (www.entrepreneur.com) features its Franchise 500 and 101 home-based businesses. Its Franchise Zone provides information on numerous franchises.

Franchise Update (www.franchise-update.com) provides information about franchise opportunities.

Inc. magazine (www.inc.com) has useful franchise information.

Institute for Franchise Management, College of St. Thomas (www.stthomas.edu).

International Franchise Association (www.franchise.org).

Disclaimer: The author is not responsible for the accuracy of the material provided in the sources of information. Some of the material is available for free, and some of the information is for sale. In no way is the list to be considered an endorsement of the sources of information or the material provided by the sources.

FUNDING INFORMATION

ACE-Net, or Angel Capital Electronic Network (www.ace-net.org), provides information about having your business profiled for potential angel investors.

Angel Investor News (www.angel-investor-news.com) provides a newsletter and information.

National Association of Small Business Investment Companies (www.nasbic.org).

National Venture Capital Association (www.nvca.org).

GENERAL INFORMATION

CCH Business Owner's Toolkit (www.toolkit.cch.com) provides various tools, templates, checklists, and advice.

Deloitte & Touche (www.dtonline.com) provides various resources, including tax tips.

Edward Lowe Perspectives (www.lowe.org) provides information on various topics.

Idea Café (www.ideacafe.com) provides information, tips, and contacts.

National Business Incubation Association (www.nbia.org).

Office.com (www.office.com) provides a number of links to other sites as well as articles.

Onvia (www.onvia.com) provides a guide on bid notices for doing business with the government.

PricewaterhouseCoopers (www.pwcerc.com) provides the Entrepreneur's Resource Center, which offers sample business plans, financial models, and approaches for soliciting venture capital funding.

PricewaterhouseCoopers Barometer Surveys (www.barometersurveys.com) enables you to access surveys about current business conditions, operating benchmarks, and so on.

Smart Online (www.smartonline.com) provides easy-to-use software for starting, growing, and managing a business.

Standard and Poor's (www.standardandpoors.com) provides financial ratios and useful data.

Workz (www.workz.com) provides useful articles, checklists, and links.

GOVERNMENT AGENCIES

U.S. Census Bureau (www.census.gov).

U.S. Department of Commerce (www.commerce.gov).

The Internal Revenue Service (www.irs.ustreas.gov) provides tax information. It also provides links to other useful sites.

U.S. Patent and Trademark Office (www.uspto.gov) provides information for inventors and describes the filing process.

U.S. Small Business Administration (www.sba.gov).

Small Business Development Centers (SBDCs) (www.asbdc-us.org), located at nearly 1000 universities in the United States, offer free counseling, training, and resources.

U.S. Small Business Administration Office of Innovation and Research (www.sba.gov/sbir) coordinates the Small Business Innovation and Research (SBIR) grant program. The office also provides an agency-by-agency listing of federal R&D programs.

INCORPORATING YOUR BUSINESS

Business Filings Inc. (www.businessfilings.com) provides a free guide to incorporating your business.

The Company Corporation (www.corporate.com) provides a process for forming a corporation or LLC in any state.

INVENTION INFORMATION

Patent Café (www.patentcafe.com) provides information on how to get a patent.

MAGAZINES

Entrepreneur magazine (www.entrepreneur.com) provides considerable information and a search engine for finding additional sites. The magazine also publishes guides, found at www.smallbizbooks.com, for starting numerous businesses.

Inc. magazine (www.inc.com) provides very useful information. Its site also includes archives of articles and sources for various business tools.

Kiplinger (www.kiplinger.com) provides useful information for growing a business.

Wall Street Journal (www.StartupJournal.com) provides advice and business tools.

MARKET INFORMATION

SRDS (www.srds.com) provides market information and media costs.

Index

ABOUT THE AUTHOR

STEPHEN C. HARPER is president of his own management consulting firm, Harper and Associates Inc. He is also the Progress Energy–Betty Cameron Distinguished Professor of Entrepreneurship at the University of North Carolina at Wilmington. Steve has worked with entrepreneurs and executives for more than 30 years. He was cofounder of the Coastal Entrepreneurial Council and served as director of the UNCW's Small Business Institute for 17 years. He has received numerous teaching awards. He has also received special recognition for outstanding service by the U.S. Small Business Administration.

Steve is the author of numerous books, including *Management: Who Ever Said It Would Be Easy?*, *The McGraw-Hill Guide to Managing Growth in Your Emerging Business*, and *The Forward-Focused Organization*. His articles have appeared in national and international magazines. Steve has served on the faculty at Arizona State University, where he earned his Ph.D. He has also been a visiting professor at Duke University.